Immigrant Subjectivities
in Asian American and Asian Diaspora Literatures

Immigrant Subjectivities
in Asian American and Asian Diaspora Literatures

Sheng-mei Ma

STATE UNIVERSITY OF NEW YORK PRESS

Published by
State University of New York Press, Albany

Printed in the United States of America

For information, address State University of New York
Press, State University Plaza, Albany, N.Y. 12246

Production by E. Moore
Marketing by Dana E. Yanulavich

Library of Congress Cataloging-in-Publication Data

Ma, Sheng-mei.
Immigrant subjectivities in Asian American and Asian Diaspora literatures / Sheng-mei Ma.
p. cm.
Includes bibliographical references (p.) and index.
ISBN 0-7914-3829-5 (hard. : alk. paper). — ISBN 0-7914-3830-9 (pbk. : alk. paper)
1. American literature—Asian American authors—History and criticism. 2. National characteristics, American, in literature. 3. Asians—Foreign countries—Intellectual life. 4. Emigration and immigration in literature. 5. Asian Americans in literature. 6. Subjectivity in literature. 7. Immigrants in literature.
I. Title.
PS153.A84M3 1998
810.9'895—dc21 97-30819
CIP

10 9 8 7 6 5 4 3 2 1

For Lien

Contents

Acknowledgments

The first draft of this book was written while I was teaching at James Madison University in Virginia, carrying a full load of four courses per semester. What sustained me throughout the project was my colleagues at Keezel Hall and the beautiful Shenandoah Valley. I benefited immensely from the friendship and advice of Mark and Susan Facknitz, and Bruce Johnson.

But above all, I am indebted to my wife, Lien Hsu; every word, every syllable within these pages entwines with her selfless love.

Portions or early versions of the following chapters have been published previously and I wish to thank these journals and publishers for permissions to reprint: chapter 2 in *Modern Language Studies* 23.4 (Fall 1993): 104–17; chapter 5 in *Ideas of Home: Literature of Asian Migration*. East Lansing: Michigan State University Press, 1997. 129–39; chapter 6 in *Positions: East Asia Cultures Critique* 4.3 (1996): 5–42; and chapter 8 in *Journal of Popular Culture* 30.1 (Summer 1996): 191–201.

Introduction: Ideology and the Representation of Immigrant

This book addresses an overlapping lacuna in current scholarship on ethnic, postcolonial, and area studies. In Asian American studies, few critics have engaged texts in order to construct immigrant subjectivities, which become the Other in the Manichean division to formulate the (Asian) American Self. In postcolonial discourse shaped by the Commonwealth legacy, the emphasis has been largely on Anglophone and Francophone literatures of Africa, Australia, the Caribbean, and the Indian subcontinent, with scant scrutiny of the Pacific Rim or its continuum in immigrant enclaves in the West. Finally, in modern China studies, scholars seem content to remain in a "cultural ghetto" and ignore, for instance, Taiwan's postcolonial condition. My project fills in these gaps by exploring the intersecting space of the three disciplines—immigrant subjectivities, with a particular focus on Chinese-speaking immigrants.

Divided into three parts, this book interrogates, in Part 1, the representation of immigrants in Asian American and, to a lesser extent, Asian Diaspora literatures. Immigrant subjectivities in these texts are frequently subsumed in the urgent need of self-fashioning and take the peculiar form of "immigrant schizophrenic" in chapter 3. Part 2 explores how the drive to "claim America" manifests itself as an eroticization of white bodies in male immigrant and minority writers. With gender and power inextricably coupled in these texts by males, the critical engagement in Part 2 draws from first-world feminist theories enriched by third-world postcolonial circumstances. Part 3 directs its attention to immigrant self-representation from the unique yet representative positionality of Taiwanese immigrants: how the nationalist impulse suppresses the postcolonial and U.S. minority conditions in overseas student literature since the 1960s; how cultural compradorism closely associated with immigration is critiqued in *Hsiang-t'u wen-hsueh* (home-soil or nativist literature) of the 1970s; and how, in recent films by immigrants, postmodernist multinational capitalism commodifies the multiplicity of immigrant subjectivities.

Throughout the following pages, "the immigrant" is shown to have become a contentious discursive site for self-definition and self-empowerment by Asian Americans and by immigrants themselves. The process of searching for identity goes beyond mere individual efforts, but it derives from as well as contributes to larger cultural ethos. Needless to say, "we" must define ourselves as opposed to, or through the *difference* from, "them"—aliens or immigrants. Inherent in any subjectivity formation, the image of the Other is required even for the founding of the United States. The construction of "American-ness" in the colonial period entails the existence of "savage" native Americans without and dark satanic forces within. The Declaration of Independence (1776) likewise elaborates on the ills of the Old World in order to demarcate the New. However, the collective memory of the United States has managed to erase the fact that "whiteness" itself is manufactured so that it becomes the invisible hegemony. As George Lipsitz puts it:

> Whiteness is everywhere in American culture, but it is very hard to see. As Richard Dyer argues, "white power secures its dominance by seeming not to be anything in particular." As the unmarked category against which difference is constructed, whiteness never has to speak its name, never has to acknowledge its role as an organizing principle in social and cultural relations. (369)

When that racial difference is created, it is rarely neutral and disinterested, but almost always a move for control, resulting in representations of the Other which are *un*consciously skewed. To explore why this distortion is unbeknownest to the one engaged in distorting, I locate my starting point in Louis Althusser's theory of the ideological interpellation of individuals as subjects:

> [I]deology has always-already interpellated individuals as subjects, which amounts to making it clear that individuals are always-already interpellated by ideology as subjects, which necessarily leads us to one last proposition: *individuals are always-already subjects.* ("Ideology and the Ideological State Apparatuses [Notes Towards an Investigation]" 175–76)

Althusser explicates the abstruse term of "interpellation" with the analogy that ideology works on individuals just as each of them feels being hailed or addressed *personally* on the street when "Hey, you there!" is called out from behind. Put another way, ideology is ubiquitous and infiltrates subjects without being perceived as an infiltration.

A vicious strain of such ideological interpellation is the national amnesia over "whiteness," which over time becomes identical with being "American." Occasional reminders of the diverse origins of Americans occur in the cliche that this is "a nation of immigrants," which is the title of John F. Kennedy's 1964 book, heralding an era of liberalism toward immigration from Asia. Kennedy bases his argument in part on writers such as Oscar Handlin, who opens *The Uprooted* (1951) with "Once I thought to write a history of the immigrants in America. Then I discovered that the immigrants *were* American history" (Introduction 3). Under Kennedy's stewardship, the anti-Asian tradition was temporarily suspended.

In the evolution of Asian America, the Immigration Reform Bill passed in 1965 contributes to the dramatic upswing of the Asian population in the United States, a consequence unforeseen by the Kennedys and lamented afterward by other liberals. As Bill Ong Hing, in *Making and Remaking Asian America through Immigration Policy 1850–1990* (1993), aptly points out, Asian America is formulated by immigration policy and Asian American demographics is dictated by U.S. policy on immigration. It is regrettable that many Asian American authors examined in Part 1, in fashioning their own identity, realign their symbiotic relationship with Asian immigrants as an adversarial one.

It becomes oppositional because of the pressures from hegemony on Asian Americans. The 1960s are marked by the civil rights and the black power movements, sensitizing minorities to their rights and inspiring the Asian American consciousness movement. Asian Americans were also spurred by the anticolonial movements internationally and, specifically, by the Vietnam War.

In institutions of higher education, student activists demanded to have Asian American studies and other academic curricula to satisfy their needs. It is important to note, however, that what is called "Asian America" arises primarily from "political and social processes, rather than . . . cultural bonds" (Yen Le Espiritu 13) at a given moment in history.

Thus, swept up in the excitement of those tumultuous decades over identity formation, Asian American writers, such as Maxine Hong Kingston and Frank Chin in chapter 2, Orientalize immigrant characters, particularly their dehumanizing physical features and pidgin English, in their shared drive to "claim America." Yet this Orientalizing or distancing proclivity toward Asians coexists with the psychic need to assert one's difference from the American majority and one's ethnic pride in these points of difference. Chapter 1 hence investigates the complex intersections of "native informants" and "ethnographic feminism" in Kingston, Amy Tan, and others. The imagining over the Asian Other also leads to the representation of the "immigrant schizophrenic" in Pai Hsien-yung, Nieh Hua-ling, Kazuo Ishiguro, and Bharati Mukherjee in chapter 3.

A vein running through a long line of texts by male writers in this book is the deployment of eroticization of white bodies as a strategy of empowerment. Part 2 devotes itself to this fusion of power and gender. Lisa Lowe in "On Contemporary Asian American Projects" describes this fusion thus: "Throughout our lived social relations, it is apparent that labor is gendered, sexuality is racialized, and race is class-articulated" (46). Since both male Asian immigrants and American males of Asian extraction are feminized in popular culture, they idolize white women in hopes of feeling masculine again. Trinh T. Min-ha's notion of woman as the "Inappropriate Other," "[n]ot quite the Same, not quite the Other . . . in that undetermined threshold place" (*When the Moon Waxes Red* 74) brings out the intricacy of how the alleged other—Asian immigrant—engages in a further othering of women, such as the quintessential object of desire—the Statue of Liberty—in Carlos Bulosan of chapter 5.

But first-world feminist theories alone will not decipher adequately this masculinist lineage of fantasizing one's possession of white bodies. Part 2 reads the long line of male texts spanning the century—from the early San Francisco rhymesters collected in *Songs of Gold Mountain* (1987) to transitional figures such as John Okada, Louis Chu, and Carlos Bulosan to contemporary authors—

against their postcolonial background in first-world ghettos or in the third world.

Part 3 concludes the book with a study of immigrant self-representation, which is not, however, separate and apart from the U.S. context where immigrants find themselves or where immigrants-to-be long to be. Social realities in the United States and elsewhere around the globe have altered considerably since the Asian American consciousness movement in the 1960s, a sea change over some three decades repeatedly elaborated in a double issue of *Amerasia Journal* as well as in *The Ethnic Canon*, edited by David Palumbo-Liu, both published in 1995. While the decade of the sixties gives birth to a multiculturalism, which, as Palumbo-Liu explains, "manage[s] and neutralize[s] conflict" (6), the ensuing years see an added responsibility for ethnic studies programs, facing up to new challenges from the conservative "Reagan-Bush agenda," the growth of "college-age population," and "the need for a newly skilled workforce" in "'nontraditional' students" (Palumbo-Liu 7). Lisa Lowe locates Asian American literature and studies in similar circumstances: "post-Fordist" restructuring of global capitalism; "changed demographics of the Asian American population" since 1965; "the colonial and neocolonial rule of the U.S. in the Asian states"; the "one-sided class war" in the United States since the 1970s ("On Contemporary Asian American Projects" 43).

These critics hold that Asian American studies must expand its territory to embrace rather than reject new demands. Lowe maintains that Asian Americans are not "exclusively determined by their 'American' histories of immigration exclusion, racism, proletarianization, and internment." Rather, today's Asian Americans include people "emerging out of colonialism and neocolonialism in Asia" (45). Sau-ling Cynthia Wong observes that Asian American studies is undergoing a denationalization and internationalization ("Denationalization Reconsidered: Asian American Cultural Criticism at a Theoretical Crossroads" 1–2). Wong's remark serves as a wake-up call both for U.S.-centered Asian Americanists and for their colleagues in other disciplines whose studies are tilted toward immigrants' home countries. Palumbo-Liu likewise expects *The Ethnic Canon* to "resist the essentializing and stratifying modes of reading ethnic literature that make it ripe for canonization and co-option" (17).

The first step in avoiding the danger of being mainstreamed is to read the texts interdisciplinarily, against the grain of their alleged literary and cultural tradition and along with the ever-shifting social realities. Part 3 hence begins, in chapter 6, by situating a particular genre of immigrant texts, *Liu-hsueh-shen wen-hsueh* (overseas student literature) since the 1960s in Taiwan, at the interface of Chinese, Postcolonial, and Minority studies. The textual privileging of immigrant characters' "Chinese-ness," which they lose in the New World, is found to be a defensive ethnocentrism reacting to the disorienting postcolonial and minority conditions. Chapter 7 examines, through writers such as Chen Ying-chen, Huang Chun-ming, and Wang Chen-ho, the nativist critique of Taiwan's compradorism implicit in overseas student literature. The last chapter updates overseas student literature through a look at its cinematic metamorphosis in Ang Lee's immigrant trilogy in the 1990s.

Similar to the ideological interpellation rendering "whiteness" invisible to Americans, ideology is at work as well, soundlessly, in the formation of immigrant subjectivities in Asian American and Asian Diasporic texts. Ponder, for instance, the paradox that while the English language, or more precisely, the acquisition of English as a second language (ESL), lies at the core of immigrant existence, rarely is it given extensive treatment either in overseas student literature or in Asian American literature. Undeniably, the educational system of the Pacific Rim with its heavy emphasis on the English language and culture has come to ensure that aspiring young men and women would feel personally summoned to go abroad and partake in the *Liu-shueh* ("study abroad" in Mandarin) culture. Grounded specifically in the English classes from junior high school, if not earlier, through college in most Pacific Rim countries, this education blossoms into a constellation of institutions: government bureaucracies and private enterprises subsisting on the supremacy of the West; popular culture featuring American TV programs, movies, and videos; English examinations administered in regular and cram schools, culminating in TOEFL; and so forth. This learning process makes possible the immigrant's lived experiences in the United States as well as literary representations of immigrants. In order to comprehend such immigrant subjectivities, one must investigate ESL education or language in general as an integral part of the ideological apparatuses of postcolonial culture in Taiwan and of the culture of assimilation in the United States. Little reflection has been given, though, to the forging of immigrant subjectivities via language in the texts studied herein. This omission is most glaring in view of the fact that white-collar, professional-class immigrants, including all the distinguished authors of overseas student literature, seem to be the "fruition" or "crown jewel" of this process, their prestige in the United States and Taiwan attained in no small measure from their mastery of the English language and the Anglo-American culture. By comparison to their "rich relations," blue-collar, working-class immigrants, such as those "native informants" in Asian American texts, are "hibernating seeds" or "pale imitations," whose incomplete absorption of the language and its related skills dooms them to a life of menial jobs. Be it "crown jewel" or "pale imitations," be it "fruition" or "hibernating seeds" that might flower in the next generation, they all receive nourishment from the same hidden roots. The oversight of this pivotal substratum in immigrant psyche arises from Asian Americans' inability to come to grips with the Other and from Asian immigrants' similar difficulty in penetrating the Self, one that is molded by the cold war and is only beginning to be modified in the post–cold war era.

However, Althusser's usage of the term "subject" can be viewed as deliberately double-edged. One the one hand, it implies subjectivity which stems partly from the human agent or self-will; on the other, it suggests being subjected to a system beyond one's control or even consciousness. The tension between human subjectivity and its subjection to ideology runs through this entire book by way of writers' conformity to hegemony juxtaposed with their resistance to it. For instance, it is irrefutable that ESL education or language more broadly, combined with other factors of the cold war, brings an entire generation of Taiwanese writers to the United States. To be specific, the institution of the International Writing Program at the University of Iowa attracted to these shores a great number of writers and artists explicated in Part 3 and subsequently either launched or solidified their careers as leading intellectuals in Taiwan. But from their texts which have come to be known as overseas student literature and nativist literature, one detects inchoate as well as full-fledged signs of self-critique of postcolonialism. To map out this invisible network stretched tautly over the Pacific Ocean, Althusser's hypothesis makes possible a theoretical connection between individual condition and cultures as well as between local specificities and the global context.

The term "immigrant subjectivities" appears to have undergone a radical narrowing in scope and definition from the first two parts to the last part. While the term in Parts 1 and 2 refers largely to Asian American literature's representation of immigrants, regardless of their national, ethnic, U.S. regional, linguistic, and socioeconomic background, one might think it unduly confined in Part 3 to two specific bodies of immigrant texts, overseas student literature and nativist literature. Both, some may protest, originate from Taiwan and are written in Chinese. But a comprehensive survey of Asian Diaspora literature in the United States at this time is all but impossible due to the lack of scholarly attention in this field. Asian immigrants to the United States exhibit diverse histories of immigration, locations of settlement, races and nationalities, languages, and social classes. This fundamental complexity and elusiveness of immigrant selfhood, among other reasons, leads Asian American writers, the group closest to immigrants in the New World in terms of biological, emotional, and political bonds, to resort to the mainstream, somewhat Orientalist, perspective in depicting Asian immigrants. Such a subsuming of immigrant subjectivities in Asian American texts makes it all the more paramount not to lapse into similar generalization and objectification in Part 3 when efforts are made to recuperate immigrant voices.

More fundamentally, to see an imbalance of magnitude between various segments of this book is to capitulate to the imperialist notion which assigns more weight to literature in English than to literatures in other languages. Asian American literature, this essentialist logic somehow intimates, occupies the metropolitan center, unmatched by literatures in other languages on the periphery. The fact that the majority of American academicians are circumscribed by English and European languages makes the emigre or nativist writers in Part 3 look rather obscure. This is quite ironic since Asian American texts continue to be regarded as a *minority*, or even *minor*, literature relegated to the controversial and often tokenized multicultural program in U.S. academe, whereas Part 3 boasts of many canonical figures in the Chinese-speaking literary scene. In fact, the possible charge against the concentration on Chinese-language texts begs the question of the definition of Asian American literature itself, which has traditionally privileged "American" texts in "English" and which has dismissed a large number of immigrant texts inaccessible to Asian Americanists as a result of language barrier. Part 3 begins to elaborate the multiethnic fabric by tracing one particular strand which extends beyond the American border and psyche. Arguably, the present status of Asian American scholarship *demands*, ethically as well as politically, a concurrent inquiry into immigrant texts ignored thus far.

Part 1

The Representation of the Asian Other

ONE

Native Informants and Ethnographic Feminism in Asian American Texts

U.S. laws designate all foreign nationals as "aliens," legal or illegal, resident or nonresident. Asian immigrants have in recent years become one of the newest waves of aliens arriving on the shores of America. But even after having been naturalized as U.S. citizens, they remain alien-ated due to, primarily, their non-Caucasian physical traits, a painful historical fact crystalizing in the internment of American-born Japanese American citizens, but not European-born German and Italian citizens in the United States, during World War II.[1] Barred by linguistic, cultural, and other barriers, these Asian immigrants rarely tell their stories firsthand in what is known today as Asian American literature; their stories are told, instead, by their children or their grandchildren. Consequently, in most Asian American texts, there exists a tense triangular relationship: Asian American raconteurs and the American market actively woo each other in appropriating alien(s') stories, the surest sign of ethnicity, as commodity. Indeed, a significant source of that ethnicity is Asian American writers' emplotment of immigrants' heart-wrenching and almost always "exotic" experiences. While these alien(s') stories contribute to rendering Asian American texts highly marketable, immigrants remain largely a blank, an absence—the voiceless, plastic other waiting to be born by their children.

The core paradox of this triangular relationship stems from Asian American writers' identity politics, most nakedly embodied in the position of *Aiiieeeee!: An Anthology of Asian American Writers* (1974), the first anthology of its kind edited by American-born Asians.[2] To establish their unique identity as neither Asians nor Euro-Americans, its editors—Frank Chin, Jeffrey Paul Chan, Lawson Fusao Inada, and Shawn Wong—in various prefaces sharply demarcate themselves from Asians, while empowering themselves in the midst of a white society through immigrant memories and the mythic Asian past. These two tactics, used indiscreetly, contradict each other, exhibiting the simultaneous urges to distance from and embrace things Asian, creating the problematics of representing the other which is part of the self. This dilemma is further exacerbated by the inability of immigrants to "write back"—to mount an oppositional discourse.

This triangular relationship of alien stories, Asian American teller, and American market will be interrogated with respect to what I call the "ethnographic feminism"[3] in texts such as Maxine Hong Kingston's *The Woman Warrior: Memoirs of a Girlhood among Ghosts* (1976), Amy Tan's *The Kitchen God's Wife* (1989), and D. Roberts' "Mei Mei: A Daughter's Song" (1989). The ethnographic myths of Fa Mu Lan, the Kitchen God, and Kuan-yin Pu-sa ("Lady Buddha") narrated by the three mother figures who act as native informants in the three texts respectively are seamlessly transposed into a feminist, Westernized context to, in part, cater to the American readership, whose appetite for exotic (hence ethnographic) and politically correct (hence feminist) readings is simultaneously satisfied. While Kingston invariably Orientalizes and objectifies China and its immigrants,[4] Tan and Roberts struggle to undo, to varying degrees of success, that very impulse inherent in the tradition of "ethnographic feminism" inaugurated by Kingston's woman warriors.

This approach of training literary *and* ethnographic gazes on a text has been practiced for some time. George Marcus' "Afterword: Ethnographic Writing and Anthropological Careers," in *Writing Culture: The Poetics and Politics of Ethnography* (1986), opens with "The task of the Santa Fe seminar from which these essays [of *Writing Culture*] emerged was to introduce a literary consciousness to ethnographic practice by showing various ways in which ethnographies can be read and written" (262). A specific instance of such interdisciplinarity is found, in that collection, in Michael M. J. Fischer's "Ethnicity and the Post-Modern Arts of Memory," which studies Kingston and other "ethnic autobiography or autobiographical fiction" in light of "textual theories of deferred, hidden, or occulted meaning" (194–95) to re-examine the notion of ethnicity. The authors in this collection no longer view ethnic literature and ethnography as two totally unrelated disciplines; instead, the terrain of the presumably objective and scientific research of primitive cultures is believed to overlap with ethnic writings, sharing similar strategies of textual production as well as of subjectivity construction.

Asian American scholars have certainly attended to this fusion of literary criticism and ethnography. Patricia Lin in "Clashing Constructs of Reality: Reading Maxine Hong Kingston's *Tripmaster Monkey: His Fake Book* as Indigenous Ethnography," for instance, applies the postmodernist approach to textuality in *Writing Culture* to illustrate how Kingston's novel approximates contemporary ethnography in terms of contending voices. Stressing Kingston's playfulness and multivalence, characteristics akin to the style of postmodernist ethnography, Lin nevertheless ignores Kingston's departure from Marcus and others in terms of their reluctance to objectify the other (alien story) in constructing one's (Asian American) subjectivity. More specifically, an Asian American author such as Kingston acquires ethnographic details of an alien people from the "native and subaltern imformants"—unfailingly the immigrant generation like the mother figure in *The Woman Warrior*—and proceeds to transcribe alien('s) stories into a feminist context, thus creating a winning formula of quasi-ethnographic Orientalism and timely, politically correct feminism, a combination which accounts for Kingston's sudden rise in the West in recent decades.

Though Kingston herself has rarely elaborated on her own success by way of its ties to market value, other ethnic writers have. The Anglo-Japanese novelist Kazuo Ishiguro has candidly linked the contextual to the textual. In an interview with Allan Vorda and Kim Herzinger, Ishiguro discusses the causal relationship between the times ethnic writers happen to live in and their rapid ascent:

> In Britain, around the time when I published my first novel [*A Pale View of Hills* (1982)], the climate had actually turned towards a great deal of interest in writers who wrote books set in that particular setting [non-Western locales]. . . . I tend to think if I didn't have a Japanese name and if I hadn't written books at that stage set in Japan, it would have taken me years longer to get the kind of attention and sales that I got in England with my first two books. (133)

The immediate acclaim his works receive in England and North America, however, does not derive from the kind of exoticism in Kingston. In fact, his works are praised by the Japanese Nobel Laureate Oe Kenzaburo as containing "excellent descriptions of life in Japan, of Japanese buildings and landscapes" ("The Novelist in Today's World: A Conversation" 164). To which, Ishiguro responds that while his depiction may be accurate, it is "very much my own personal, imaginary Japan" (164). He would like to be regarded, professes Ishiguro repeatedly, as an "international" rather than ethnic writer (169). An intriguing contrast to Kingston's phantasmagoric Orient, Ishiguro's exquisitely realistic Japan, when identified as such, has to be elevated to a universal level. Both betray, in varying ways, the unease Asian minorities in the West feel about themselves: one resorts to Orientalism to prove how un-Oriental she is, the other Universalism. Their Asian heritage is portrayed as an incidental, almost negligible appendix to their Western and cosmopolitan identity.[5]

Despite their contrasting styles, Ishiguro's career in Britain in the early 1980s repeats the pattern of Kingston's success in the United States in the mid-1970s. Both novelists have clearly provided something the reading public demanded. With regard to *The Woman Warrior*, its stunning success stems, as stated earlier, from the exotic China Kingston creates in conjunction with the feminist message she interjects into that wondrous landscape—a universe where the misogynist, corrupt culture forces the "No Name Woman" to give birth in a pigsty; where a mother allegedly cuts her daughter's frenum; where Hong Kong's Kung Fu films as part of American popular culture are superimposed on contemporary politics of the madding crowd of red guards at Tiananmen Square; where Fa Mu Lan's bare back is tattooed with Yueh Fei's words;[6] and where countless other fantastic tales bedevil the reader. Such blatant Orientalism notwithstanding, Kingston's reflection on the "cultural mis-readings" of her text takes the form more of a critique of the reading public than of her own complicity in cultural misrepresentations. In reviewing the reviews of *The Woman Warrior*, Kingston finds the otherwise complimentary commentaries aggravating in their highlighting of her interracial marriage. She believes that her last name served in the seventies to dilute the sense of defamiliarization American audiences were likely to feel when confronted with ethnic literature, for a marriage with a Western man suggested and continues to suggest to the public a sensibility already assimilated.[7] (In which case, "Hong," no longer a forbidding sign, actually increases the appeal of the exotica.) A shrewd analysis on her part, Kingston nonetheless neglects to mention the fundamental fact that such "cultural mis-readings" catapult her to the status of the premier Asian American writer. More significantly, these mis-readings may come partially from Kingston's own mis-representations of the Other—China and Chinese.

Amy Tan, Kingston's heir apparent in Chinese American literature, burst into the literary scene in 1989 with the publication of *The Joy Luck Club*. Tan's handling of ethnographic materials has "mellowed" somewhat along with the softening of attitude toward China and its immigrants during the two decades since *The Woman Warrior*. Asian Americans no longer have as urgent a need as before to distinguish themselves from Asians due to the influx of immigrants in their midst as well as the change of political, cultural climate. Elaine Kim argues in her foreword to *Reading the Literatures of Asian America* (1992) that since the transformations in the political relationships between the United States and Asian countries and in the U.S. immigration policy of the mid-1970s, "[t]he lines between Asian and Asian American, so important in identity formation in earlier times, are increasingly being blurred" (xiii). With a broad stroke meant to encompass the world, Frederick Buell in *National Culture and the New Global System* (1994) has characterized this shift as moving from a consolidation of bounded, separate ethnic identity to an expansion of a more heterogeneous, hybrid self:

> There has been a transformation from speaking against to speaking with and to; from a sense of cultural communities as separate to an awareness of their complex interlocking; from a cultivation of opposition to a grappling with the possibilities and limitations of interaction. (236)

Under such improved atmosphere regarding ethnicity, Tan has taken leave of Kingston's hostility toward native informants, although traces of Tan's own Orientalism still persist. A case in point is the highly sensationalized story delivered by one of the four mothers in *The Joy Luck Club*. An-mei Hsu, to impart "shou" (codes of behavior) to her American-born (therefore uncivilized) daughter, narrates how An-mei's mother commits self-immolation: she cut a piece of her own flesh and cooked it in the medicinal soup in hopes of reviving her dying mother-in-law in China (48). The stark contradiction of the mother's intention of conversion to respectability and her means—a horrendous and macabre account about the last generation—bespeaks Orientalism which views the East as inscrutable and antithetical to the West.

But Tan's much more cordial position toward ethnographic elements in her text can be seen most clearly in the romantic refrains of Chinese-ness toward the end of that novel. Jing-mei Woo (the only daughter who, in addition to her English name June, has a Chinese first name) begins the story, replaces her mother after her death at the club, and ends the fiction by taking a trip to China to meet her twin sisters. Jing-mei's journey back reads almost like a "homecoming" in its reiteration of how she feels Chinese once her feet touch Chinese soil, how her Chinese genes are instantly activated, and how her Chinese side is "waiting to be let go." Though not without some foreshadowing throughout of Jing-mei's urges to seek her roots, such ethnic, even nationalist, assertions remain slightly melodramatic. However, Tan's somewhat maudlin attitude toward China and Chinese immigrants illustrates the divergence of the two leading Asian American writers: while Kingston fixes her distant and rather cold gaze on the Orient, Tan at least finds a tender place in her heart for it.

Tan may have gone to the other extreme, though. While the interracial protagonist, Olivia Bishop, in *The Hundred Secret Senses* (1995) confesses that "[i]t's hip to be ethnic" (157), the emphasis falls on "hip" rather than "ethnic." Opting for the slang "hip," Tan unknowingly reveals the irony of her status as an ethnic writer. Part of the novel resembles a travelogue set in Changmian, China, a traveloque disguised as yet another "homecoming" to ethnic roots. This journey to the backwaters of China, a journey back in time literally since Olivia revisits her former life at that remote village as a Western missionary around the turn of the century, has more to do with the New Age spiritual concerns in the States here and now than with the exotic, mythologized China. Ethnicity is thoroughly romanticized by Tan because it is "in."

It is perhaps inevitable that these writers, to various degrees, Orientalize the East. Shirley Lim's "Assaying the Gold: Or, Contesting the Ground of Asian American Literature" puts it eloquently in the vein of Foucauldian and Saidian analysis of power and discourse:

> The "problem" of ethnicity becomes "resolved" in the writers' facility and ease with majority rhetoric and aesthetics, and the "danger" posed by the unfamiliar and alien is thus

> defused. Instead of defamiliarization, that radicalizing technique by which the complacent majority are made uncomfortable, Asian American writers who have mastered the resources of American English literariness are able to elide the alien in Asian American culture and make it accessible to American audiences. . . . One technique by which they do this is to posit themselves not as advantaged insiders of the Asian culture but as similarly disadvantaged as their Anglo readers in finding that Asian component bizarre, distasteful, and difficult to comprehend. . . . Another is to abstract, intellectualize, and refine upon ethnic experience in a fairly logocentric manner, so that the ironizing distance parallels the white reader's cultural distance from the ethnic materials. (161)

The references to "American audiences" and "Anglo readers" suggest a minority discursive practice targeting and addressing the dominant population. This concern for the particular kind of market drives the practitioners to identify with or at least acquiesce to the Orientalist perspective, thus following the paradigm of Orientalism in terms of the binary opposition of Self and Other, of subjectivity and objectivity, and, most of all, of the power structure inherent in such a dichotomy. In addition to such a collaboration with the majority culture, these writers also thrive in the American market as a result of an alignment of their texts with one of the dominant current ideologies in the West—feminism.

The manner in which Kingston and others ingeniously join feminism with ethnography is their deployment of "the theology of the oppressed." Indigenous to Chinese folk beliefs are Kingston's woman warrior such as Fa Mu Lan, Tan's Kitchen God, and Roberts' Kuan-yin Pu-sa ("Lady Buddha"). But these folk deities are given a contemporary feminist spin to empower the oppressed female characters in China as well as in America. Kingston, for instance, reconfigures the myth of Fa Mu Lan in *The Woman Warrior* in order to found/inherit a feminist lineage based on the legendary heroine and the strong-willed, barefoot-doctor mother character, Brave Orchid. Yet quite revealing about Kingston's ambivalence toward her native informants is that once the feet of this mother figure, to paraphrase Tan, touch American soil, she deteriorates into a stubborn, superstitious, and ignorant old woman, who is nothing but a quaint embarrassment to her American-born children. The protagonist Brave Orchid has lost her antagonist, such as the "Sitting Ghost" in the Cantonese folk belief system, whose existence is essential for the demonstration of her heroism; she herself becomes "the other," an alien "ghost" in America and to her own children. Brave Orchid's ways are judged to be out of date and out of place, symptomatic of her ineffectual adaptation to the New World. This native informant, initially providing a feminist prototype through her deeds, has since declined into a negative example whom the daughter-narrator must shun rather than emulate in America. Kingston's delineation of Brave Orchid, in fact, borders on an image of immigrants as "schizophrenics," who fail to cohere the two halves—American and non-American—of their experience and who consequently lose touch with the American reality. This split personality culminates in Moon Orchid, Brave Orchid's feeble sister, who goes insane in the United States.[8]

Tan also utilizes "ethnographic feminism," but in a reverse fashion. Tan first presents in *The Kitchen God's Wife* the indigenous informants—Winnie Louie, Helen (or Hulan), and Grand Auntie Du—in a light as unsavory as, but definitely more comical than, Kingston's; nonetheless, these emigre mothers grow in stature in the narrative. (The equivalent to these evolving female immigrant characters in *The Hundred Secret Senses*, of course, is Kwan, Olivia's half-sister.) Grand Auntie Du, whom Pearl, Winnie's Americanized daughter, haphazardly dismisses to be long dead, turns out to be Winnie's savior from a Shanghai prison. Helen, seemingly an illiterate scatterbrain, adroitly fabricates the lie of her brain tumor to secretly coerce the mother and the daughter to confide in each other the unsettling truth. Finally, Winnie appears to be unreasonable and "negative-thinking" (152) only because of her horrible sufferings at the hands of her monstrous first husband, Wen Fu. In fact, the persevering spirit of Winnie gradually unfolds in this novel until she becomes all but a deity herself—"the Kitchen God's Wife." Despite their similar strategy of feminizing folk beliefs that originally privilege the patriarchy, Tan's text aspires to present the Orientalist knot tied by Kingston, a self-proclaimed "outlaw knotmaker" (*The Woman Warrior* 190), in a far more light-hearted, charming, and "lawful" mode. Even though they both immortalize the peripheral female figures in Chinese culture, they draw from contrasting aspects of the Oriental mystique. Kingston deploys images of a "hard-core," unrelenting Orient to distance the reader from it, whereas Tan renders China endearing through a melodramatic, tragicomical plot.

Beyond the manipulation of ethnographic materials gathered from native informants, another consequence of "ethnographic feminism" is male backlash—the criticism of reverse stereotyping and objectification of male characters in the texts. While immigrant mothers are portrayed as enigmatic so that their daughters can begin to make sense of themselves, Chinese and Chinese American men, so the accusation goes, are likewise swathed in mystery and their psychology simplified in the writers' fervor of reinventing female subjectivity. Men rather than women now serve as the background props against which females define themselves.

The male backlash against "ethnographic feminism" is spearheaded by the contentious Frank Chin, who takes on the myth of Fa Mu Lan in his "Come All Ye Asian American Writers of the Real and the Fake."[9] In this article, Chin, as bellicose as ever, argues against what he sees as Kingston's exploitation of this legend, which is alleged to misrepresent the Asian tradition as misogynist. To claim authority on the Chinese source, Chin even takes pains to quote verbatim—in classical Chinese—an anonymous poem considered to be the culminating expression of the Fa Mu Lan myth. This might be an exercise in futility since no evidence suggests that either Chin or his opponent is a competent reader of classical or even vernacular Chinese; however, a Chinese tale has been elevated to the site of present-day struggle between Asian American writers over feminism and its backlash. Both tellers reshape their source stories in his/her image in the name of reclaiming the authentic Chinese heritage, while veiling their design for control of discourse and representation. Indeed, to borrow Edward Said's theories in *Orientalism* (1978), such discourse concerns only with the exteriority of the other—immigrants and Asian culture—as Asian Americans see fit to project.

Chin's retaliation is motivated by a wounded male ego, signifying male rage over being consistently ignored by the American academy and market. It might be more sensible for Chin and other like-minded writers to take on the literary establishment and the mainstream sensibility rather than to vent their fury on Asian American feminists. But the kind of public indifference suffered by Chin has also struck Kingston's career. Kingston has long asserted that she was compelled to put the materials on Chinese males into *China Men* (1980) for the sake of coherence of *The Woman Warrior*. But this sequel to *Warrior* never achieved the fame of her first book; the critical and the commercial receptions have been lukewarm for this text on the historical travails of Chinese males written in a style much less extravagant. This lack of interest testifies to the power of "ethnographic feminism," without which, even Kingston flops.

Moreover, Chin's complaint concerning the representation of males is not entirely without merit, provided one is able to see through Chin's emotionally-charged, mad-prophet pose. Males are de facto excluded from, for instance, Tan's imaginary world. The mah-jong club in *The Joy Luck Club* proceeds devoid of any major male participation. By the same token, the men in *The Kitchen God's Wife* receive stereotypical depictions at best. The male protagonist in *The Kitchen God's Wife*, Wen Fu, the epitome of Chinese patriarchy, rarely acquires psychological depth other than a demonic kind. To Tan's credit, she does attend to this inadequacy by intimating the practical inability of Winnie the narrator to probe into her tormentor's psyche in a male-dominated society. Tan skillfully delineates Winnie's maturation via her change from blaming Wen Fu's mother for his wrongdoing to blaming the true culprit himself. An additional indication that this flaw is being ameliorated is the well-developed male protagonist, Simon Bishop, in Tan's most recent novel, *The Hundred Secret Senses*. But the irrefutable fact remains that far too many blanks exist when it comes to male characters, particularly in *The Kitchen God's Wife*. Why is Wen Fu such a sadist? Is he not fearful of being punished by Jiaguo, his immediate superior and Helen's husband? Would Jiaguo's sense of guilt over impregnating and causing the death of Helen's sister be sufficient to reform him from a heartless military officer to a kind and loving, yet now impotent, husband? Why does Jimmy Louie, Winnie's second husband, convert to Christianity after being forced to leave China, his new-found faith supposedly contributing to his decreased passion for Winnie? The best incarnation of the disjointed images of males is found in Winnie's father, who falls from a wealthy, self-assured man to a collaborator with the Japanese invaders and a derelict after the war, crippled by a stroke. The two halves of the father's face allegorize males: the normal half retains his past dignity, while the other, paralyzed, betrays the dark and insidious self. Males in this novel are stereotypes of extremes rather than living beings like Winnie and Pearl who never cease to surprise readers.

In a miniature version, Roberts' radio play, "Mei Mei: A Daughter's Song," which won the 1989 George Foster Peabody Award for Broadcasting Excellence, exhibits "ethnographic feminism" in a manner less antagonistic to the Other than Kingston and less melodramatic than Tan, resulting in a moving story that lingers in the air long after it is gone. Produced the same year *The Kitchen God's Wife* was published, Roberts' play also resembles

Tan's novel in its initial emotional quandary between the mother and the daughter and in its denouement of a happy reconciliation. In this well-crafted, twenty-seven-minute-long play with fugue-like echoes and refrains, Roberts interweaves the American-educated Mei Mei's "confession," her interviews of her immigrant mother, and sound effects to construct this tapestry of voices on the impossibility and inevitability of communication between the mother and the daughter.[10] One such strand of this complex composition is the tumultuous relationship of the two women, reflected in the perpetual modifications of statements from the outset. While the title suggests a daughter's story, the first line foregrounding the mother's presence—"Just remember," the narrator, Mei Mei, announces, "this isn't about me. It's about my mother"—undercuts the title. Moreover, despite Mei Mei's attempt at detachment by insisting on the stilted address of "mother" (already complicated by the background cries of "Mommy" of a Taiwanese girl), she subconsciously reverts back to the term of endearment, Mama, halfway through the play, a term which corresponds to the loving name of Mei Mei (little sister or daughter). These narrative strategies demonstrate how the stories of the immigrant mother and the Asian American daughter intertwine, ideally, into one. Indeed, for Asian American literature, this wedding may herald a more inclusive identity politics, forgoing the radical othering of Asian heritage advocated by the *Aiiieeeee!* anthology, practiced implicitly by Kingston, and sugarcoated by Tan. This bittersweet merging of the mother and the daughter, of the native informant and the Western feminist, occurs most visibly in, once again, "the theology of the oppressed" in the play.

The mother in her teens, illiterate and abused in war-torn Taiwan, finds strength in her faith in Kuan-yin Pu-sa or "Lady Buddha," the Goddess of Mercy prevalent in Chinese folk beliefs closely linked to Buddhism. She claims that Kuan-yin Pu-sa dissuaded her from suicide by taking her on what seems to be a mental journey to heaven and providing her with a vision of beatitude, hence abrogating the mother's glimpse of female ghosts "with the tongue roll[ing] down from her mouth"—the fate of the mother had she taken her own life. The juxtaposition of heaven and cemetery, both fantastic manifestations of the soul, is not a mere ethnographic footnote to the Taiwanese mother's traumatic experience. Rather, this contrast is inextricably tied to feminism in the specifically American context. The vision in heaven, according to the mother's pidgin English, is of "all different color people," hence befitting the multiethnic fabric of the host society. As for the feminist lineage, Kuan-yin Pu-sa is as much a savior for the mother as the mother is for Mei Mei. As it turns out, the mother's "superstition" empowers not only herself but the daughter as well: the narrator at one point accepts the deity's might in stopping her own parricidal drive. Heaving a sigh of relief, the daughter reflects: "Maybe Buddha was there for her [mother or daughter?] that night." Buddha stayed the mother's suicidal hand as well as the daughter's homicidal one. More significantly, the play ends with the myth of the Dragon King—also from the mother's folk belief system—when a peasant girl and the king's daughter join in a duet to augur rain, thus ending the drought. This chorus follows in the wake of, and against the backdrop of, the mother and daughter's peals of laughter, like drops of rain falling on the wasteland, over their inability to communicate. Their lack of communication is resolved in a true communion of the souls. The theology of the oppressed is hence enacted both in terms of the mother's reliance on Kuan-yin Pu-sa and in terms of the daughter's similar appeal to that deity and to her mother, now a goddess of sorts, immortalized by the artistry of the radio play.

The tense triangular relationship of alien story, Asian American teller, and American market is epitomized in the "ethnographic feminism" in Kingston, Tan, and Roberts. That relationship is highly problematic and Orientalist in Kingston. With Tan, the Asian Other turns so innocuous and "good" that that image may saturate the collective consciousness of the American public more effortlessly than Kingston's pugnacious one. "Secret senses" exchanged between two women, Olivia and Kwan, are after all more enticing and less intimidating than woman warriors' fragmenting stories. Roberts appears to have sustained a creative and potentially egalitarian tension among the three forces in her radio production. Implicit in such complex interfaces, however, are a host of pending issues: alien in relation to American identity, ethnic-specific or mainstreaming positionality, and male as opposed to female subjectivity, among others. But the evolution of Asian American literature within the context of contemporary American culture points toward a less embattled and divisive milieu regarding these points of contention, in part due to the globalization of economy and its impact on how one perceives the other. Another encouraging sign is that this fin-de-siècle of ours has witnessed the coming of age of Asian American literature, one of the fastest-growing ethnic literatures, evident from the stream of Asian American anthologies, fictions, plays, poetry, films, and works in other genres. The amazing outburst of creativity from this traditionally silenced group is long overdue. Exactly because of their increasing standing, it is incumbent upon Asian Americans to engage in a conscientious self-critique on the problematics of canonization and commercialization.

TWO

Orientalism in Chinese American Discourse: Body and Pidgin

Edward Said in his *Orientalism* (1978) offers a sweeping panorama of how Western scholarship treated the area of the Near East—the Arab world. Orientalism is described by Said as a means for the West to grasp and domesticate the Other; it refers to one culture's attempt to control the other by fashioning it, a malleable object, according to one's own imaginings. Metaphorically cast as a white gaze at the nonwhite object, Orientalism distorts within its field of vision whatever that is inconsistent with its scheme of things.[1] Indeed as Michel Foucault explains, knowledge becomes in the case of Orientalism a vehicle of power to manipulate a novel and frustratingly impenetrable part of the world. Just as a network of power relations lies at the core of Foucault's analyses of various institutions and human knowledge, Said employs the same methodology to expose the relationship of domination inherent in the corpus of Western learning we have come to call "Orientalism."

There exists, of course, "the other" Orientalism on the "Far East," which Said acknowledges but refrains from discussing, for that area falls outside the purview of his book. In addition, Said seldom ventures to study the impact of Orientalism on "the Orient," nor on Asian minorities living in the West. This lack is justified by Said as he narrowly defines Orientalism as "a field of [Western] learned study" (49). This chapter will try to extend Said's work on Orientalism by examining a subtle variation of the Orientalizing tendency in Chinese American discourse. I wish to discover how cultural representations of the other Orient—the Far East—has infiltrated every segment of the American society, specifically amongst Chinese Americans themselves.

Simply put, Chinese Americans frequently take on the white gaze at their nonwhite object. Depicted as born and brought up in the United States, many Chinese American characters in fiction internalize, as do Jewish anti-Semites explicated in Sander Gilman's *Jewish Self-Hatred* (1986), the Orientalist cultural assumptions, which obliterate the differences between Chinese and themselves. Considering themselves, thus, inferior or nonmainstream, many seek to assimilate by adopting the white gaze and by projecting onto China and Chinese immigrants Orientalist—often racist—stereotypes. By so doing, they separate themselves from what thcy deem to be the *true* Other, China and Chinese immigrants, creating the impression that they could identify with mainstream America. Therefore, a large number of texts in Chinese American discourse Orientalize China, its immigrants to the United States, and ultimately American-born Chinese. This divorcing of oneself from one's ethnicity bespeaks a disguised self-hatred.[2]

To borrow Foucault's example from *Discipline and Punish* (1977), while an inmate in J. Bentham's notion of a Panopticon prison becomes "the object of information, never a subject in communication" (200),[3] Chinese Americans reverse their confining, Orientalized roles from the object of cultural practices to the subject supposedly operating these practices. They aim to empower themselves as practitioners rather than recipients of these cultural assumptions. This transformation of the self is, however, an illusion; Chinese Americans are in fact enmeshed even more deeply in the network of power once they try to elevate themselves in this manner. Their effort not only exposes their self-hatred but considerably damages the Other—China and Chinese.

A second reason for Orientalization is that a number of Chinese American writers deliberately employ the Orientalist view in order to debunk it. A strategic maneuveur, this reaction against the hegemonic culture is self-empowering rather than self-loathing. This self-affirming act, however, is tinged with ambiguity. Being products of the West themselves and raised on twentieth-century American popular culture, Chinese Americans frequently conceive of China in the Orientalist way. The very terms they use in defining themselves descend partly from the colonial discourse. Maxine Hong Kingston coins the phrase "talk-story" to justify her exotic reveries. Her phrase bears strong resemblance to pidgin English; her stories smack of the white gaze through "yellow" eyes. David Henry Hwang is obliged to feature in the bulk of *M. Butterfly* (1986) the dainty Madame Butterfly with all the trappings of Orientalism before he can put in his spin in the last scene. In using pidgin English and in smashing the myth of Oriental woman, these writers try to create their own ethnic identity. But this in-between status involves an excruciating dilemma: their unique Americanness derives in large measure from a resistance to the Orientalist discourse, which in turn presupposes an acknowledgement and even an internalization of the vocabulary of Western constructions of themselves.

This simultaneous disavowal and embracing of one's otherness can be found in the preface to *Aiiieeeee!: An Anthology of Asian American Writers* (1974), one of the earliest attempts to define Asian America. The four editors of this anthology, Frank Chin included, testify with one voice that to Asian Americans, China and Japan come from "the radio, off the silver screen, from television, out of comic books, from the pushers of white American culture that pictured the yellow man as something that when wounded, sad, or angry, or swearing, or wondering whined, shouted, or screamed 'aiiieeeee!'" (xii). The choice of "aiiieeeee!" as the title of the collection shows the editors' effort to secure power from a cry of powerlessness. But this power relation buys into the essentialism of race based on the color of the skin ("white culture" versus "yellow man"), the stereotype of the other as the perennial victim reduced to primal emotions, and, lastly, to the linguistic Orientalism of a scream (and perhaps a pain) unintelligible to the West. Among other things, this manifesto exposes the essentialism of the body and the linguistic reductionism the editors have implicitly accepted.

For the focus on body and language in my analysis of the preceding citation as well as of this entire chapter, I am greatly indebted to Sander Gilman's *The Jew's Body* (1991). Gilman explains in his "Preface: The Fall of the Wall":

> Thus I am not speaking here about "realities" but about their representations and the reflection of these representations in the world of those who stereotype as well as those who are stereotyped. In this volume I am not interested in determin-

> ing the line between "real" and "fabled" aspects of the Jew. This can be done only by ignoring the fact that all aspects of the Jew, whether real or imagined, are the locus of difference. (1–2)

To apply the same strategy to the study of Orientalism, it is thus not my concern that whether Chinese immigrants' bodies are always crooked and disgusting, whether their English is always garbled pidgin (for the answer is clear); rather, I inquire into the intentionality of manufacturing and magnifying these assumed physical and linguistic differences. For in Chinese American discourse, the Chinese body and pidgin English are often taken to be the indicators of the Oriental's alienness and at times degeneracy. By demarcating themselves from this foreign group, Chinese Americans empower themselves, albeit in an ambiguous manner. As a result, the act of divorcing from the Chinese body and pidgin English is repeatedly followed by or coexists with an opposite act of wedding, of priding oneself in one's physical features and Creole heritage, an ambivalent move to consolidate the Chinese American sense of identity.

In *The Jew's Body*, Gilman almost entirely ignores the female body, a choice in gender attributed to what he sees as the simple fact that "the male Jew, the body with the circumcised penis . . . lies at the very heart of Western Jew-hatred" (5). Such an approach resembles Foucault's in *The History of Sexuality* (1978) in terms of subsuming gender differences into cultural, class, or other supposedly larger schemes, for which Foucault has been severely criticized by feminists.[4] To explore Orientalism in Chinese American discourse, however, one does not have the luxury of overlooking gender. A case in point is David Henry Hwang's 1979 play *FOB*, in which he casts FOBs (Chinese immigrants Fresh Off the Boat) as:

> Clumsy, ugly, greasy FOB. Loud, stupid, four-eyed FOB. Big feet. Horny. . . . High-water pants. . . . Someone you wouldn't want your sister to marry. If you are a sister, someone you wouldn't want to marry. . . . They are the sworn enemies of all ABC—oh, that's "American Born Chinese"—of all ABC girls. (6)

Characteristically, as in most Chinese American texts when the topic is the Chinese, Hwang opens with a physical depiction of the uncouth immigrants, who are likened to merchandise recently unloaded and whose full humanity is called into question. Moreover, though by no means pidgin English, the use of acronyms indicates a willingness to push beyond the linguistic horizon. Steve, an FOB in the play, embodies this bent most visibly in his pidgin conversation with the ABC Dale. Pidgin is a language that alienates in and of itself. Hwang has given vent to a paradoxical obsession in Chinese American discourse: A Chinese American playwright exhibits his alleged power in image-making, in Orientalizing Chinese physically and linguistically, while both the image and the power are perpetuated by Orientalism against people like himself in the first place.

Most significantly, both corporal and dialectal deformities serve to bring out FOBs' imagined lust and to caution ABC women against them. This charge of FOBs' lecherousness in fact reflects ABCs' anxiety over their own masculinity. The Orientalist assumptions imposed upon Steve the FOB only expose the insecurity of manhood plaguing Dale the ABC. Orientalism, in other words, is inextricably entwined with gender; it is predicated on a gender dialectic. Both Orientalism and gender politics grow out of the same infrastructure of power which casts the dominated, either the East or the woman, either Steve the alien or Dale the alienated, in the role of the "weaker" sex.[5] Clearly, Chinese American writers are compelled to react toward this ideology which effeminizes and enfeebles them. Yet their response to hegemonic Orientalism is complicated by skirmishes against each other—the other sex in the Chinese American literary scene—in the form of sabotaging or espousing feminism. For instance, both writers examined herein, Frank Chin and Maxine Hong Kingston, take not only Orientalism but each other to task. Chin accuses Asian American feminists of contributing to the gelding of Asian American men; Kingston condemns the misogynist Asian tradition inherited by most Asian American men in her fiction. A war between the sexes is waged perhaps more fiercely than the war against Orientalism.

Yet to understand the Orientalization of the Chinese body and pidgin English in Chinese American discourse, one needs to search for the fountainhead of this phenomenon—the Western image of Chinese. Despite the immense output of Asian American female writers, most critical works in this area do not begin from feminist theories, and they tend to investigate the male rather than the female body. Elaine Kim's "Images of Asians in Anglo-American literature," the opening chapter to her *Asian American Literature: An Introduction to the Writings and Their Social Context* (1982), serves as an enlightening guide.[6] Kim amasses an amazing amount of materials, through which the openly vicious or the thinly veiled racism of both low-brow and high-brow Anglo-American writers is exposed. She discovers that two archetypes dominate the image of Chinese males: Fu Manchu, created by Sax Rohmer; and Charlie Chan, developed by Earl Derr Biggers. The former epitomizes the "bad" Chinese, who in public imagination is multiplied into "the sinister villains and brute hordes," only to be destroyed by the West. The latter represents the "good" Chinese, who often metamorphoses into "the helpless heathens to be saved by Anglo heroes or the loyal and lovable allies, sidekicks, and servants" (4). The simplistic cartoon stereotypes of good and evil fulfill the need of the West to define itself as a superior force in relation to China, thought to be backward, ignorant, and unredeemable.

Kim also asserts that broken, hilarious pidgin English is an important feature in Anglo-American representation of the alien Chinese. Often a source of comedy, pidgin English is characterized by "high-pitched, sing-song tones, tortured syntax, the confounding of *l*'s and *r*'s, the proliferation of *ee*-endings, and the random omission of articles and auxiliary verbs" (12). Chinese American discourse adopts the same strategy to imitate the speech of Chinese characters, usually for the same comical effect.

Frank Chin, considered by some as the "godfather" of Chinese American plays, dramatizes this distaste for the Chinese body and pidgin English. Chin and some like-minded writers have established the Combined Asian Resources Project (CARP) to promote Asian American literature. They have contributed admirably to the publication of many long-ignored works and to the formation of an Asian American canon (Kim's *Asian American Literature* 175). But this effort, at least in the case of Chin, originates in part from a dubiousness of identity illustrated above. In one of his letters to Frank Ching, the editor of *Bridge*, Chin states: "I'm not shunning immigrants. I'm stating a fact that I am not Chinese. I am not shunning Albinos, elephants, dwarves, and midgets either. But call me one and I'll just have to set you straight" (qtd. in Kim 176). This seems to be a starting point for the construction of Asian American consciousness as opposed to immigrants, with whom they are constantly being confused. But this self-empowerment entails immigrant-bashing, comparing immigrants to one animal and three groups of people, each marked by a specific physical handicap. Such aliens are then conceived as having a certain kind of corporal deformity as the locus of their difference. To distance himself and other

Asian Americans from immigrants is, to Chin, to avoid weaknesses intrinsic to the bodily makeup of that foreign group.

This phobia of debility is manifested as the anxiety over the male body in Chin's critical and creative works. Such a fear is certainly rooted in socioeconomic reality. As Amy Ling demonstrates in *Between Worlds: Women Writers of Chinese Ancestry* (1990), Chinese men have long been emasculated in the New World due to the professions they are allowed to enter: they "serve the white master through the demeaning work usually relegated to women—cooking, washing, and ironing" (145). In the same vein as Ling though with quite a different agenda in mind, Chin and other CARP members, militant and contentious, direct their attack against the castrating American culture. They first blast the stereotype of Charlie Chan as "the fat, inscrutable, flowery but flub-tongued effeminate little detective" "walking with 'the dainty step of a woman'" (Preface to *Aiiieeeee!* xvi). They further protest against the gelding of Chinese men, which is claimed to be caused not only by Anglo-American imaginings but by Asian American women's abandonment. To prove that Asian American manhood is being seriously challenged from within as well as from without, they cite reports that in 1972 "50 percent of Japanese American women were marrying outside their race" (xii–xiii). Indeed, the preservation of the "race" is presented as at stake. This criticism against Asian American women and their alleged betrayal has been sustained over the years, culminating in the fury over the commercial and critical success of Chinese American female writers, particularly Maxine Hong Kingston and Amy Tan, in the introduction to *The Big Aiiieeeee!: An Anthology of Chinese American and Japanese American Literature* (1989). The Asian American women's disloyalty is reiterated as recently as in the 1991 preface to the Mentor edition of *Aiiieeeee!* in which the editors rehash yet again the threat to Asian American masculinity from within that ethnic community: "In both Chinese American and Japanese American writing, by yellow male and female wordsmiths, yellow men are not sexually attractive to yellow women. The only Asian American writers to lay a few words in praise of yellow male sexuality are Eurasian women" (xl).

In Chin's own plays, the urgency of salvaging Asian American manhood finds expression in the male characters' torturous search for a father figure and the anxiety over their effeminate body. His *The Chickencoop Chinaman* (first produced in 1972) presents the filmmaker Tam(pax) Lum (note the female nickname) looking tirelessly for Charley Popcorn, the alleged Afro-American father of an ex-boxing champ, Ovaltine the Dancer, on whom Tam is producing a documentary. His pursuit brings him to the black ghetto of Pittsburgh, where his close friend Kenji the "BlackJap" buries his identity among another minority group. Charley runs a dilapidated porno movie house, a constant reminder of the decaying manliness of the Asian American characters.

Lee, a woman of mixed Chinese blood passing for white, accuses Tam and Kenji of being "chicken," "little vulnerable sea animals born with no shells of their own," "mama's boys and crybabies," "not a man in all your males" (24). The subtext of her reproach is, as decoded by Tam, that Chinese men are feminine. Lee's ex-husband is said to fail to fulfill Lee's "lesbian fantasies" (23). Lee also dares Tam to embrace her by taunting, "Come on, I'm just one of the boys" (25). Most revealingly, Tam and his double, Tom, a Chinese American who is possibly Robbie's father with Lee, dwell on the Orientalist stereotype:

TAM: What're ya talking about. What's bein Chinese gotta do with "homosexuality"?
TOM: In American eyes we don't appear as he-men types.
TAM: Oh, we look like queers!
TOM: Yeah.

While proceeding to deny this stereotype, Tam is clearly poisoned by it. To confirm his manhood, he seeks a father figure not only in Charley Popcorn but more directly in the old Chinese dishwasher. Telling the story of the dishwasher to Robbie, a Chinese American boy seeking a father in Tam, Tam betrays his own obsession with the Chinese body and its perceived lack of masculinity. Tam recalls with intense emotion the passing away of this dishwasher who wore underpants in his bath for fear of "white old ladies peeking at him through the keyhole" (16). The dishwasher's neurosis over his sexuality is inherited by Tam, who wears "boxer type swimming trunks" (15) to shower. In part to commemorate his symbolic father, Tam's unusual shower habit overcompensates for an alleged ethnic deficiency by subconsciously associating oneself with the macho activity of boxing, with which both the dishwasher and Tam are obsessed.

For Tam and Kenji, two Asian American men with low self-esteem who liken themselves to chickens, their relationship with women veils a hierarchy of power. Tam, feeling superior to Asian women, constructs the Hong Kong dream girl, with the body of a china doll and a sweet voice which parrots male fantasies. Dressed as a cheerleader (rooting for the male ego?), this stewardess's hands are said to "hold, not to speak of twirl a baton. Yessir, hands like greased smoothbore cannons" (6). With her body parts and voice cast in sexual metaphors, this Chinese woman is molded after the fantasies of submissive and exotic picture brides from the Orient.

On the other hand, feeling puny when with Western women, Kenji imagines the gigantic and overwhelmingly powerful body of a blonde:

> Aww, man, if I'm going to go to all the trouble of mind to get a white girl, man, she's going to be all white. And tall. And giant, huge tits man. And blonde. The scariest kind of white girl there is, man, none of this working my way up for me. Blonde hairs all over her head. Tall . . . and tits, man like when I walk up to her and get my little nose stuck in her navel, man, and I look up at her belly, I feel like I'm on the road with you and see two Giant Orange stands across the road from each other. (28)

Kenji, a shell-less sea animal, idolizes a larger-than-life blonde as a white goddess. This exposes the schizophrenia over the inferior Oriental body. Indeed, both Kenji and Tam once married white women, a subconscious choice to merge with an alleged source of power and to become assimilated into American society.

A more graphic dramatization of the Chinese body and pidgin English is found in Chin's *The Year of the Dragon*, first produced in 1974. This play is set in New York's Chinatown, where the family reunion of the Engs is about to take place on the eve of the Chinese New Year. Pa, the patriarch of the family, wishes to hold onto the old ways, whereas Sis, the daughter who married Ross, a Caucasian, and moved far away, represents the escape from one's ethnicity. Fred, the eldest son and a Chinatown tour guide, is somewhat torn between Pa's request that he stay and take over the reins of the family and Sis's invitation to flee to Boston with her. Due to his lack of courage, Fred remains in Chinatown after Pa's death and shows signs of Pa's corruption and possessiveness, but he does advise his younger brother Johnny to leave.

The Engs are presented as rather unsavory characters. Fred's body, for instance, is repulsive and his behavior vulgar and incomprehensible. In the first act, Fred returns from his tour and takes off his shoes according to the stage direction: "*Sits and takes off shoes and socks near* CHINA MAMA. *He holds up his feet for her to sniff, after he sniffs*" (79). This bizarre behavior with a distant allusion to foot-binding is repeated throughout the play, implying how archaic Fred's ideas are. Not only is he eccentric, but he is also libidinous. Toward their adopted mother who is an American of Chinese descent, both Fred and Johnny reveal an incestuous infatuation, in part showing their assimilationist urge:

FRED (*up and after* Ma): Last night I dreamed you were naked, ma. Your body was so . . .
JOHNNY (*overlapping* Fred): I dreamed I took off all your clothes by myself, ma. . . . (100)

The Orientalizing of characters will not be complete without Pa's pidgin English and his Charlie Chan "spitch." This tyrannical and absurd Pa speaks in a pidgin which alienates both through accent and through content: "I wanna talking allaw body in a room togedders up. When Johnny home, I essplan naysun family aww togedders up" and "Okay! No talking! (*Waits for calm*) I'm Pa. I been longtime Californ moses obba life. Den I know I die dis year obba Dragons. Tahm chenj. I gotta die Chinese" (87, 99). An absolutely estranging presence, Pa understands neither the English language nor the American lifestyle. His lingo even deteriorates, at the urging of Ross, to a faking of the fake Chinese, Charlie Chan, taking over not only the botched grammar but some familiar lines of the famous detective. With Pa's inevitable demise at the end of the play, the whole Chinatown culture seems outdated and moribund.

Frank Chin's concern over Asian American masculinity has somehow been intertwined with Maxine Hong Kingston's career. Feeling threatened by Kingston's and other female writers' message and success, Chin has launched frontal assaults against them, to which Kingston has responded with no less than the lengthy novel *Tripmaster Monkey: His Fake Book* (1989).[7] Amy Ling offers a firsthand account of the connection between the combative Chin, in real life, and Wittman Ah Sing, the character in *Tripmaster*. Ling writes that Kingston has admitted in a private conversation with her that Wittman is indeed inspired by Chin along with other men in Kingston's life (*Between Worlds* 149). Even without this admission, Kingston in *Tripmaster* is obviously satirizing Chin's stage alter egos, who are extreme and compulsive, as well as Chin's views, which are radical and divisive. But it would be unfair to attribute all the representations of the Chinese body and pidgin English in *Tripmaster* to Kingston's contempt for Chin. First of all, the generic differences between plays and novels allow Kingston in her fiction great leeway to explore the connotations of the body, achieving a more detailed and more loaded description than in Chin. Kingston's elaboration on her characters' physical attributes simply goes beyond its sketchy equivalent in Chin's dialogues and stage directions. Secondly, the Chinese body and the alien Cantonese dialect have long been a Kingston trademark. Rather than discovering these specific representations in Chin, Kingston actually recycles her own portrayal of Chinese and injects it with Chin's belligerent flavor. In sum, Kingston's depiction of body and pidgin is not a simple act of feminist vengeance against Chin; rather, she actively Orientalizes Chinese to establish Chinese Americans as a people apart and distinct from the alien immigrants.

The rendering of the bizarre Chinese behavior runs through Kingston's career. In *China Men* (1980), Ah Goong, the narrator's insane grandfather, used to display his penis on the dinner table, "shook his head and clucked his tongue at it," and worried that "this sausage" would not produce a daughter after four sons (21). Note that this perversion is brought out in terms exactly like Hwang's delineation of Steve the FOB and Chin's portrayal of Fred, Tam, and others. The Chinese body is presented as the locus of difference, concealing a depraved sexuality, enunciating disorienting sounds such as the clucking of the tongue. Kingston's manufactured memory of a faraway land heralds *Tripmaster*'s street scenes in San Francisco's Chinatown.

In addition to the debased Chinese body as in *China Men*, the marked physical differences between the emaciated, aging Chinese immigrants and the vivacious, confident Chinese Americans recur throughout *The Woman Warrior* (1976). Brave Orchid, the narrator's stubborn mother, is absolutely shocked when she observes from afar at the San Francisco airport her long-lost sister Moon Orchid, now an old and shriveled woman. Yet to Brave Orchid's Chinese American children, this aunt brings an added embarrassment to their already unpresentable immigrant family. In the airport, the children shamefacedly "slunk away" (136). In fact, "since they were babies," in order to escape from their parents, Brave Orchid's children "had burrowed little nests for themselves in closets and underneath stairs" (149). They wish to block out their parents from their life. Now with an even more neurotic Chinese aunt, the children reached the boiling point and "told each other in English": "[Moon Orchid's] driving me nuts!" (164). Finally, they declared: "Chinese people are very weird" (183), a clear denial of their background. Chinese American self-hatred comes through indirectly in these remarks. Moreover, their outburst is made in English, a language their parents are not well versed in but the only language they can competently use in communication, thus marking the chasm between the generations.

The gulf between Chinese and Chinese Americans is exposed even more poignantly during the confrontation between Moon Orchid and her husband after years of separation. Her husband is now a successful medical doctor practicing in the United States with his other Chinese American wife and the sisters pretend they are patients near his clinic.

> "What is it?" he asked. "What's wrong?" These women have such awful faces. "What is it, Grandmothers?"
>
> "Grandmother?" Brave Orchid shouted. "This is your wife. I am your sister-in-law."
>
> Moon Orchid started to whimper. Her husband looked at her. And recognized her. "You," he said. "What are you doing here?"
>
> But all she did was open and shut her mouth without any words coming out.
>
> "Why are you here?" he asked, eyes wide. Moon Orchid covered her face with one hand and motioned no with the other. (176)

A painful family reunion, the age gap between husband and wife may be due to the antiquated Chinese custom of marrying a young son with an older woman. This social explanation aside, the physical deterioration and helplessness of the Chinese woman contrast sharply with the assertiveness of the Chinese American man, a juxtaposition borne out not only through their opposite physical qualities but through the language they use. Moon Orchid is addressed as "grandmother" by her own husband. She can do nothing but utter the most rudimentary sounds of weeping. Finally, she censors herself from speaking out of shame. On the other hand, her husband demands an explanation over and over again, despite his own fault of abandoning the family in China.

Frequently, a Chinese American character, like the heartless medical doctor, would attempt self-cleansing by projecting self-hatred onto another person. For instance, the young narrator at the end of *The Woman Warrior* ruthlessly tortures a Chinese American classmate, the narrator's "alter ego . . . who represents the fragility and softness of the victim" (Kim's *Asian American Literature* 205).

> "You're going to talk," I said, . . .
>
> I reached up and took the fatty part of her cheek, not dough, but meat, between my thumb and finger. . . . "Talk," I said. "Are you going to talk?" Her skin was fleshy, like squid out of which the glassy blades of bones had been pulled. . . . Her skin seemed to stretch. I let go in horror. What if it came away in my hand. . . . I squeezed one cheek, then the other, back and forth until the tears ran out of her eyes. (204–6)

The fragile girl symbolizes all that is wrong with the narrator herself in accordance with the Orientalist stereotype: a soft and passive body, voiceless and will-less. Furthermore, the flesh of the other acquires an otherworldly, marine quality. The narrator has irrevocably internalized the Orientalist assumptions and therefore reacts violently toward a girl who, like a mirror, reflects what she perceives to be her own image.

Preceded and prepared by these earlier vignettes, the Chinese body and pidgin English receive the fullest treatment in Kingston's most recent novel *Tripmaster Monkey: His Fake Book*. In the first chapter, Wittman Ah Sing, a Berkeley graduate, a sixties angry young man and a word-drunk playwright-dreamer, observes a family of "uncool" immigrants:

> a Chinese dude . . . hands clasped behind, bow-legged, loose-seated, out on a stroll—that walk they do in kung fu movies. . . . Following, straggling, came the poor guy's wife. She was coaxing their kid with sunflower seeds, which she cracked with her gold tooth and held out to him. "Ho sick, la. Ho sick," she said. "Good eating. Good eats." . . . Mom and shamble-legged kid were each stuffed inside of about ten homemade sweaters. Their arms stuck out fatly. . . . Next there came scrabbling an old lady with a cane. . . . On Granny's head was a cap with a pompon that matched everybody's sweaters. The whole family taking a cheap outing on their day offu. Immigrants. Fresh Off the Boats out in public. (4–5)

A biting caricature, the immigrant's unwholesome body becomes the butt of mockery. It is repulsive with the bowed legs and gold tooth. Ridiculously clad in layers of sweater and a pompon to match, it neither moves nor behaves properly—it straggles or scrabbles rather than walks. Auditorily, from the semihuman body are uttered alien sounds—"Ho sick, la. Ho sick," as if a hen is calling her chicks. This Cantonese statement is then deliberately translated into awkward English "Good eating" "Good eats"—along with the pidgin "offu"—to heighten the foreignness of the immigrant object, to distance the perceiver who masters English from the immigrant who mangles it. Ultimately, Wittman deprives these immigrants of their full humanity in order to confirm his own differences, despite his similar physical characteristics to the Western undiscerning eyes.

Wittman's antagonism against "Orientals" continues unabated in this novel. An "embarrassingly short" Hong Kong man tells bawdy jokes to Americans in a party, while thumbing at a group of "pretty chicks" from Asia (58). On the bus, Wittman encounters a pushy Chinese woman with a "flat profile," who changes into a "blue boar" along the way, whose "tusks" flash as she speaks (74, 79). Wittman, painfully self-conscious, distorts Asians because he dreads being reminded of his otherness. This self-despising man would idealize only those women who appear to have crossed the racial barrier. When he woos Nanci Lee, for example, he worships this Berkeley beauty queen who could be "part Black or white Southern, Korean, Scotsman, anything—and also rich." More bluntly, Wittman muses that "she was no China Man the way he was China Man" (12). Wittman adores Nanci Lee for the false assumption that she is able to break away from the ethnic bondage. Yet even Nanci is stereotyped by her Oriental face in the film industry. Her make-up artist, Nanci confesses, once shrugged his shoulders in despair and commented: "There's just so much we can do about these eyes" (24).

As in Chin's plays, Kingston portrays the Chinese body as the source of Asian American self-hatred. Both Wittman and his Japanese American friend Lance, like Tam and Kenji in *The Chickencoop Chinaman*, are pathologically sensitive to the inadequacy of their physical attributes and compensate by marrying Caucasian women. A union with these white goddesses symbolizes one's being accepted by the American mainstream. Beyond aesthetic perfection and social approval, white women are, as in Chin, eroticized; Wittman is fascinated with his wife Taña's blonde hair: "He stroked her arm. The hairs stood up and moved back down. More so than the hair on her head, this light hair on the arms was to him Caucasian" (155). While Oriental femininity is associated with the hen-mother's repulsive gold tooth as well as the blue boar's sparkling tusks, Caucasian femininity is found in the attractiveness of the light blonde body hair.

Bearing out Asian Americans' simultaneous acceptance and disavowal of Orientalism, Kingston increasingly in *Tripmaster* employs a strategy of empowerment to attack Orientalist representations of the Chinese body and pidgin English. Consequently, counterpointing the derision of the immigrant's body at the beginning of the novel, Wittman proceeds to debunk the racist myth toward the end of this nearly four-hundred-page quasimonologue.

> "The full line," said Wittman, "is, 'Is it true what they say about Chinese girls' twats?' They think they're sideways, that they slant like eyes. As in *Chi*nese *Jap*anese *Koree*an." He put his fingers on the tails of his eyes, and pulled them up, "*Chi*nese," pulled them down, "*Jap*anese," pulled them sideways, "*Koree*an." . . . White men let little yellow men overhear that twat joke to make them littler and yellower. And they fuck over the women too. Kick ass, Wittman. "The King of Monkeys hereby announces: I'm crashing parties wherever these jokes are told, and I'm going to do some spoilsporting. Let me educate you, Mr. and Mrs. Potato Head, on what isn't funny." (317)

To undermine racial epithets based on the assumed physical differences of "Orientals," Wittman is forced to first repeat them. The distortion of eyes is coupled with a virulently sexist turn, namely, Asian women's vulvas are said to slant the same way their eyes do. The fascination with the exotic other moves from what is exposed to what is concealed, aligning both the seen and the unseen with racist misconceptions. But Wittman has ventured beyond Fred Eng's and Tam Lum's self-hatred in that he perceives the power relation inherent in Orientalism. He correctly diagnoses that such racial slurs as well as the invasion of Asian women's bodies by Caucasian males serve the purpose of making "little yellow men . . . littler and yellower."

In revolt, Wittman turns the physical stereotype around and slights the mainstream Americans as "Mr. and Mrs. Potato Head." As for the question of "are you *Chi*nese or *Jap*anese," he fumes over the naked bigotry, because the answer is expected to contain

> something obscene, something bodily. Some disgusting admission about our anatomy. About daikon legs and short waist or long waist, and that the twat goes sideways, slanting like her eyes. They want me to show them the Mongolian spot on my ass. They want to measure the length of my ape arms and compare them to Negers' arms. (317)

Wittman preempts the racist rhetorical strategies, cataloguing and resisting all the pejorative distortions of the Chinese body. Poised against such stereotypes, Wittman awakens Asian American consciousness by declaring the Asian American face as most perfect and by condemning those who undergo eyelid operations to have double-lidded eyes like Westerners. Wittman seeks to undo Orientalism from its foundation, calling for ethnic pride in one's body.

Chin and a number of Asian American male writers undoubtedly feel besieged both by Orientalist stereotypes and by feminism, which threaten to reduce them to the status of disenfranchised women. To restore their masculinity, they Orientalize Chinese to demonstrate their distinct Americanness, on the one hand, and they attack Asian American feminists, on the other. Similarly, Maxine Hong Kingston and other female writers, in the attempt to empower themselves, perpetuate the estranging Chinese body and pidgin English, and prosecute the misogynist, male-oriented Asian tradition. Juxtaposing the two Chinese American writers, this chapter has concentrated on the representation of the Chinese body, male or female, as an Orientalized, undesirable object. However, feminist theories, which, after all, should be partly anchored in Kingston's woman warriors, Tan's female-only joy luck club, and other female writers' texts, introduce troubling complications into this reading. For instance, how does the feminist critique of the female body as a desirable object arrested by the male gaze come into play? Do Chin's plays harbor so much male fantasy that they lend themselves more appropriately to a feminist than to an Orientalist approach? Is the body in Kingston's texts engendered more by its creator's gender than by Orientalism? To what extent should one elevate sexual politics within Chinese American discourse over cultural representations across racial boundaries as the most fruitful area for study? The intersection of Orientalism and feminism blurs the focus on body and language; Part 2 of this book, "Male Subjectivities through Eroticism," attempts to map out this largely uncharted crossroads.

THREE

Immigrant Schizophrenic in Asian Diaspora Literature

Though there is hardly any clinical evidence to demonstrate that immigrants are more prone to schizophrenia than either the population of their homeland or that of their adopted land, the representation of the Asian immigrant *as* schizophrenic and, oftentimes, schizophrenic suicide continues to proliferate. This peculiar bent of literary imagination is shared not only by Chinese, Japanese, and Indian diasporic writers but also by their Asian American counterparts. I select from the broad spectrum of writers implicated in such a representation four writers—Pai Hsien-yung, Nieh Hualing, Bharati Mukherjee, and Kazuo Ishiguro—who are all participants of Asian Diaspora, with Ishiguro as a child of Asian Diaspora. (I have discussed their Asian American counterparts elsewhere and will review briefly some examples.) The first three migrated to North America as somewhat established or at least committed writers, despite the difference that the two Chinese writers continue to create in their native tongue, whereas Mukherjee, a self-professed "Hindu Bengali Brahmin" (Carb 651), the Westernized elite of a postcolonial country, writes in English. Ishiguro arrived in England at the age of six with his Japanese family in what turned out to be a permanent sojourn. This Anglo-Japanese novelist has been considered part of the "New Internationalism" in British literature and regarded as "writ[ing] about their native lands or the immigrant experience from within the mainstream of British literature" (King 193). By the same token, Mukherjee occupies a central position in Asian (North) American literature. Pai and Nieh, on the other hand, enjoy tremendous prestige in Chinese-speaking areas but not in the United States, due to the language barrier posed by their fiction.

Those Asian American writers more squarely situated in the ethnic canon as well as American culture often opt for the identical formula of schizophrenic when it comes to the depiction of immigrants. Salient examples can be gleaned in leading Asian American writers. In Maxine Hong Kingston's *The Woman Warrior* (1976), Moon Orchid, a weak and traditonal woman ill-adapted to the New Land, winds up institutionalized. Even her headstrong elder sister, Brave Orchid, is so entrenched in her thinking that she appears to her Americanized children to be the opposite of her former self, a romanticized Kung Fu master cum barefoot doctor in China. To use Kingston's own language, she changes from a Fa Mu Lan in a mysterious Orient to a cranky laundress in San Francisco's Chinatown. The irreconcilably split personality associated with past glory and present shabbiness of immigrant mothers surfaces in Amy Tan's novels as well, except that Tan offers more space, the bulk of *The Kitchen God's Wife* (1991) practically, to the mothers to explain their incomprehensible actions and patterns of thought. Similarly, immigrant schizophrenics recur in Asian American male writers. John Okada's *No-No Boy* (1957) features a schizoid immigrant mother who commits suicide along with an alcoholic, self-destructing father. Frank Chin's Chinatown derelicts and their descendants, those castrated chicken-males, compel the theatergoers to suspect the integratedness of these characters' ethnic selves.

These Asian American and Asian Diaspora writers somehow are drawing from the same cliched notion that Asian immigrants and Americans of Asian extraction have "split personality" or "buried self." In its most vitriolic form of representation by whites, this strain of pop psychology casts Asian Americans as the "unassimilable aliens."[1] Such a motif repeats itself in Asian American writings as well and can be traced back to as early as, if not earlier than, Sui Sin Far (Edith Eaton) around the turn of the century. In "Leaves from the Mental Portfolio of an Eurasian," she confesses to her readers: "I do not confide in my father and mother. They would not understand. How could they? He is English, she is Chinese. I am different to both of them—a stranger, tho their own child" (222). This public confession, which privileges the English-speaking side of her heritage, seeks to compensate for the lack of a private one, but it remains doubtful whether the writer is any less a stranger to her readers.

Some Asian American critics have in fact seriously studied this phenomenon of a divided self. Sau-ling Cynthia Wong's immensely important chapter "Encounters with the Racial Shadow" first sketches the history of Western scholarship on "the double, variously known as the alter ego, the shadow, the Doppelgänger, the second self, the anti-self, the opposing self, the secret self" (*Reading Asian American Literature* 77). Wong then reads the recurrence of the racial shadow in Asian American literature against this history. In this erudite and densely written essay, Wong makes the tactical decision to "exclude cases of so-called split, dual, or multiple personality" in order to make her project "manageable" (80). As a consequence, she focuses on "the *spatial* coexistence of selves (whether 'real' or 'imagined') in the double" rather than "the *temporal* alternation of the split personality" (80). A legitimate move, Wong's strategy, nevertheless, leads to a theoretical framework superbly suited to an analysis of U.S.-born Asian American characters, as her primary example is drawn from Maxine in the schoolyard torture episode of Kingston's "A Song for a Barbarian Reed Pipe," complemented by other Asian American characters such as in Monica Sone's *Nisei Daughter* (1953), Lonny Kaneko's "The Shoyu Kid" (1976), and David Henry Hwang's *FOB* (1979). When it comes to immigrant characters, Wong's paradigm falls short, for immigrants constantly stand for the reprehensible Other in Asian American texts and Wong's model does not lend itself to an examination of, so to speak, *the double of the double.* In fact, she summarily dismisses any likely fisson in the double—immigrant characters. "We might note that it is the American-born Maxine who is troubled by an alter ego," comments Wong, "the psyche of her immigrant mother remains relatively intact, despite a trying physical existence" (91). As I have argued elsewhere, to suggest Brave Orchid possesses a "relatively intact" and reasonably integrated personality is to ignore the abundant evidence pointing to Kingston's representation of her and other immigrant characters, such as Moon Orchid and the scholar-turned-laundryman father, as latent schizophrenics with splintered lives. Calling all the writers to whom she refers, with the exception of Sone, "beneficiaries of the Asian American consciousness movement of the 1960s," Wong believes that they have "learned to be suspicious of both the rhetoric of ethnic split ('best of both worlds') and ethnic schizophrenia ('torn between two cultures')" (111). The prevailing minority ethos of distrust of majority values notwithstanding, this volume seeks to demonstrate that the schemata of ethnic schizophrenia persists in Asian Diaspora texts, which may or may not have been influenced by the 1960s. Yet to separate "canonical" Asian American writers from their Asian Diasporic colleagues in terms of the former's higher sensitivity to the pitfalls of ethnic stereotypes simply overlooks the discursive infrastructure of ethnic schizophrenia in Kingston and other Asian American writers.

Wong may be quite sagacious not to bring the issue of schizophrenia to bear on the immigrant dilemma, a juxtaposition offensive to many in the minority community. But the term "immmigrant schizophrenic" renders explicit what is already implicit in literary imagination; it also brings to the fore some stunningly uncanny connections between psychiatric studies on schizophrenics and the immigrant condition. It is far from the intention of this book to investigate psychiatry at great length. As Louis A. Sass aptly describes in *Madness and Modernism: Insanity in the Light of Modern Art, Literature, and Thought* (1992), "[t]he history of modern psychiatry is, in fact, practically synonymous with the history of schizophrenia, the quintessential form of madness in our time" (13), and it is beyond my capability to conduct such a study. Similar to A. Alvarez's assertion, "[t]he more technical research I read, the more convinced I became that the best I could do would be to look at suicide from the perspective of literature to see how and why it colours the imaginative world of creative people" (Preface 13). My subject likewise is to investigate this persistent trope of immigrant as schizophrenic in Asian Diaspora literature.

Any discussion on schizophrenia has to, at some point, consult R. D. Laing's classic definition:

> The term schizoid refers to an individual the totality of whose experience is split in two main ways: in the first place, there is a rent in his relation with his world and, in the second, there is a disruption of his relation with himself. Such a person is not able to experience himself "together with" others or "at home in" the world but, on the contrary, he experiences himself in despairing aloneness and isolation; moreover, he does not experience himself as a complete person but rather as 'split' in various ways, perhaps as a mind more or less tenuously linked to a body, as two or more selves, and so on. (*The Divided Self* 15)

"Peter," Laing's schizophrenic patient, labels the separation from the world disconnection and the separation from the self uncoupling. These two rifts in the mind of the schizophrenic are defense mechanisms against a world too hard to bear. With immigrants, they cease to be *mental reactions* to external reality, but the reality itself. Immigrants are constantly separated, in space, from their loved ones and, in time, from their memories of the past (self). The present strange world as well as their former existence lay a siege against immigrants in Asian Diaspora literature, resulting in their schizophrenic tendency. It is almost eerie to note that as Laing's patients try to depict their mental state figuratively, that self-description turns out to be the exact immigrant condition—literally.

"Meeting you [the physician] made me feel like a traveler who's been lost in a land where no one speaks his language," quotes Laing from his patient "Joan." "Worst of all, the traveler doesn't even know where he should be going. He feels completely lost and helpless and alone. Then, suddenly, he meets a stranger who can speak English" (178). A metaphorical linguistic maze used by Joan to portray her state is in fact the experience of many immigrant schizophrenics in the texts, who *should* have difficulty expressing themselves in English. I use the subjunctive mood because all four writers under study fail miserably in sketching the linguistic web entrapping immigrants, a shared flaw to be revisited at the close of this chapter. Suffice to note, for the moment, that even Joan articulates what is supposedly an inarticulate and inarticulable situation. Herein perhaps lies the ultimate paradox of language, whose service we require even when we try to capture what is fundamentally beyond language.

Before proceeding any further in associating certain immigrant characters with schizophrenia, the reservations of Laing and others in labeling someone schizophrenic should be taken to heart, especially to call attention to the implications of this motif in Asian Diaspora literature. Laing cautions in *The Politics of Experience* (1967) that schizophrenia is a political construct:

> There is no such 'condition' as 'schizophrenia,' but the label is a social fact and the social fact a *political event*. This political event, occurring in the civic order of society, imposes definitions and consequences on the labeled person. (83–84)

Laing redefines schizophrenia not as a disease of which to be cured but as a normal response to a world of alienation and madness. This reconceptualization culminates in the conclusion of the essay "The Schizophrenic Experience," where Laing urges reading into this term "its etymological meaning: *schiz*—'broken'; *phrenos*—'soul' or 'heart'" (90)—a compassionate ending consistent with Laing's writings and a fitting portrayal of immigrant schizophrenics' shattered lives.

This chapter, therefore, tries to rehabilitate the metaphor of schizophrenia in ethnic studies without being weighed down by its "baggage"—the stigmatization of mental disorder. To advance an argument on such a precarious theoretical position, one must realize that to label someone else schizophrenic entails the assumption of a well-integrated personality of that labeling subject, which is in itself a political act. No one is without some clefts in consciousness. Such clefts oftentimes become salient or even are made to stand for one's entire identity as a result of imbalance of power between those who diagnose disease and those who are diagnosed as having disease, which in turn justifies social control. Moreover, in view of the preceding contrast between immigrants' and schizophrenics' sense of alienation, it should give one pause to use the term *schizophrenia* in the portrayal of ethnic characters in any way other than as a metaphor. Even though all four writers depict characters who are literally insane, that insanity is to be taken by readers as a trope for the immigrant condition and in no way reflects the actual state of mind of every immigrant in real life.

The stigmatization of schizophrenia is also attacked in other scientific research. Sue E. Estroff makes the observation that schizophrenia belongs to what she calls "I am" illness, including "epilepsy, diabetes, alcoholism, hemophilia" (256), as opposed to "I have" illness, such as arthritis and multiple sclerosis. The "I am" illnesses are "more stigmatized" and carry more blame for the patient than the "I have" illnesses (257), as a result of

> Western notions of the nature of schizophrenia (and perhaps other chronic, debilitating conditions) combine[d] with Western notions of the self and identity to produce "I am" Illnesses, a fusion of self with sickness, of diagnosis with identity—in *consequence*, chronicity. (257)

To be an immigrant schizophrenic doubles the sense of taboo and blame. An immigrant says: "I am an immigrant," which is one's unenviable identity, only to have it eroded irreparably if one is forced to confess: "I am an immigrant schizophrenic."

His shrew and passionate analysis of schizophrenia notwithstanding, Laing has never addressed the immigrant issue directly. How valid are his views when applied to *immigrant* schizophrenics? Fortunately, Laing's critiques of the mainstream on behalf of the marginalized are preceded by another psychiatrist who happens to be an exile in France and Algeria in the midst of decolonization—Frantz Fanon. Unlike Laing, Fanon has firsthand experiences of being caught in the crossfire of races and cultures from the vantage point of the disempowered minority. In his introduction to *Black Skin, White Mask* (1967), Fanon announces that he aims to demolish the "massive psychoexistential complex" created by "the juxtaposition of the white and black races." He hopes "by analyzing it to destroy it." Conceding that many "Negroes" and many whites may not experience such a problem, Fanon immediately follows with a typical touch of poetry: "But the fact that I feel a foreigner in the worlds of the schizophrenic or the sexual cripple in no way diminishes their reality" (12). At first blush, the shift of tone of voice from scientific discourse to poeticality is difficult to follow, but Fanon's claim that the majority's incomprehension of a mad world does not lessen the reality of madness for the inflicted few seems plain enough. It is uncanny with respect to the project at hand that Fanon would use a phrase such as "the schizophrenic or the sexual cripple" to describe cases of black psychosis, for while the splitting of the self between "the fact of blackness" and the urge to be white causes schizophrenia, frequently manifesting itself sexually, the whole description fits the immigrant schizophrenic impeccably. After all, Asian immigrant schizophrenics are literally, from their own standpoint, "foreigner[s] in the worlds of the schizophrenic or the sexual cripple," a Western world both disorienting and, in the words of John Fowles's *The French Lieutenant's Woman* (1969), "highly-sexed." It is not the immigrant but the New World which seems to be deranged, where everyone appears to be either a psychotic or a sexual pervert or both. But is not that intoxicating novelty, with its concomitant material well-being, personal freedom, and sexual emancipation, part of the appeal which first attracted immigrants to these shores? Hence, their own pursuit of happiness brings on the disintegration of the self, aggravating the sense of self-blame.

A discursive thread running through the gradual decline of immigrant schizophrenics is that the narrative routinely begins with a semivoluntary fleeing from the confines of the old, only to terminate in cultural alienation and sexual perversity in the new, best illustrated by Pai and Nieh's works from the 1960s and 1970s. Even when acculturation is apparently achieved, as it is by Ishiguro's immigrant mother in *A Pale View of Hills* (1982), past sin returns to create a schism in her consciousness, compounded by the suicide of her immigrant daughter, the victim of her failings as a mother. Prior to suicide, or, in Mukherjee's *Wife* (1975) and *Jasmine* (1989), homicide, characters exhibit classic schizophrenic symptoms of a skewed perception of the external world and of themselves, one marked by microscopic and macabre details signifying a fracturing psyche on the verge of self-annihilation.[2]

The Ambivalence of Fleeing; The Entrapment in Alienation and Sexuality

> *Without the threat of punishment, there is no joy in flight.*
>
> —*Kobo Abe, The Woman in the Dunes*

The epigraph suggests that to artists probing into human experiences, the darker recesses of the mind can be accessed only by those who venture out of the boundary of security—in this case, by immigrants. In a rather romantic vein, the possibility of losing oneself in an alien land renders the departure risky, ambivalent, and so much more exhilarating. The leave-taking in Pai Hsien-yung and Nieh Hua-ling is also ambiguous due to the larger context. As spokespersons for an entire generation of overseas Taiwanese Chinese students, they represent the cold war exodus of young men and women from the third world to the Metropolitan West. For many, it might not be a conscious decision but an unconsicous following of the crowd. This movement away from "Chineseness" and into the West ironically coexists with or even amplifies a Chinese ethnocentrism, which lies at the heart of their fiction as well as of Chinese readers' warm reception of them. As a consequence, characters' physical departure from Chineseness is presented as a reaffirmation of some inalienable Chineseness. When they come to the agonizing realization that the core of their being—some Chineseness—is beyond retrieval in a foreign land, their mental state regresses visibly.

Both Pai and Nieh are champions of the *Liu-shueh-shen wenshueh* (overseas student literature) which arose in Taiwan in the

1960s. Born in China and fled to Taiwan after the Communist takeover, they were already established writers by the time they moved to the United States. In his short stories, written between the mid- and the late-1960s and set in Chicago and New York,[3] Pai Hsien-yung describes almost exclusively overseas Taiwanese Chinese students—how their dreams turn to nightmares in the dystopia of the United States and how they become rootless souls adrift in an alien land. Disillusionment sets in as a result of the rude awakening to one's alienation from the Chinese roots and the defamiliarization of the American setting. The losing of Chinese roots is conspicuous in terms of the physical distance from home, the death of family members, and, ultimately, the protagonists' own demise.

Initially, suicides in Pai as well as in many other Asian Diaspora texts appear to belong to what Emile Durkheim categorizes as "anomic" suicides in his *Suicide: A Study in Sociology* (1898). A. Alvarez uses literary analogies ingeniously to distinguish the three types of suicides in Durkheim: "Egoistic and altruistic suicide differ much as the world of *Catch 22* differs from that of the *Kamakaze* pilots. Beyond them is the anomie of, say, Kafka's *Metamorphosis*" (115). Alvarez characterizes anomic suicide as "the result of a change in a man's social position so sudden that he is unable to cope with his new situation. . . . He kills himself because, for better or for worse, his accustomed world has been destroyed and he is lost" (114). Durkheim limits his analysis of social causes of anomic suicide to a sudden change of fate, such as the loss of fortune. Somewhat contrary to Durkheim's definition, these deaths in Pai come on the heels of modest achievement by immigrants, hence further underscoring characters' deep ethnocentric yearnings despite the change of fate for the better. In other words, anomic suicide alone fails to explain fully these deaths; egotistic and altruistic tendencies are locked in battle as the suicides realize their ambitions at the expense of the integrity of their "Chineseness."

"Death in Chicago" (1964) portrays Wu Han-hun, whose first name puns with "Chinese Soul," taking his life soon after obtaining a Ph.D. in English literature at the University of Chicago—surely an enviable attainment by any standard. At the juncture of earning his doctorate, he learns that his mother has died, and he recalls with infinite sadness his only girlfriend who married someone else after having waited for him for three years. In total dejection, Wu drowns himself in Lake Michigan. In "The Tale of a Fallen Angel" (1965), Li Tang, nicknamed "China" by the other three upper-class women going abroad together, commits suicide during a trip to Venice.[4] Her death is similarly foreshadowed by the loss of family and its fortune as a result of the Communist takeover. To these immigrants, the very things which bring pride remind them of how much they have lost. Material comfort comes to equal materialistic greed; Americanized sophistication exudes depravity.

Indeed, immigrant characters' downfall is foreshadowed by their sexual corruption. When the new Ph.D. in "Death in Chicago" begins to see his apartment in the basement as a tomb and his books as corpses, Wu flees by venturing into the other side of Chicago and of himself which he has never visited—an overnight journey to nightclub, alcohol, black jazz singer, androgenous dancers, and Laura the prostitute. Far from offering the emasculated Wu sexual pleasure and validating his manhood, Laura turns out to be, literally, the grotesque of a woman:

> Under brighter light, Wu Han-hun realizes that Laura's shoulders exposed outside her white slip resemble layers of folds on the surface of milk. Laura turns around and switches off her fire-red wig. Pressed tightly underneath is her scraggly, hemp-like hair. (235; translation mine unless otherwise noted)

The dark soul of America echoes his buried sexuality. As Chicago, "an Egyptian sarcophagus," corrodes millions of "the living and the dead" (238), Wu takes his own life as well. Another type of promiscuity is found in the student turned bar girl, Huang Feng-yi, in "Lamentation on a Fallen Angel" (1969). Huang first describes in the correspondence to her mother in Taiwan her carefree life in New York. The latter half of the story portrays Huang's profession. Dubbed a "Mongolian princess," she flirts with a customer, calling herself "a vampire" while sipping a bloody Mary (325–26). These falls from originary innocence seem to diverge based on the character's gender: males are castrated, females so emancipated as to appear degenerate and monstrous.

As Pai's stories are too short to offer sustained depiction of immigrant schizophrenic, one turns to Nieh's *Sang-ching yu tao-hong* (Mulberry and Peach: Two women of China or Mulberry Green and Peach Red 1976), where the ethnocentric protagonist's faculty gradually dwindles, accompanied by her drifting away from Chineseness. The story is fragmentary and allegorical, weaving together certain historic moments in modern China. Part 1 depicts the protagonist, Mulberry Green, along with a number of other passengers stranded in a ferryboat on the Yangtze River en route to *Ta-hou-fang* (the Great Interior) in southwest China to join the anti-Japanese war effort. Part 2 focuses on Mulberry Green and her husband Shen Chia-kang returning to Peiping (Beijing) during the brief interval between Japan's defeat in 1945 and the Communist takeover of mainland China in 1949. Part 3 portrays the Shens, having retreated to Taiwan with the Nationalists, hiding with their eight-year-old daughter in an attic to escape police detection due to the husband's crime of embezzlement. Inserted into every part is Peach Red's—Mulberry Green's schizophrenic other—interview with and letters to the officers of the U.S. Immigration and Naturalization Services.

Professing in an interview that she is "more obssessed and involved with the Chinese" now she is physically away from China at the University of Iowa, Nieh sees the protagonist of her novel as exhibiting the "split personality" of twentieth-century Chinese (Nazareth 11). This tendency of pathologizing expatriate Chinese is of course intrinsic in C. T. Hsia's infamous coinage of "obsession with China" in describing modern Chinese writers, since whoever is obsessed with a particular time and place would heed the immediate surrounding only tangentially. Nieh merely takes this alleged dissonance to its extreme end—schizophrenia. It is interesting that all those theorizing and practicing this "obsession with China" appear to transform what is usually regarded as pathology into a laudable trait, one that testifies to an unremitting devotion to "Chineseness." Schizophrenia undergoes a thorough romanticization in such an immigrant text manufacturing Chineseness as Nieh's. Peach Red's censoring of Mulberry Green, her Chinese self, serves paradoxically to highlight what she attempts to erase.

This "obsession with China" manifests itself in Peach Red's subconscious attempt to acknowledge her previous self by sending the INS officer Mulberry Green's diary entries from 1945 through 1959 detailing the three pivotal events. While eluding the INS, Peach Red leaves a trail for the agency to follow, for the seemingly unattached Peach Red, traveling across the continent, yearns subliminally to be captured by the authority and hence reunited with her diasporic identity. This dual theme is borne out by the juxtaposition of the three parts on China and Taiwan with the stream of letters to the INS. The three parts on the ferryboat, the besieged Peiping, and the low attic deal with entrapment with a heightening level of bondage and paranoia, culminating in the schizophrenic present, a psychological rending now complete because of the total severance from Chinese soil. The young Mulberry Green with her vibrant companions on the boat are still able to enjoy themselves. Her future husband Shen Chia-kang, a fellow passenger, appears to be a gallant young man. The situation is enlivened especially by the down-to-earth presence of the ferryman and the Peach Flower Woman, both symbolizing the "primitive life force" of the Chinese (Nieh's foreword 3–4). In Peiping, the joy of family reunion is eclipsed by the moribund mother-in-law who heralds the disintegration of the old order through her illness as well as her deathbed refrain of "[t]he Nine Dragon Wall is falling down." In Taiwan's attic, the impending crisis unfolds in a claustrophobic atmosphere, turning the couple into a suspicious, hate-filled one in the course of the two-year hideout. The ailing Shen Chia-kang decomposes physically; Mulberry Green collects tabloid clippings on ghost and fugitive stories; the daughter crawls around in the low attic, prompting her mother to wonder whether she could stand straight and walk at all. This dehumanizing experience leads Peach Red to disown her previous self. Yet despite her carefree and brisk demeanor on U.S. highways, Peach Red clings desperately to the past.

In the prologue and four letters to the INS, the illegal alien Peach Red presents herself as retracing the American myth of mobility by moving incessantly from the East Coast to the West.[5] Though the American psyche seems invigorated by the movement and its concurrent oblivion to the European ancestry, Peach Red's sole reason for existence and motion is to suggest how astray she has become from her former Chinese identity. The sketchy delineation of Peach Red as opposed to the "thickness of description" devoted to Mulberry Green betrays the weightlessness of immigrant subjectivities in Nieh's mind. The immigrant self is assumed to be one of voidness, at once an escape from and a pursuit of "Chineseness." Nieh's ethnocentric view resulting in the lopsided presentation of the Chinese self and the immigrant other invalidates the possibility of fashioning a new immigrant identity anchored not in fixed locale and memories but in a series of ever-shifting subjectivities, something Leo Lee in "On the Margins of the Chinese Discourse" advances following his criticism of "the nihilistic mood" of *Mulberry and Peach*. Lee finds in Nieh's most recent novel *Chianshan wai shuichangliu* (Beyond the myriad mountains flows the river 1985) "a more affirmative tone" in moving beyond the depiction of exile as "utterly traumatic, dark, and without hope" (217).

Guilt, Repression, and Schizophrenia

Nieh's immigrant schizophrenic reappears in Kazuo Ishiguro's *A Pale View of Hills* (1982), the premier of a distinguished career which also includes *An Artist of the Floating World* (1986), *The Remains of the Day* (1989), and *The Unconsoled* (1995). The theme of guilt and repression runs through Ishiguro's novels. While all the protagonists seek to conceal the erroneous ways of their past—collaboration with the Japanese military during World War II, acquiescence to an anti-Semitic, Nazi-abetting employer, or emotional stunting due to a Butler's professionalism—only in *Hills* does the narrator seem unconscious of her distancing from the former self, rendering her a potential schizophrenic.

The narrator of *Hills*, Etsuko, tells of her friendship with Sachiko in war-torn Nagasaki. Like all the other Ishiguro narrators, she is unreliable, guarded about the past yet obsessively hinting at it. Etsuko's story, for instance, is fraught with inconsistencies pointing to the possibility that Sachiko is in fact Etsuko herself, and Mariko, Sachiko's weird daughter, is Keiko—Etsuko's daughter supposedly unborn then. Etsuko subsequently remarries a Mr. Sheringham and is widowed; the young and rebellious Niki is the daughter of this interracial marriage. The mystery of the identification of Etsuko and Sachiko is never fully resolved, masterfully sustained throughout by Ishiguro's understated and restrained style. Not far below the "surface quietness" of this novel ("The Novelist" 169) seethe pain and turmoil; Etsuko, after all, is compelled to confess to Niki about the past in the wake of Keiko's suicide, an immigrant herself, one who has been terribly neglected and abused since childhood by Sachiko-Etsuko. (For the sake of convenience, the ensuing discussion will use, whenever possible, "the mother" for Sachiko-Etsuko and "the daughter" for Mariko-Keiko.)

Consonant with the ambiguity of fleeing in Pai and Nieh, the mother tries to flee Nagasaki, a city in ruins, to the West, but she is conscious that she has to stoop low to achieve this. Akin to overseas student literature is the sexual indiscretion involved in the protagonist's ambivalent flight. Her hope hinges on an American soldier, Frank-san, a drunkard who, with the help of a saloon girl, squanders the mother's money for transportation to the United States. More revealingly, however, is Mariko's graphic description of Frank-san. In the novelist's typical style of refrain and crescendo, Mariko repeats, over the course of half a page, "Frank-san pisses like a pig. He's a pig in a sewer. . . . He drinks his own piss" (85), even as the mother glares and slaps the daughter. Such strikingly vulgar language so *a*typical of childhood and of Ishiguro's understated style reflects how the daughter has been immersed in a surrounding where she grows immune to sexual perversity. Indeed, Mariko may well be a victim of sexual abuse as a consequence of her mother's negligence. The mother literally abandons Mariko in pursuit of Frank-san in the city. Upon her return, Mariko has been defiled: "Mariko had been lying in a puddle and one side of her short dress was soaked in dark water. The blood was coming from a wound on the inside of her thigh" (41). The description of the source of blood is given vaguely, almost euphemistically, by Etsuko in an attempt to hide the horrible truth behind the blood stain and Sachiko's guilt—her own guilt.

The mother's sexual indiscretion and its devastating repercussions on the daughter are only part of the cause of her guilt. Textual evidence suggests that the mother's heartlessness gradually kills the daughter. Repeated images of the killing of the young in bombed-out Nagasaki—"child murders" (100), "little girl found hanging from a tree" (156), a woman's drowning of a baby (74)—pave the way for the mother's own drowning of Mariko's pets. Robbing Mariko of the only friends she has, this act becomes much more chilling because of its touch of "casual-ness":

> She put the kitten into the water and held it there. She remained like that for some moments, staring into the water, both hands beneath the surface. She was wearing a casual summer kimono, and the corners of each sleeve touched the water. (167)

The "surface quietness" in Ishiguro's writings resembles the surface calm of the water, with the only unseemly detail in the wet sleeve corners. But under the surface, a young life struggles in the stifling darkness. So does the young life above water, witnessing this execution. The daughter's complete lack of external empathy signals the dual layers of tranquillity and turbulence in Ishiguro's book.

> The little girl was standing at the top of the slope, watching with the same blank expression. On seeing her mother's face turn to her, she moved her head very slightly; then she remained quite still, her hands behind her back. (167)

A nonchalant pose, it harks back to her air of indifference as she foulmouths Frank-san and as she is found violated. The flatness of affect is adopted at an early age by this traumatized girl as a defense mechanism, a strategy she employs after being taken against her will to England. The daughter, now a young immigrant, completely shuts herself off, locking herself in her room, putting the laundry outside the door occasionally, leaving the family to live in Manchester by herself, and eventually hanging herself in a rented room. Knowing her daughter as well as she does—at least the outer trappings, the mother's "first thought" is to "wonder how long she had been there like that before they found her" (54). The mother's initial reaction proves how much she understands her daughter's alienation and how deeply she herself is implicated in creating that alienation.

Another recurring metaphor suggesting the mother's complicity in the suicide is the rope. Cognizant of what the mother is capable of doing, the daughter grows tense over any sign of threat from her. The first such reference to rope occurs when Etsuko's ankle is tangled by a piece of rope, which makes a "rustling noise as if a snake were sliding in the grass" (83), a sound so sinister in its association that Mariko runs away. The second time a rope emerges is toward the end of the story where the facade of separation between Etsuko and Sachiko is about to collapse. Etsuko's voice now assumes more of Sachiko's harshness and, once again, Mariko flees after repeatedly asking "Why are you holding that?" (173). At last, the noose the mother has symbolically bequeathed to the daughter encircles Keiko's neck in a room in Manchester.

Certainly not as ethnocentric as Nieh's double, Etsuko's elaborate scheme, nevertheless, originates from an urge to expiate past sin while preserving present serenity. Etsuko, hence, projects the disgrace of a fallen woman and the guilt of a failed mother onto Sachiko in order to protect her own image as a kind, conventional, and maternal Anglo-Japanese. This tactic is highly problematic, of course, judging from the final "punch line" which exposes the schizophrenic's charade. Reminiscing the outing to the neighboring hills of Nagasaki which the pregnant Etsuko allegedly took with Sachiko and Mariko, Etsuko says to Niki: "Keiko was happy that day. We rode on the cable-car. . . . No, there was nothing special about it. It's just a happy memory, that's all" (182). Either a slip of the tongue or a subconscious confession to the only family she has, Etsuko identifies Mariko with Keiko. But even if this were an admission of guilt, it is a selective, if not fabricated, moment of happiness to defuse her role in the suicide. Whereas the immigrant mother manages to remain self-deluded, the immigrant daughter takes her own life. To inquire into how the world collapses for a potential immigrant schizophrenic such as Keiko, Bharati Mukherjee's *Wife* (1975) offers a detailed case study.

Microscopic and Macabre Details; Suicide and Homicide

The representation of immigrant as schizophrenic finds its most complete trope in the characters' distorted vision of microscopic and macabre details of themselves and their world, leading to suicide or homicide. The defamiliarization inherent in such schizophrenic perception of the world echoes the famous artistic principle of Russian formalists. In describing the premonitions of schizophrenic attack, Louis A. Sass borrows from the techniques of defamiliarization advocated by Viktor Shklovsky, the leader of the Russian formalists:

> taking a very distant or else fragmentingly microscopic perspective on an object, avoiding standard causal/narrative schemas of meaning, and describing an object in terms of its mere existence or geometrical form (that is, by avoiding use of its name and suppressing all references to its usual functional role in human life). (63)

Shklovsky, in fact, offers an apt depiction of the immigrant schizophrenic's reaction to the new land. Rather than deliberately practiced as an artistic expression, the "distant or else fragmentingly microscopic perspective" and the unfamiliarity of "standard causal/narrative schemas of meaning" of things are deployed in Asian Diaspora literature to embody the immigrant character's miserable condition. In the restrained prose of Ishiguro, one only sees hints of that defamiliarization in Etsuko's reminiscences of Keiko, the immigrant suicide. Both Pai and Nieh utilize such a strategy, while Mukherjee's text traces meticulously the gradual decomposition of the mind of an immigrant schizophrenic. All of these writers have their immigrant characters dissect the environment in morbid minutiae, a move foreshadowing their doom.

Wu Han-hun in Pai's "Death in Chicago" perceives his roomful of books after receiving his Ph.D. as "a pile of carcasses of various colors. The stench in the room seems to emanate from those corpses. Wu Han-hun feels nauseated, like smelling preservative in a dissecting room" (227). The normal association of books is replaced by death imageries; even as Wu escapes from his basement apartment, the city itself resembles an Egyptian "sarcophagus" fitting for Wu's final act. Similarly, Nieh Hua-ling's Peach Red repeatedly asserts that Mulberry Green, her double, is dead. This severance of her former self is portended by Mulberry Green's near-deranged obsession while in hiding in the Taiwanese attic. Metaphors of cannibalism overwhelm the fugitives' thoughts: rats supposedly gnawing her body; zombies devouring the inhabitants of the entire island of Taiwan; and the erosion of the Shens' sanity and physical condition. The atmosphere of horror and paranoia is achieved through some unconventional means, such as long vertical lines of loaded words and drawings done by the eight-year-old daughter. Cannibalism continues to haunt the "new" self, Mulberry Green, fleeing the INS: she recounts "tales of cannibalism about the Donner Party" stranded in the snow in 1846 (Wong's *Reading Asian American Literature* 127).

Mukherjee develops more thoroughly the strategies of defamiliarization by means of trivial yet gruesome details to embody the protagonist's dementia in *Wife*. The name Dimple, a "chic name for Indian girls in the early 1970s," is used to suggest, as Mukherjee puts it, "slight [mental] disturbances" (Hancock 42) of the protagonist. Dimple begins as a lovelorn young girl in India anxiously awaiting Prince Charming to arrive. Her romantic reveries gradually darken in New York, culminating in a ceaseless devising of ways to commit suicide. C. L. Chua describes the protagonist as "a weak-minded Bengali woman" whose "sensibilities become so confounded by her changing cultural roles, the insidious television factitiousness, and the tensions of feminism that, ironically, she goes mad and kills her husband" (54–55). Put another way, Dimple's unresolved dilemma between her wish to remain a traditional Indian wife and the irresistible influences of the New World, particularly feminism, leads to her insanity. Dimple's desire to be a traditional wife, however, must be qualified by her subconscious move to return to the naivete and romanticism of girlhood, after being disillusioned by marriage, pregnancy, and, of course, sexuality.

The destabilizing of her world begins sexually and continues with a strong link to sexuality. Her intercourse with her husband, Amit, reminds her of a "baby lizard" with "grunts and gurgles" (23). The tendency toward grotesquerie in conjunction with sexuality is established. After she becomes pregnant, she "catalogu[es] ways to rid herself of *it*" (32). A ritual whereby she cleanses herself of worldly contamination, disgorging becomes the rehearsal for the ultimate act of purification—aborting the fetus, which symbolizes her entry into the adult terrain. Her reluctance to take leave of a teenager's romantic daydreaming is so desperate that she applies the same glamorizing techniques of youthful dreams to her marriage in disarray. Even her vomit takes on a glossy quality which fascinates her as she scrutinizes, microscopically, the "brownish liquid from her body, . . . the solid debris of chewed cauliflowers and lentils that sank fast [in the toilet]" (31–32). The abortion itself is ushered in by Dimple's killing of a mouse and her subsequent anatomization of the corpse, which "look[s] pregnant" and whose head is "[h]orribly misshapen, bloody from the blows . . . the rodent body covered with hair balls, well, black and matted. It had a strangely swollen body. A very small creature with a fat belly" (36). Finally, Dimple succeeds in expelling the unwanted fetus from her body, thus keeping herself, at least in her crazed mind, immaculate and untainted by sexuality.

Her yearning to return to naivete and innocence is further thwarted by the couples' emigration to New York, with the pressure of a strange environment exacerbated by a self-centered, traditional Indian husband, on the one hand, and her equally self-centered, feminist friends, on the other. Her vomiting or purging of impurities becomes an obligatory response to every visit by her feminist friends such as Ina Mullick and Leni. Caught in a double bind, Dimple is too traditional and polite to refuse her feminist visitors, but their ideas literally nauseate her, evidenced by her retching in secret. She even pathologically grows to love the sensation of vomit when she escapes from Ina and Leni's radical views into the refuge of kitchen and the making of Darjeeling tea: "Vomiting could be pleasurable; thinking of all the bathrooms she had vomited in she felt nostalgic, almost middle-aged" (150).

Dimple's urge to throw up is preceded by her microscopic observations and macabre associations of Leni, the feminist "grotesque," whose "large and squishy" mouth resembles "the baby calf liver under plastic wrap at the Grand Union" (147). Leni is all the more monstrous because she is not only a hunchback but also toothless. Such distorted physiognomy bespeaks Dimple's fear of being forced to reexamine her traditional role. But Dimple's facade of femininity fails to hold up when Dimple pours the tea all over the floor unknowingly—after hiding her repulsion by retching in the kitchen, after performing her duties of preparing and serving tea. The selfishness of her feminist friends is apparent in the fact that they flee from Dimple rather than stand by her, a woman in clear distress. Nor does her American lover, Milt Glasser, stand her in good stead, once Dimple inquires rather indiscreetly what his profession is at the end of their love-making.

Failed by all her acquaintances, including her husband, lover, and female friends, Dimple manifests signs of a mental breakdown. She experiences insomnia at night and sleeps most of the day; she begins to confuse TV shows and reality; she talks to herself. She muses that if the water allegedly inside the head of her neighbor's retarded boy in India "had come spurting out in yellowish sprays and had hit the passengers" (162) when he was run over by a car. Similar to her own expulsion of fetus and half-digested food, her imagination acquires morbid specificities. An atmosphere of doom and eventuality shrouds the lens through which she inspects the world. For instance, her eyes are keen in picking out mold in the refriegerator: "marveling at the greenish blue color and soft texture. It was shaped like a flower, she thought. . . . There were too many images of corrosion within the apartment" (127). Deterioration of another kind is suggested through the slight variation of the word *mole,* which Dimple notices on the left side of Amit's neck, the spot she stabs. She also notices the hairs on two joints of Amit's fingers (167), whereas Milt has "acne scars on his nose" (169) and "no hair on his finger, but the veins stood out on the back of his hand like maps of the Ganges" (170).

The final eruption of Dimple's schizophrenia is the murder of her husband, an ironic twist of *sati,* the traditional self-immolation of an Indian wife on the funereal pyre of her husband. This ironic commentary on the Indian culture is augmented by the method by which Dimple commits homicide: she stabs her husband "seven times in repudiation of the seven ritual steps taken to seal the Hindu marriage bond" (Low 14). Psychologically, however, suicide and homicide may stem from the same roots. George Simpson in his editor's introduction to Emile Durkheim's *Suicide: A Study in Sociology* maintains that

> suicide is most often a form of "displacement"; that is, the desire to kill someone who has thwarted the individual is turned back on the individual himself. Or technically stated: the suicide murders the introjected object and expiates guilt for wanting to murder the object. The ego is satisfied and the superego mollified through self-murder. (24)

By murdering Amit, Dimple fantasizes that she would be emancipated, becoming an unbounded individual as well as part of the luring consumerist culture. The novel concludes on Dimple's thought that "women on television got away with murder," demonstrating how her girlish fantasies with a twist of American capitalism are retained as coping strategies, strategies which so blur the thin line between reality and illusion that the consequences are devastating.

Conclusion: The Absence of the Linguistic Maze

What kind of linquistic difficulty does Dimple have watching American TV? Does the concluding line of *Wife* suggest how minimal and reductive Dimple's absorption of soap opera is? Or is the concluding line itself a minimalist and reductivist effort to gloss over the linguistic maze in which Dimple is arrested? Such a lack of attention on language is contradicted by Mukherjee's own analysis of the protagonist's dilemma. In an interview, Mukherjee describes Dimple as "an isolated woman because she doesn't speak much English. . . . She tells herself that she is learning American English and getting to know Americans by watching TV" (Hancock 43). Mukherjee at times does provide, though haphazardly, limited portrayal of immigrants' Tower of Babel, which ultimately contributes to their breakdown. At one point, the newly-arrived Dimple tries to buy "five hundred grams of cheesecake" (59) at a Kosher store and is flatly reprimanded by the shopkeeper. But in addition to a few explicit textual references to Dimple's broken English,[6] this fiasco in shopping is about all Mukherjee does to represent one of the most acute problems for immigrants from non-English-speaking backgrounds.

This oversight derives from Mukherjee's own privileged background, a background which entitles her to gain entry into the English-speaking First World without the most fundamental obstacle experienced by certain immigrants who could not make themselves understood in English. When Mukherjee rages at the fact that some Canadians think of her as a "Paki" "after the imported idiom of London" (Healey 41), at least she does not have to acquire anew the idiom and mannerism of London. Being English-educated and, in Gayatri Chakravorty Spivak's words, a member of the "privileged native informants of liberal third world feminists" (*In Other Worlds* 256), Mukherjee simply fails to, as she asserts, tell the story of Dimple's "traumatic changes—cultural, psychological" in Dimple's own language (Hancock 36).

By the same token, Etsuko in Ishiguro's novel speaks such perfect English in England that one is hard put to imagine her as ever having any language hurdle. Moreover, her English is virtually indistinguishable from her urbane conversations in Japanese in Nagasaki. The same confusion arises in Pai and Nieh's Chinese texts where the reader must visualize characters speaking excellent Chinese speaking stilted or even nonstandard English. Presumably, for great stylists of prose such as Ishiguro and Pai, for an English-speaking postcolonial elite such as Mukherjee and a Chinese-speaking, ethnocentric Nieh, it is nearly impossible to unlearn English or Chinese, their respective native tongues.[7] Novelists construct verbal art, but the delineation of the universe of immigrant schizophrenic entails the *undoing* of verbal art, the stripping of craftsmanship to its bare minimum, and the forgoing of what at first appears to be logical and rational—a herculean task few have undertaken, let alone accomplished.

Part 2

Immigrant Subjectivity through Eroticism

FOUR

Interracial Eroticism in Asian American Literature: Male Subjectivity and White Bodies

There is no Chinese woman I could marry, and no American lady who would marry me.[1]

—*Yung Wing, the first Asian graduate of an American university (Yale, Class of 1854)*

This is apt but not singularly postcolonial, since the subject is always *constituted at the* interface *between subjection and subjectivity.*

—*Tejumola Olaniyan, "Narrativizing Postcolony: Responsibilities" (52)*

White female bodies[2] have consistently served, in Asian American literature by male writers, to help define male subjectivity. The fact that male writers regularly choose to essentialize and objectify Caucasian rather than Asian American or Asian women signifies the troubling intersection of race and gender, an issue which has haunted in a different way many feminists, particularly women of color.[3] This convergence of race and gender has to be traced back to imperialist ideology and colonization, despite the context of the present pursuit, which is ethnic studies. In fact, strong links exist between postcolonialism and minority discourse,[4] and throughout this chapter I will continue to shuttle between the two disciplines, a choice in part justified by Sara Suleri's assertion:

> Where the term [postcolonialism] once referred exclusively to the discursive practices produced by the historical fact of prior colonization in certain geographically specific segments of the world, it is now more of an abstraction available for figurative deployment in any strategic redefinition of marginality. (759)

Postcolonial and ethnic theories together, therefore, provide a more comprehensive framework to situate women's marginalization by a marginalized minority within the United States.

In addition to the dual critical angles of postcolonialism and ethnic studies, a third grid with which these male texts can be examined is that of feminism. But first-world, middle-class feminist theories alone may prove less fruitful when untempered by social realities experienced by these immigrant and minority writers, as Shirley Lim warns in "Asians in Anglo-American Feminism: Reciprocity and Resistance":

> In order to write an essay on feminism, a term made popular and authoritative by Anglo-American women, I have first to understand wherin and why my relationship to feminism is tangled with those early cultural ideals of gratitude and obligation, and how those ideals, embedded in a Confucianist/ Malayan/Catholic background, a colonized/British imperialist mentality, and an Asian patriarchal society, still command the relations between western feminists and, in my case, an Asian woman. (241)

Lim incisively foregrounds the influences of "Confucianist/ Malayan/Catholic" traditions to sharpen "'colorless' feminism," which she sees as "ignor[ing] the place of cultural and racial difference in women" and "an expression of Anglo-American-centric colonialist theory" (249).

The precarious connection of race and gender in the West must be understood, as Lim proposes, in the context of the Western imperialist and neoimperialist ideology. To illustrate, Sander Gilman in "Black Bodies, White Bodies: Toward an Iconography of Female Sexuality in Late Nineteenth-Century Art, Medicine, and Literature" offers an insightful analysis of the "white man's burden." Gilman views the colonial mentality as having become the white man's "sexuality and his control, and it is this which is transferred into the need to control the sexuality of the Other, the Other as sexualized female. The colonial mentality which sees 'natives' as needing control is easily transferred to 'woman'" (237). To a European male in the late nineteenth century, the context of Gilman's argument, the other races and the other gender are almost interchangeable, whose feminine and/or foreign body requires subjugation. The fact that men of color can be regarded as feminine is further proof that "race," to borrow the quotation marks Henry Louis Gates, Jr., uses when editing the special issue of *Critical Inquiry, "Race," Writing, and Difference*, is socially constructed, rather than biologically based, a distinction similar to gender versus sex in most feminist discourse.[5]

Evidence of race and gender as social constructs abounds, but one in particular relates closely to Asian Americans: the U.S. miscegenation laws since the nineteenth century. Such legislation outlawing interracial sex and marriages targeted primarily men of color with white women, but the racial category as applied in the American West grew from the Chinese in the 1860s to the "Mongolian" race in order to accommodate the second wave of immigrants—the Japanese, and then the legislators were compelled to include the "Malay" race to ban Filipino men from marrying white women. While the miscegenation laws were being "perfected," white men had free access to women of color, provided property or inheritance did not become an issue of contention.[6] Clearly, the problematic of interracial eroticism is interwoven with the notions of race and gender, yet these very building blocks are subject to change as a result of the fluctuation of power in the human society. A modest Foucauldian archaeology is in order here to unearth the infrastructure of domination which underlies interracial eroticism, and more specifically, Asian American males' fascination with white female bodies.

It is indeed ironic that while Asian American males are being stereotyped, they practice reverse stereotyping against the supposedly "weaker" sex of the dominant race. In other words, as male subjectivity changes from Euro-American to Asian American, from the hegemonic group to a peripheral one, the strategy of empowerment remains the same, namely, the subjugation of women. But it is essential to excavate Asian American males' motives in this dubious quest for control. Collectively as a minority group, Asian American males have been emasculated by American culture through popular images such as the good yet feminine Charlie Chan and the evil yet a-sexual Fu Manchu as well as through distortions in canonical texts such as those by Jack London and Frank Norris.[7] To empower themselves, Asian American writers adopt and revise the age-old tactic of constructing male subjectivity by treating women as object and as other. The subconscious rationale appears to be that even though Euro-American white males maintain control, their power can be usurped somewhat by an interracial liaison with white women. Asian American writers hence consider white women not as, in Josephine Donovan's term in "Beyond the Net: Feminist Criticism as a Moral Criticism," "seats of consciousness" (40). They instead create diametrically opposed stereotypes of the maternal Mary and the seductive Eve for women, whose value rests solely in the ability to aid or detract males in their enterprise, that is, in the production of Asian American male identity.

Any identity formation within the minority group is an act of radical self-assertion, of recognizing the self's differences from as well as resemblances to the majority, a recognition distinctly at variance with the definition given them by the hegemony. This drastic deviation from what is considered the "self" ties in with the notion of "eroticism" as Georges Bataille conceives it in *Eroticism* (1962). Bataille views eroticism in a way much broader than its usual definition, signifying an act of transgression against social taboos, particularly those on sex and violence.[8] While Asian American literature does not display an exaggerated obsession with these two oldest taboos, the urge of male writers to violate racial/sexual demarcations by consorting with Caucasian women is transgressive by nature, which surfaces as much in the texts by early immigrants as in those by contemporary Asian American writers. The movement of such a cultural attitude, shared by immigrant and ethnic writers, leaves in its wake an abiding trajectory of defining male subjectivity by objectifying the opposite sex from the opposite race.

This configuration of interracial eroticism in fact extends beyond Asian American discourse to other minority and postcolonial literature. Frantz Fanon writes:

> I wish to be acknowledged not as *black* but as *white*. . . . who but a white woman can do this for me? . . . When my restless hands caress those white breasts, they grasp white civilization and dignity and make them mine. (63)

Similar blending of male and racial fantasies recurs in the persistent gaze at *shikse* (Yiddish term for a non-Jewish girl) in Philip Roth's fiction. This longing for Caucasian women represents, among other things, the disadvantaged group's fallacy of assimilation. Caucasian women, as a result, take on the role of "Occidental Madame Butterfly" to fulfill the need for security and power.[9] The imagination of the disposssessed projects the craving for self-empowerment onto the body of Caucasian women. By possessing the white female bodies, they see themselves as temporarily merged with the center. White bodies thus become not only an exotic physical entity whose fair skin and corporeal features captivate in an essentialist manner Asian American men but also a political symbol within which lies the promise of power yearned by the ostracized. Caucasian women evolve, therefore, into a mythical figure, simultaneously harboring uninhibited and often perilous sensuousness, angelic motherhood, and the spirit of freedom and democracy. They serve as a solace to the deprived and the downtrodden, yet also as a threat for more deprivation.

My argument follows the unremitting trajectory from male immigrant to Asian American male writers who eroticize white bodies; it then ends with a contemplation on the absence of interracial eroticism within the Asian American literary canon by female writers. But before plumbing the immigrant writer's psyche and the American social forces that shape it, it is necessary first to explore the Asian cultural heritage pertaining to skin color, which immigrants carry with them upon arrival on these shores. This seeming digression in fact pinpoints the other source—the "nativist" fountainhead as opposed to the Western imperialist one—of interracial eroticism. Though the following examples come exclusively from Chinese texts, in no way am I suggesting in an ethnocentric fashion that Chinese culture represents Asian attitude in general. But it is simply beyond the scope of this chapter to cover every Asian literary tradition to prove this ethos on light complexion predating the onslaught of colonialism with its hierarchy of race. Consequently, I choose to examine Chinese literature, one of the most prominent Asian traditions, which is replete with allusions to light-colored complexion as a prerequisite for feminine beauty. This project conceivably can be expanded to other Asian traditions by critics more capable in those fields.

In Chinese culture, the axiom *Yi-pai-ch'o-san-ch'ao* ("Whiteness covers up three times of ugliness") bespeaks the prevalent yardstick in evaluating the other sex. What is most telling in this adage, however, is the stratification of class. "Dark-complexioned" becomes a code word for peasant or working class, and is therefore scoffed at. This bias is borne out, amazingly enough, even by Asian

American texts, such as Amy Tan's *The Joy Luck Club* (1989). One of Tan's narrators characterizes her husband's concubine in prerevolution China in deprecating terms:

> He [the husband] brought home a new wife, a low-class girl, dark-skinned, no manners! Bought her for a few dollars from a poor village family that makes mud-brick tiles. And at night when he can no longer use her, he comes to me, smelling of mud. (258)

"Dark-skinned" is associated with mud, filth, degeneration; the narrator feels betrayed by her husband who finds her supposedly fairer skin and its related qualities not much different from the peasant girl's. The narrator, an abused woman, tranfers much of her hate against her husband to spite against another woman of similar fate, a move not unlike disenfranchized Asian American males' objectifying of Caucasian women.

What is most striking is that an Asian American, one generation removed from China, accurately reports to us this preference for fair skin. While cultural residuals are hard to quantify in children of immigrants, one can say with certainty that Tan is well aware of such attitudes. This further strengthens the linkages between postcolonial and minority studies, since writers themselves manifest blurrings of the two—prejudice against working class in semicolonial China in conjunction with white dominance over peoples of color in the United States.

Fair skin, in Chinese culture, also constitutes an integral part of feminine eroticism. The quintessential classical beauty, Lady Yang Kuei-fei, concubine to a Tang emperor, is described by Po Chü-yi (772–846) in his celebrated poem "The Song of Everlasting Sorrow" as follows: "On cool spring days she bathed in the Flower-pure Pool, / Her soft creamy skin laved by the smooth, warm waters" (Liu Wu-chi 93). "Creamy" suggests the delicate texture and the whiteness of the skin. Moreover, one of the most memorable episodes in Wu Cheng-en's sixteenth-century masterpiece *Journey to the West* (*Hsi-yu chi*)[10] relates the male pilgrims' encounter with the "spider-sirens," who charm not with their song but with their voluptuousness. And when that fails, they would spin out web-like ropes from their navels to capture their prey. These Medusas are cast in a five-syllabic poem as exposing "soft breasts white as silver / jade bodies tender as snow" (translation mine, from chapter 72). In addition to bearing witness to how widespread Chinese preference for fair complexion is, such formulaic phrases function both as a signifier for innocence and, once misused as by the spider-sirens, for evil. This literary trope appears in many later texts, such as Lao She's novel *Rickshaw* (1936–37), in which the legendary prostitute is nicknamed "White Flour Sack" after her "two enormous pendulous breasts . . . which she could flip up and onto her shoulders" (231). These references to fair skin indicate the cultural attitude sedimented in language and are easily invoked whenever the writer needs to portray a desirable female, celestial or diabolic.

This nativist tradition of valorizing fair skin is compounded by postcolonialism, the Asian bias reinforcing the aesthetics of imperialists.[11] One of the results is early immigrants' twisted view and frequent idolization of Caucasian women, a phenomenon which also has to be historicized. Due to the discriminatory U.S. immigration laws since the late nineteenth century, the hardships of an alien's life, and the patriarchal Asian tradition, the majority of Asian immigrants in the early decades of this century were males, either unmarried or having left their wives behind in Asia. The most poignant depiction of Asian bachelors' personal and socio-historical dilemma can be found in Louis Chu's *Eat a Bowl of Tea* (1961), set in the New York Chinatown in the forties and fifties. The predicament of the bachelors in America revolves around the absence of heterosexual partners and the lack of power. Ghettoized and ghettoizing themselves, they flock around gambling houses, endlessly exchanging gossip about liaisons and scandals, belying their obsession with sexuality. The impotence of these Chinese sojourners is epitomized by the inability of the protagonist, Ben Loy, to have intercourse with his wife, Mei Oi, a tragedy attributed to his promiscuous past with white prostitutes, the only women available to low-class laborers. Representing a whole generation of castrated Chinese immigrants, Ben Loy's inadequacy is diagnosed as "psychological," and he eventually undergoes a miraculous recovery upon return to the source of Chinese America—San Francisco's Chinatown—to "eat" a traditional herbalist's mysterious tea.

But first, in order to marry a proper woman, Ben Loy is charged by his family to journey back to China to meet Mei Oi, regarded as more decent than "*jook sing* [American-born Chinese, or ABC] girls," who run around "naked" and "have no respect for the elders." This fear over the younger, Americanized generation comes from the belief that they have been contaminated by a land from which the immigrants feel estranged. Marlon K. Hom's collection of San Francisco Chinatown's Cantonese rhymes in the chapter "Songs of Western Influence and the American-borns" from *Songs of Gold Mountain* (1987) records the mentality of early immigrants, a meticulous testimony of the coexisting repulsion by and attraction to "*jook sing* girls" and Caucasian women. The perception of Caucasian women as carefree and uninhibited underlies the outrage against American-born women:

> They [the young generation] stroll together, hand-in-
> hand; their infatuation is mutual.
> Imitating the barbarian women,
> She plays house with him at her pleasure. (227)

Sexism is evident as the speaker's wrath is directed toward young women rather than men, who are engaged in the same act. As is the case in any collection of folksongs, there exists counterevidence to this condemnation of ABCs. But the prevailing tone remains that the Western influence has corrupted the next generation. Accompanying this sense of dismay, a number of Hom's collected verses reveal the craving of immigrants for white bodies:

> Girls of the Flowery Flag nation [the United States], all
> superbly beautiful and charming;
> By all means, have a taste of the white scent while
> there's time. (257)

"Flowery" is a Chinese word laced with erotic connotation, such as in the maxim, "I would rather die amidst the flowers; then even as ghost I could still be licentious." "[H]ave a taste of the white scent" is a pale imitation of the sensuousness of the original language (literally translated, "savor the white race taste") with its mental imagery of chewing and relishing. Women are practically transformed into a morsel of food, the whiteness of the race as something tangy and mouth-watering.

Though arriving on the West Coast decades after the San Francisco rhymesters, Filipino immigrants exhibit similar passion for white bodies. Carlos Bulosan in *America Is in the Heart* (1943, 1973) chronicles how the protagonist is transformed from a typical Pinoy (Filipino migrant worker) at the time into a union organizer and writer. The Mary-Eve stereotype of woman is once again deployed in Bulosan; American women are portrayed either as Florence Nightingales who tend to him in the hospital or as entrancing, statuesque "nudes." Working as a domestic, the young protagonist first overhears Americans accusing Asian males of being obsessed with white women, and then the narrative, as if to substantiate the charge, follows up with his first exposure to a Caucasian nude:

> "And I won't have a Filipino in my house, when my daughter is around," said one of the women.
>
> "Is it true that they are sex-crazy?" the man next to her asked. "I understand that they go crazy when they see a white woman." . . .
>
> The lady of the house was still in bed. She got up and went to the bathroom when she heard me knock on the door. She came back to the room without clothes, the red hair on her body gleaming with tiny drops of water. It was the first time I had seen the onionlike whiteness of a white woman's body. I stared at her, naturally, but looked away as fast as I could when she turned in my direction. She had caught a glimpse of my ecstasy in the tall mirror, where she was nakedly admiring herself. . . .
>
> "Get out!" She pushed me into the hall and slammed the door.
>
> I did not forget her for a long time. (141)

In circumstances resembling Yang Kuei-fei's upon entry into the text, the nude's red hair serves to accentuate the "onionlike whiteness" of her body. The highlighting of exotic colors and traits of a white body is a recurring motif in the male gaze throughout Asian American literature. But the narrative strategy relies on two incredulous points: the coincidence between the racist dialogue and the protagonist's "initiation"; the mistress' outburst of anger after being utterly oblivious to the servant at first. These incongruities weave together a Filipino's ill-concealed longing for an object of taboo and thus of intensified desire.

Bienvenido N. Santos came to the U.S. not as a migrant worker but a *pensionado* student. His descriptions of Caucasian women in *Scent of Apples* (1979; a collection of stories written from the fifties through the seventies) are more fleshed out than Bulosan's. Caucasian women are romanticized as "Occidental Madame Butterflies," emanating maternal warmth as well as sexual charm. Never delineated except in broad strokes, the women's physical attributes which do receive emphasis are likewise those focusing on their race—their blond or red hair, their height and light complexion. While Oriental women are viewed in Western culture as obedient, submissive, sensuous, and eager to please, their Occidental counterparts tend to become carefree, passionate, seductive, and often with loose morals.

In his introduction to *Scent of Apples* (1979), Leonard Casper writes that Filipino immigrants used to be dubbed "blonde chasers" (x), through whose eyes Santos profers glances of American women to silhouette his compatriots' aspirations and quandaries. The narrator-author's own position with respect to blonde chasers and interracial eroticism is ambiguous:

> I stood there [at the Lincoln Memorial] speechless and awed by the magnificence of his words, carved into stone: FOURSCORE AND SEVEN YEARS AGO, and glimpses of my childhood came rushing back: my voice rising above the din and clatter of a Tondo evening as I recited Lincoln's Gettysburg Address . . . how many of these boys had made the pilgrimage, how many of them had taken time out of their many empty hours to look into the sad eyes of Lincoln, to read the words again in silence? . . . Meaningless . . . meaningless. In spring and summertime, they have walked in the parks, and have posed for pictures, little brown man in an expensive suit, arm around the waist of a smiling—often a little taller—American girl, the Lincoln Memorial for background or the dome of the Capitol rising above the trees, or the Washington monument tall against the skies. (58–59)

Typical colonial mentality in a melodramatic mood, the narrator reveres Lincoln due to the colonial history of the Philippines. His attachment to the United States goes back to his childhood when he distinguished himself by reciting Lincoln's speech. In addition to what Fanon would call the "inferiority/dependency complex" of the colonized,[12] this passage also betrays Santos' sense of superiority over Pinoys, whose outing with American women at the national mall in Washington, D.C., is called "meaningless," revealing their blindness to the magnificence of the site and their amnesia for the colonial upbringing. Caucasian women, montaged with key American institutions, come to symbolize assimilation. Santos taunts the simple-mindedness of these Pinoys trying to blend into the American mainstream by hugging American women and posing at these locales. Prefacing his mockery with the Gettysburg Address on liberty, Santos implies that these Filipino expatriates await psychological emancipation. But the writer himself is trapped in colonialism as well as interracial eroticism; the narcissism with which Santos reminisces his childhood performance testifies to his bondage to U.S. imperialism. Furthermore, when Santos narrates a failed romance between a Filipino man and an American woman, Fay, in "Quicker with Arrow," the immaculate and self-sacrificing Fay is eulogized: "She's a very good girl, noble, honest. She's *white through and through*" (153, emphasis mine). There is no sense that Santos is critiquing such maudlinism and sentimentality expressed here by a *manong*-like character, Dr. Mendoza; he means what he writes. Indeed, consistently throughout the book Santos has never been averse to metaphors such as Dr. Mendoza's: a Caucasian woman is idealized as a shaft of light, glowingly transparent from the exterior of fair skin to the interior of virtues.

Moving from immigrant to ethnic literature, the same veneration of white bodies persists, symptomatic of the grip of postcolonialism not just of the third world where Bulosan and many others come from but of the Asian American minority. John Okada's *No-No Boy* (1957, 1979) is situated at the juncture of immigrant and ethnic literary tradition. Okada is entirely ethnic with the wisdom of hindsight, but his sense of identity is problematized by the historical fact of being designated as "enemy alien" and interned during World War II. While exploring the agonizing aftermath of the internment of Japanese Americans, Okada contrasts the images of the protagonist Ichiro Yamada's Issei mother with his Japanese American girlfriend, Emi. His immigrant mother is unseemly:

> She came through the curtains a few minutes after, a small, flat-chested, shapeless woman who wore her hair pulled back into a tight bun. Hers was the awkward, skinny body of a thirteen-year-old which had dried and toughened through the many years but which had developed no further. (10–11)

Almost every repugnant physical attribute of this immigrant is counterbalanced by Emi: "Emi was several inches taller. . . . She was slender, with heavy breasts, had rich, black hair which fell on her shoulders and covered her neck, and her long legs were strong and shapely like a white woman's" (83). This sharp contrast of the perceptions of these two women closest to the protagonist manifests the Japanese American's self-hatred as a result of the humiliation inflicted upon them. Ichiro subconsciously shuns his unintegrated mother and embraces Emi who em-bodies Americanness.

Even without the ethnic experience of being imprisoned, however, the same juxtaposition occurs, for instance, in Chinese American writers. Apparently, even the civil rights movement in the sixties, with ethnic pride as one of its principles, did not drastically revolutionalize the Asian American male's *sub*consciousness. David Wong Louie's "Pangs of Love" parallels the narrator's monkey-like immigrant mother with his sensuous American partner. Intertextually in Asian American drama, David Henry Hwang's Ama and Popo, two venomous Chinese crones in "Family Devotions," clash with Frank Chin's white goddess in the shape of a gigantic billboard or pin-up girl in "The Chickencoop Chinaman."

Jeffrey Paul Chan's "The Chinese in Haifa" likewise showcases a captivating Ethel Goldberg, the protagonist Bill Wong's Jewish neighbor, with whom he is committing adultery. The title is deceiving: Bill Wong is not Chinese but Chinese American, whose only tie with Jewry is the secret romance. Ethnicity in the integrated neighborhood where the story is set submerges into an undercurrent beneath the calm, bourgeois facade. Numerous allusions to "Jap" terrorists by Ethel's cuckolded husband foretell the possibility of an ugly racial strife if the affair ever comes to light. More relevantly, Bill and Alice Wong's impending divorce is suggested to be connected with the couples' divergent viewpoints on ethnicity. In one of the last telephone conversations between the estranged couple, Bill Wong, an assimilationist, expresses resentment that their children are sent to Chinese schools and taught a language he himself could not speak. As opposed to Alice who reminds Bill of his differences, Ethel Goldberg offers the prospect not merely of sexual gratification but also of psychological acculturation.

It is perhaps fitting to conclude this narrative of Asian American male writers' interracial eroticism with David Mura's *Turning Japanese: Memoirs of a Sansei* (1991), for Mura, culturally and geographically, demonstrates how far Asian Americans have come or how bogged down they are, as if they have traveled in a full circle, back to where their ancestors embarked. Unlike early immigrants or transitional figures such as Okada, Mura proves to be a well-assimilated, middle-class, highly-(Western)educated, third-generation Japanese American, whose family name was anglicized for convenience by his father. The usual quarrels in any long-term relationship notwithstanding, he is happily married to Susie, a Jewish

American. His memoir details the Muras' one-year stay in Tokyo on a U.S./Japan Creative Artist Exchange fellowship. With the unfolding of the narrator's search for his lost heritage, the texture of his book grows intricate yet taut, strained over discovery of his sexuality and the light and shadow it sheds on the relationship with his beloved wife.

A case in point is that after referring to the interracial romance in Alain Resnais' film *Hiroshima, Mon Amour* (1959), Mura contemplates with remarkable candidness and lucidity:

> The city [Hiroshima] had somehow made me aware of our [the Muras'] racial differences in a rather disturbing way; after all, I felt, it's partially because she's a white gaijin that the Japanese doctors like her so much. She's like a prize to them. Immediately a voice inside echoed: "And to you." (119)

That Mura casts his confession at a remove as "a voice inside" addressing "you" attests to the wrenching nature of this confession. Mura proceeds to admit that Susie's physical attraction lies in part in those racial characteristics. When they were college students, David Mura used to dye Susie's hair: "The dye will make the hair blonder, streak it, give it a cheapness she will hate and I will want more of" (166). Despite her reluctance, Susie puts herself through the ordeal of being "cheapened" for the sake of love, quite a reversal from immigrants' fantasies of domination through the patronizing of prostitutes. Yet the driving force behind the deeds of the immigrants and David Mura remains, to different degrees, an enigmatic interracial eroticization. Mura, however talented a poet he may be, is still a product of the environment, and, microcosmically, of his family upbringing.

Upon discovering his father's *Playboy* magazine, an experience so common in boyhood that it appears, among other texts, in David Henry Hwang's *M. Butterfly* (1986), Mura muses:

> Of course, if she were black or brown or yellow . . . but she is white, her beauty self-evident. I sense somehow that she must be more beautiful than Asian women, more prestigious. But the forbidden quality of sex overpowers any thought of race. (125)

This passage is one of the few rare occasions where the narrative strays from its style of precision. After stating that whiteness makes the woman more alluring, Mura adds that race is not of primary concern. But the violation of racial taboos in all likelihood has led to an intensification of "the forbidden quality of sex." This dubious symbiosis of the racial and the erotic bears upon Mura's own speculation about his father in the wake of the release from the internment camp:

> Does he admit to himself his desire for the white girls in his classes [at Western Michigan University]? . . . My father never slept with a white woman. . . . Still, I know he must have thought of crossing that line, must have been aware it was there to cross. (123–24)

This transgressing, racially and sexually, goes beyond a mere physical act and makes the infraction all the more thrilling. As much a meditation on his father as on himself, Mura is certainly aware that he has crossed that line. Intergenerationally, a secret thought has blossomed into a fait accompli; an unspoken ethnic lineage has finally come of age—the dream of possessing not just the body but the soul of Caucasian woman.

Asian American female writers constantly enact their male counterparts' enthrallment with white bodies—often in a parodic way. From a feminist standpoint, Karlene Faith in "Resistance: Lessons from Foucault and Feminism" sees the "female body, as a central, socially invested site of male domination, render[ing] virtually all women vulnerable to the fear if not the actuality of violation" (39). One of the strategies, in Faith's terms, of "[r]esistance to [such] [g]endered power relations" is to resist "traditional discourses which have controlled women's bodies" (58). Asian American writers such as Gish Jen hence seek to oppose traditionally male discourses by caricaturing male desire. Jen's *Typical American* (1992) presents the newly-arrived Chinese student, Ralph Chang, under the spell of Cammy, the secretary of Foreign Student Affairs. Not only is he christened "Ralph," "a kind of dog," by Cammy, but his cultural and sexual initiation consist of becoming obsessed with the "colorful" clerk's "[o]range hair, pink face, blue eyes. Red nails. Green dress. And under the dress, breasts large and solid as earthwork" (11)—all of them imagined characteristics of the Caucasian race.

Even when interracial romance does occur in Asian American female writers, it rarely takes on the thematic prominence seen in their male colleagues. Presented in a realistic fashion, love between a mixed-race couple is utterly devoid of the embellishment of erotic fantasy. Joy Kogawa in *Obasan* (1982) matter-of-factly recounts how Stephen marries a Parisienne and flees from his ethnic past to Europe and Western classical music. Amy Tan's protagonist, Pearl, in *The Kitchen God's Wife* (1991) marries a Caucasian for no apparent reason of race. Even a story most inclined to be eroticized becomes in the hands of a female writer a story of compassion. Hisaye Yamamoto's "Epithalamium" in *Seventeen Syllables and Other Stories* (1988) delineates the doomed, somewhat sadomasochistic, love between a "*hakujin* [white] alcoholic" and the "plain-faced," self-deprecating Yuki Tsumagari. Yet the aesthetic form of this story, imposed especially through the refrains of Gerard Manley Hopkins' poetry, endows the failing relationship with immense spiritual tension. While it is nearly impossible to decide specific influences of feminism on Asian American female writers' portrayals of interracial romance, one can say with some degree of confidence that, as the title of Josephine Donovan's essay suggests, these female writers are gravitating "[t]oward a Women's Poetics" as a result of common denominators such as experiences of oppression, confinement to the domestic sphere, and many physiological similarities.

The trajectory of interracial eroticism from immigrant to ethnic writings by males validates the methodological collapsing of postcolonial and minority discourse. To conclude with one of the epigraphs which opened this chapter, the subject, either an immigrant from ex-colonies such as Bulosan or a sansei-poet such as Mura, "is *always* constituted at the *interface* between subjection and subjectivity," a human condition neither "singularly postcolonial" nor ethnic. Yet, ironically, male writers have to a large measure erected their subjectivity by tacitly acknowledging and submitting to the hegemony's image of themselves. Despite the evolution of ethnic consciousness for the past several decades, the collective unconscious of Asian American males seems to stagnate. Though Mura's sense of ethnicity has evolved into a far more advanced and self-reflexive form than that of Santos, though Jeffrey Paul Chan's Chinese cuckolder emerges as more virile than Louis Chu's ghettoized immigrants, the social construction of race and gender continues to haunt these writers' texts, propelling them to forge male subjectivity through the labyrinthine move of eroticizing white female bodies.

FIVE

Postcolonial Feminizing of America in Carlos Bulosan

There is a beautiful lady surrounded with swords.[1]

—*Tagalog riddle*

I.

Ronald Takaki in *Strangers from a Different Shore* (1989) cites this Tagalog riddle to exemplify how *manongs*—first-generation Filipinos—cautioned their fellow countrymen newly arrived in the United States.[2] This riddle splits America into two halves and genders them as the beautiful lady (with the spontaneous association of the Statue of Liberty), for whom male immigrants yearn,[3] and as the masculine phallic symbols which forbid any communion with the "essence" of America—its femininity. To borrow from R. W. Connell's "The State, Gender and Sexual Politics: Theory and Appraisal," a "male state" with its apparatus of domination—government, bureaucracy, and the economic system—is described by *manongs* as occupying a land cast in maternal metaphors.

The attraction for the "imagined community"[4] of a feminized America manifests itself as the persistent theme of postcolonial interracial romance in works by writers such as Carlos Bulosan, only to be repeatedly repulsed by a racist, largely "masculine" America. This erotic desire stemming from the colonial complex intriguingly intersects with Bulosan's Socialist activism against the masculine America. These two seemingly contradictory dimensions—the feminized, fetishized Eden versus the masculine, capitalist hell—complement each other in postcolonial consciousness like Bulosan's: the harsher the persecution by American men in the form of owners of factories and farms or police force along the West Coast, the more desperately the victims would embrace the escapist icon of Caucasian women. Eroticizing America appears to offer Filipinos a minimum sense of masculinity—through, ironically, turning their desires to and only to idealized white women—in a land where they have been all but emasculated.

This complementariness of social formation and sexual fantasy has been explored, among other works, by *Nationalisms and Sexualities* (1992).[5] The blurring of "lines of national affiliation and sexual attachment" (Introduction 2) observed by the editors of the collection exists both in the minds of Bulosan's Pinoys longing to merge into America and in those of Pinoy haters—American males who justify their discrimination against Filipinos in the name of national, racial, and sexual integrity. Indeed, the anti-Filipino sentiment in the United States during the Depression years often exhibits itself as racism characterized by sexual anxieties. For instance, the indignation of white California males over miscegenation focuses on what is regarded as aberrant Filipino sexuality, evident from the string of virulent statements quoted in Takaki: "The Filipinos are hot little rabbits, and many of these white women like them for this reason," a union greatly feared, for it would allegedly propagate a "new type of mulatto," an "American Mestizo" (328–29). Elaine Kim likewise details the paranoia over yellow peril, which maintains that interracial marriages benefit Asians by endowing white racial characteristics on the yellow but eventually mongrelizes and devours the white race (*Asian American Literature* 10). Gad Horowitz and Michael Kaufman in "Male Sexuality: Toward a Theory of Liberation" define such pornographic paranoia as a "fixation, not only on the object of sexual desire, but also on the object of fear, and this fixation has to do with 'castration' anxiety" (97). In other words, white males' xenophobia stems from the fear of losing control, signified by the masculine sex organ. Bulosan bears out the horrendous consequence of this Freudian interpretation when the protagonist, Leroy, in his story "Life and Death of a Filipino in the USA," the narrator of *America Is in the Heart* (1943, 1973), and the courier, Felix Rivas, in *The Cry and the Dedication* (1995) are brutally castrated by white males. In fact, Hassim, the leader of the Huk guerrilla unit in *Cry* is implied to have had his testicles crushed as well. The recurring motif of castration befalling Bulosan's characters reinforces the episode in his autobiographical novel *America* whereby the narrator himself undergoes that horrible torment (ch. 28, or p. 208). It is impossible to decide whether Bulosan experienced this crime himself or he is drawing from the collective Pinoy sufferings. (Just before the narrator's testicles were smashed, the assailants had singed his friend José's private parts.) But while it may simply be a psychological complex for white males, it is castration, literally or figuratively, for Filipino males. White males' warped fear turns into warping lived experiences for Pinoys. As white males castrate others because of the fear of being castrated themselves, Fililpino male writers such as Bulosan eroticize white females to validate their own masculinity.

However, Leroy's profession as a union activist and the latter two text's Socialist leaning suggest the psychological reading alone obfuscates the economic cause of the persecution. The targets chosen for these heinous crimes indicate that economic and social insecurity lies behind an avowed public concern over sexual mores and racial purity. The link Bulosan tacitly establishes between the victims' mutilation and their profession/conviction reflects the writer's own traumatized life and pro-union career in the United States. He devotes a major portion of his short life to social activism, writing for and editing union publications to fight for the exploited workers. His Socialist disposition can be traced back to his own background. He grew up in an impoverished peasant family in the Philippines, a childhood meticulously recorded in his magnum opus, *America Is in the Heart*. This autobiographical fiction gradually moves from his individual to the collective Filipino experience in the New World. Bulosan's dispossessed background sets the stage for his later conversion to union activism, as he relates easily to the plight of workers in a capitalist country in terms of his own origin. This transformation from a common laborer to an activist is chronicled in *America*; moreover, Bulosan makes outright assertions about his Socialist conviction: "What I am trying to do . . . is to utilize our [Filipino] common folklore, tradition and history in line with my socialist thinking" (qtd. by E. San Juan, Jr., in *Bulosan: An Introduction with Selections* 18; Bulosan's letter dated January 8, 1950, see *On Becoming Filipino* 181). The exact contour of Bulosan's political affiliation remains elusive, though. While clearly harboring Communist sympathy and Marxist ideology, he rarely refers to them explicitly in his own writing, except the posthumously published *The Cry and the Dedication* (1995). The word he constantly resorts to in characterizing his literary enterprise, as shown above, is "Socialist." This might be an act of self-preservation in the anti-Communist atmosphere permeating the United States throughout his stay here—from the Depression to World War II to the McCarthy Era. Granted that these three terms—*Marxist, Communist, Socialist*—have drastically different meanings, a nontheoretician operating in tight censorship as Bulosan did might have sensed some overlapping in their definitions and sought to exploit that accordingly.

Statements such as the one on his "Socialist thinking" notwithstanding, Bulosan was, as P. C. Morantte testifies in *Remembering Carlos Bulosan: His Heart Affair with America* (1984),

> a bit too sentimental to be a bigoted Marxian doctrinaire and he always kept open his heart to the entry of noble souls high in the political and social ladder even though they happened to be of a different ideological persuasion from what he himself professed. (22)

It may be the biographer's own bias to stereotype Marxists as "bigoted" "doctrinaire[s]," but Bulosan's political stance is correctly diagnosed as ambiguous. His ambivalence comes through most vividly in terms of the fusion of body politic and white bodies, of the interlocking of his faith in socialism and his obsession with Caucasian women. Long before socialism enters the consciousness of the teenage Filipino protagonist struggling with poverty in *America*, the pattern of entanglement of social commitment to the downtrodden and of sexual fantasy for white women has materialized: amidst the protagonist's misery, Mary Strandon from Spencer, Iowa, descends like a guardian angel to deliver him. The deification and fetishization of white women are strengthened by Strandon's story of Abraham Lincoln who liberated the slaves. Strandon's physical presence supposedly foretells the narrator's own emancipation; a woman's corporeality meshes with the histories of the colonizer and the colonized on both sides of the Pacific Ocean. As *America* proceeds to reconstruct a Pinoy's brutalized life in the underworld on the West Coast in the 1930s and 1940s, the protagonist's Socialist awakening converges unrelentingly with the Caucasian female savior, whose clone-like duplications are variously named "Mary Strandon," "Judith," "Marion," the sisters "Lily and Rosaline," "Dora Travers," "Harriet Monroe," "Alice and Eileen Odell," and so forth. (The only exception in *America* is Helen, a strike-breaker who sabotages union leaders' efforts.) The politicized and the eroticized strands eventually become inseparable, since women are portrayed as, among other roles, mentors introducing him to a wide range of readings to raise his consciousness. This model of union activities interwoven with colonial romance continues unabated throughout the book. Susan Evangelista has pointed out that white women offer some kind of saving grace in the hostile land of *America*, but this "redemption" is premised on the "purgatory" or even "hell" associated with the male side of America, which triggers Bulosan's Socialist reaction. Elaine Kim views white women in Bulosan as representing America, both good and evil (*Asian American Literature* 51–57), whereas I argue for a sharp split between gender for good and evil.

The source of the gendering of two Americas and the resultant attraction/repulsion lies in the postcolonial condition. Bulosan inherits in fact a Filipino tradition of blending anticolonial politics with procolonial personal neurosis. A quick comparison with José Rizal's career reveals this contradiction.[6] Rizal is known as the national hero who fueled the decolonizing movement against Spain, and his novel in Spanish, *Noli Me Tangere* (1887), is usually credited with initiating the form of modern novel in the island-nation. Lilia Quindoza Santiago's "The Filipina as Metaphor for Crisis" focuses the attention on the mestiza heroine, Maria Clara, in *Noli*. It is ironic, Santiago observes, that this patriot-nationalist's heroine is a half-breed.[7] Born out of wedlock of a Filipina mother and a Franciscan priest, Maria Clara exhibits Western physical features. Carmen Guerrero Nakpil in *Woman Enough and Other Essays* describes Maria Clara as having "fair" skin, "curly" hair, "European nose," and "round and long-lashed" eyes rather than the "Oriental almond eyes" (33–34). The powerful yet invisible interpellation of colonial ideology in its subjects is obvious from the fact that even a national hero's literary imagination is obsessed with mestiza heroines. The leading contemporary Filipino writer Nick Joaquin defends Maria Clara against feminist criticism: "They [Rizal's critics] are dismayed that Rizal should have made a mestiza his heroine; but seem quite undisturbed that his hero should also be a mestizo" ("The Novels of Rizal: An Appreciation" 36). This defensive posture denotes the wide gap between the readings of the two genders; it also calls into question any nationalist or nativist attempt when the culture launching that attempt is already hybridized.

Bulosan's literary precedent and the mestiza prototype help explain the widespread phenomenon amongst his Filipino contemporaries who iconize white women. Filipino immigrants then were called "blonde chasers," which did not come entirely from white racist paranoia. Filipinos themselves admit to as much; Morantte explicates this mentality:

> Carlos felt insecurity, tinged with indignity, in his relationship with white girls. Like his countrymen Carlos liked white women. Filipinos tend to like white women insofar as they represent a type of feminine beauty of Hellenic standards: stately form, fair skin, light or blonde or brown hair, shapely nose, limpid blue or brown eyes, sensual lips. (18)

Quite tellingly, the verb tense shifts from the past tense with regard to Bulosan's specific case to the present tense as Morantte universalizes one Filipino's sexual preference, a move indicative not so much of Morantte' personal views of Bulosan but of a sentiment shared by many of the expatriates. The physical description of the ideal "Hellenic" femininity illustrates the extent postcolonialism pervades people's lives, including that of a union activist grappling with the hegemony which legitimizes the dominance of a particular ethnic group, along with its aesthetics. Such a colonial complex of inferiority surfaces unremittingly in Morantte's memories of Bulosan:

> Carlos loved America. However, it was a kind of idealistic love, with a tinge of romanticism, as one would love a beautiful girl above one's station in life—a rich girl, endowed with fame and power and glory, seemingly beyond the reach of ordinary mortals like him. . . . He was inwardly excited at the sight of Lady America holding a torch in one hand and a book of freedom and justice in the other. The symbol portended not the hopelessness of the situation but the promise of fulfillment of the dreams of all those coming to her shores. (95)

Rather than be taken in by such luring romanticism (which, at any rate, deconstructs itself subliminally—"the hopelessness of the situation"), one might see that the infatuation with Caucasian women comes from the fact that they symbolize America—its affluence and power, euphemized as enlightenment ("torch"), "freedom and justice." Put another way, even sexual preferences, guarded as the core of the private self, are not immune from the intervention and regulation of public discourse, such as the racial and cultural ideology of imperialism. Similar to the drive for domination underneath white racists' rage over miscegenation, Filipinos' fascination with white women is likewise rooted in political economy, which disguises itself as interracial eroticism.

Interracial eroticism is indisputably Bulosan's lifelong obsession and one of his paramount literary motifs. He writes about it extensively but still faults himself for not capturing it in the texts. This sense of inadequacy recurs in his correspondence. In a letter dated 2 November 1949, Bulosan writes:

> I have a secret dream of writing here a 1,500–page novel covering thirty-five years of Philippine history . . . I owe it to the Filipino people. But this is only one of a series of four novels covering 100 years of Philippine history. This one I am working on now covers 1915–1950. One will cover the period from the birth and death of Rizal. Another from his death to the outbreak of the first war. And the fourth will cover 1951–1961, which I consider will be a great crisis in Philippine history. And there you have the whole panorama of my project.
>
> There is really a need for a novel covering the ideal friendship, courtship and marriage of a Pinoy and an American white woman, but the pressure for a novel about the Philippines at this stage of human civilization is demanding. (San Juan's *Bulosan* 152)

Bulosan digresses from a contemplation of his masterpiece on Philippine history to dwell on his favorite topic of interracial eroticism. The proximity of the two projects leads one to speculate that they may be one and the same in the author's subconsciousness. The nationalist-Filipino sentiment directed against a masculine foreign occupying power (both in the Philippines and in the United States) is intertwined with the urge to unite with the feminine half of that power. In another letter dated 24 September 1945, Bulosan claims that his "recent poetry reflects the agonies of a Filipino lover loving a white woman in America, using the racial conflicts in California as a background" (San Juan's *Bulosan* 146). Whether "recent" in 1945 or at any given moment in his career, this theme of interracial romance proliferates with amazing frequency and intensity.

While these women in *America* function as *deux ex machina* to rescue the protagonist, Bulosan's short stories exhibit an identical yearning for and frustration over these female icons. "As Long as the Grass Shall Grow" revolves around an American woman, closely resembling Mary Strandon in *America*, who volunteers to teach Filipino children how to read and write—in English, needless to say. The idolization of Caucasian women commences early in childhood through their alleged kindness.[8] "The Soldier" deals with the romance between a Filipino soldier and a Caucasian woman in the midst of a racist climate. In the quasi-autobiographical story "The Time of Our Lives," one of the characters, Morantte (Bulosan's biographer), asks a Caucasian woman bluntly: "Would you marry a Filipino?" (San Juan's *Bulosan* 49). The story ends on an ominous note as "the small Filipino with the tall blonde" (San Juan's *Bulosan* 52) whom the narrator and Morantte met in the bar is murdered. "Sometimes It's Not Funny" delineates the bankruptcy of the interracial dream as several Filipinos perfunctorily take turns proposing to Margaret, an American woman, who accepts every advance as perfunctorily. This trivialization of human emotion constitutes the initiation into this culture for the innocent narrator ready to propose to Margaret himself. Margaret and other women like her, by virtue of their seductress image, begin to complicate the stereotype of Virgin Mary (Strandon). These two contrasting images form the opposite ends of a spectrum of women deployed to chart Filipino desires in Bulosan. Finally, the image of heartless temptress is best represented in "The Romance of Magno Rubio" by a white "goddess," Clarabelle, worshipped by Rubio, "*Four-foot six inches tall. Dark as a coconut. Head small on a body like a turtle's*" (San Juan's *Bulosan* 59; italicized in the original). This woman swindles the hard-earned savings of the Filipino laborer, who, burdened by his subhuman self-image, bears no grudge against his idol.

On the contrary, whenever Bulosan portrays females in the Philippines (seldom in the United States, for there were few Filipino women here during and after the Depression), they usually live in squalor. The lengthy depiction in *America* of the narrator's mother and sisters marks Filipino femininity with hunger and pain, as opposed to Caucasian women associated with emancipation and well-being. Despite their resourcefulness, these Filipino women could not revert the social forces in the Philippines eroding their lives, from which the protagonist only wishes to flee. Indeed, the protagonist leaves for the New World in *America* and, in "Homecoming," takes his leave yet again after returning from the United States an ailing man. Even in *The Laughter of My Father* (1942), where America and its legendary females are noticeably absent, Filipino femininity epitomized by, once again, the young narrator's mother and sisters is already fated to endure misery, which derives, in addition to all the instruments of feudalistic oppression in the island-nation, from the husband who exhibits at times magical power in outwitting the rich, yet who, alas, is frequently unemployed, irresponsible, and drunk. Filipino women are portrayed as the ultimate victims, occasionally at the hands of their peasant husbands.

II.

That the momentary respites in the narrator's dreadful vagrancy in Bulosan's corpus are almost always blessed with the company of angelic women is symptomatic of postcolonial desires. At first glance, *The Cry and the Dedication* (1995), his last work and published posthumously,[9] seems to be an exception to Bulosan's consistent erotic imaginings, with the text's unmistakably Communist ideology and its focus on a group of underground insurgents in the Philippines. In other words, its overt political scheme rather contests the claim of inextricability of the public and the private. But while the Philippine setting of *Cry* pre-empts any appearance of Caucasian women, the trope of feminizing the land, the "mother earth," is equally deployed.

Annette Kolodny in *The Lay of the Land* (1975) describes the impulse of the genre of American pastorals as having "the central metaphor [in] . . . the metaphor of the land as a woman" (54). The discovery of America, observes Kolodny, makes possible the actualization of a human fantasy, namely, that the land is a maternal, giving mother. To European settlers, they came to realize that "*[t]his* paradise really existed" (5) due to the intersection of "at least two accidents of history—the discovery of the new continent . . . and the reawakening of archetypal patterns derived, finally, from human biology and the human condition" (154). European settlers could afford to regard America as a virgin land because they did not see native Americans as equal human beings already inhabiting and cultivating the land, whereas Asian immigrants must contend with a white race already claiming the New World as their own. Asians, therefore, can not imagine a feminine land to be possessed; they must transfer the metaphorical conceptualization of "land-as-women" into the metonymic one of "woman-as-land."

Europeans use the patriarchal metaphors as the justification for the violence committed against the land and its people, whereas Asians draw from a pale metonymic imitation of Caucasian woman as land to cope with violence committed against themselves. For early colonists, it is a fantasy realized as lived experiences. For Asians, it remains an unfulfilled fantasy to relieve the pain of lived experiences.

Undoubtedly drawing from the legacy of patriarchy, male immigrants are, nevertheless, forced to adopt this strategy as, to borrow from L. M. Grow's essay title on Bulosan's "The Laughter of My Father," a "survival kit." Bulosan hence objectifies women by coalescing them with the promised land in his writing about the New World. For instance, the object of desire in "Five Poems for Josephine" readily merges with America, in accordance with the notion of "motherland." That the land does not consider the narrator a native son ironically intensifies his urge to possess it by possessing its woman:

> Now I contemplate this our land, flowing
> With her full breasts into hamlets and villages,
> Full of life and strength, with her arteries
>   Running along the Mississippi;
>   With her blue eyes in the Great Lakes,
> And her fertility in corn and wheat and grapes
> . . .
> And my new country! And my new paradise!
> O Josephine! O Josephine! O Josephine!
> (Evangelista 98–99)

The central metaphor rather befits the poem's expansive, romantic impulse. Yet even during the bleakest moments prior to *Cry*—moments antithetical to the verse's utopian vein, the dual gendering of America as a literary deployment serves to compartmentalize Bulosan's experience, thus safeguarding the mother earth's innocence and impunity: "And this land . . . is not yet denuded by the rapacity of *men*. Rolling like a beautiful woman with an overflowing abundance of fecundity and murmurous with her eternal mystery, there she lies before us like a great mother" ("Be American" in San Juan's *Bulosan* 37; emphasis mine). The dark hours of the writer's experience is attributed to "the rapacity of [American] men," whereas femininity harbors both seduction and security.

Cry follows this pattern of separating a mother earth from its male occupants. Despite the masculinist, action-oriented veneer of the novel, the theme of homecoming to a ravaged motherland, crystalized in the female protagonist, Memeng, a disfigured virgin, demonstrates the yearning to return to one's place of origin. This yearning is intensely male in its effort to eroticize local landscape through male gaze, culminating in the union of Dante and Mameng, between an exhausted male returning from the United States and his nurturing homeland:

> There was a rise on the hillside below them where a tuft of grass was like rice heavy with grain. They were looking at it now . . . focused on the gravitating rise, the symbol resolved itself into a phallic truth. For the rise became a woman in repose, undinal and containing the orgiastic truth of life . . . ululant now and vibrant with life. . . . The femaleness of it, the fecundity of it all. (54)

The imaginary intercourse of a stalk of rice rising and flowing into a feminine earth sets the scene for their consummation.

The story follows seven "Huk"—Communist guerrillas in the Philippines, a term never mentioned in the text perhaps due to the McCarthy Era and similar paranoia in his home country—fighters trekking across the island to the city of Manila to rendezvous with Felix Rivas, a courier from the United States bringing them instructions to obtain funds for the Communist cause. This journey proves to be a prolonged homecoming for the guerrilla members, as each of them visits his or her hometown to see what is left of the family and village and to convert the peasants to the Communist cause. More significantly, this book is Bulosan's own wish-fulfillment of homecoming and of a successful proletarian uprising in his homeland, two thwarted dreams which remain unrealized until his death in 1956.

Jingoistic and didactic at times, cinematic and suspense-filled elsewhere, this novel, unique in Bulosan's corpus, thrives on military action—assassinations, ambushes, sabotages, getaways. Its plot of an indigenous struggle leads one to assume that it has little to do with America and *manong*'s psyche. But America remains the subtext of this novel on the Communist rebellion in the Philippines. Dante, a member of the group, befriended Felix while in the States and hence is the only person who can identify the courier. Not only are Dante's experiences intimately entwined with America, but both Dante and Felix are spinoffs of the narrator in *Amer-*

ica. Both migrated to the New World in a similar fashion as the narrator; both suffered immense hardships and were hospitalized; Felix was castrated by racists and was nursed back to health by Caucasian women who brought him books and new horizons of consciousness—episodes based closely on the plot of *America* and on what appears to be the "master narrative" of Bulosan's literary imagination.

There exists unquestionably an intensified bitterness in Dante against America, where men and women "destroyed [his] humanity." The American dream conceived in *America* via the perfect bodies of angelic females has turned nightmarish over a decade later as Dante makes love—for the sake of the mission, which is never adequately explained—with Memeng, who scarred her own face to repulse Japanese soldiers trying to rape her. Memeng the female fighter stands for the beloved nation pristine in spirit yet long defiled. Bulosan's disillusionment with America, however, is rendered in a highly problematic manner: Dante dies toward the end without identifying Felix, and the mission grinds to a halt. Because the success of their assignment relies on, yet again, a promise of delivery/deliverance from America, America continues to, like its females, frustrate just as it entices. This may or may not be the end intended by Bulosan (who died just months after the text's alleged completion in 1955), since no sense of closure informs the concluding chapters except Dante's foreboding demise. But as a narrative of a political revolt in the Philippines as well as a sexual one against the romanticized white femininity, it is significant that both occur in Bulosan's fantasy. The latter, in particular, represents not so much a total refutation of his lifelong obsession with the feminized America; rather, it reaffirms the pattern of desire for and disenchantment over America, the ensuing melancholy bound to accompany any excessive romantic longing.

The pliant myth of a feminine America proves too strong to resist even for some of Bulosan's critics. In addition to chapters and passages rightfully assigned to examine Bulosan's relationship with white women in their respective works, a number of Filipino/Filipino American/American writers appear to compose in terms and metaphors akin to Bulosan's postcolonial romance. P. C. Morantte casts his biography of Bulosan in the trope of the writer's "affair with America"—part of the subtitle. Postcolonial aspiration continues to be treated as an unadulterated romance between a Pinoy and "a beautiful girl above one's station in life," whereas the material conditions formulating the private drive go uninterrogated. The colonial complex created by the infrastructure of power seems to plague Bulosan's critics as much as it does Bulosan himself. The Marxist critic E. San Juan, Jr., for instance, opens his *Bulosan: An Introduction with Selections* (1983) with a photograph of Bulosan and a white woman. No explanation is offered as to who that woman is and in what manner she is important enough to merit the limelight. But perhaps that is exactly the point: her personal identity does not matter. The fact that she is white and slightly taller valorizes her as the symbol of Caucasian females adored not only by Bulosan but by the collective postcolonial psyche.

Part 3

Immigrant Self-Representation

SIX

Immigrant Subjectivities and Desires in Overseas Student Literature: Chinese, Postcolonial, or Minority Text?

To rephrase Gayatri Chakravorty Spivak's famous question, can the *immigrant* speak? The immigrants' apparent silence in the U.S. academic discourse derives from an overlapping lacuna in current scholarship on ethnic, postcolonial, and area studies. The preceding chapters are engaged in demonstrating how Asian American discourse Orientalizes Asian immigrants and Occidentalizes white bodies. In the effort to retrieve immigrant subjectivities, this chapter turns to focus on one particular thread of Asian Diaspora literature—*Liu-hsueh-shen wen-hsueh* (overseas student literature)—which has been neglected not only by Asian American scholars but also by postcolonial and China experts as well. This absence of attention is perplexing, for the bonanza of a cluster of middle-class immigrant subject positions can be found, since the 1960s in Taiwan and, increasingly, Hong Kong and elsewhere, in overseas student literature, which I intend to situate at the interface of Chinese, Postcolonial, and Minority texts. This body of texts, most conspicuous in recent years as films, has consistently been regarded as a genre in Chinese literature, a categorization based on the Chinese language with which these texts are produced and the exclusively Chinese audience at home and abroad they seem to address. But these texts are produced by and find their subject matter in a growing segment of the heterogeneous American society—the middle-class naturalized professionals and their previous "incarnation" as foreign students. The term "overseas student literature" is somewhat of a misnomer, for the writers may no longer be students and their writings may touch on student life only tangentially. On the other hand, this misnomer is amazingly accurate in suggesting the genre's characteristic of social class. To become an overseas student in the postwar United States and, subsequently, a naturalized professional there, after all, signify the subjects' middle-class status. The rise and the longevity of overseas student literature are consequently tied to Taiwan and the Pacific Rim's postcolonial condition amidst the cold war era and beyond, as well as, specifically, to changes in U.S. immigration policies in the 1960s and the ensuing U.S. minority problematics.

A nice counterpoint to the middle-class positionality of overseas student literature can be located in working-class immigrant writings, but it presents a task too herculean for this project to take on. Furthermore, writers arriving on these shores from the People's Republic of China since the late 1970s duplicate some of the sentiments and paradigms established by overseas student literature. Once again, the overseas PRC writers can not be included at the present time.

Critical attention heretofore on overseas student literature has come exclusively from China specialists in the Pacific Rim and North America and has focused exclusively on the immigrant characters' losing of their Chinese roots. (Most of these specialists residing in the West, in fact, share similar backgrounds and concerns as the characters depicted in this genre.) The postcolonial condition of this genre as well as the immigrant subjects' minority status in the United States have been suppressed by sinologists, by postcolonial theorists, and by Asian American critics. In fact, the two latter groups show minimum interest in this genre, which has, with its Chinese text and immigrant perspective, the potential to reconfigure radically postcolonial and minority discourses dominated by English-language texts. A territorial protectionism lies at the heart of this genre's being sinologized within and without modern China studies: China specialists are thus satisfied that overseas student literature is their terrain; postcolonial and Asian American experts are satisfied that it is not. For to believe otherwise would entail interrogating some fundamental self-assumptions of these three disciplines: the Chinese roots may be a historical fact *and* a fabricated obsession; postcolonialism may occur to diverse regions not previously under Euro-American imperialism; and Asian immigrant literature may require as much care from Asian Americanists as do English-language texts by U.S.-born authors.

Chinese, Postcolonial, or Minority Texts?

Even though overseas student literature has been widely discussed in the Pacific Rim, particularly Taiwan and Hong Kong, that chapter of literary and cultural history will have to be left untold here; detailed description can be found, for instance, in Sung-sheng Yvonne Chang's *Modernism and the Nativist Resistance* (1993). Instead, modern China studies in the United States becomes one of the three disciplines investigated, for the reason that, due to the postcolonial condition of much of the Pacific Rim, what transpires in American academia may trickle down to the other side of the Pacific. Chang, after all, produces her book on Taiwan's literary scene within the American academia. Similarly, many literary figures active in Taiwan and Hong Kong are exactly the ones dominating modern China studies in the United States.

Of the three disciplines, modern China studies in the United States has the longest institutional history, established during the cold war to "know thine enemy."[1] Energy in this field has inevitably been directed toward mainland China; consequently, any attention to Taiwan literature, including overseas student literature, has long been subsumed in the area studies on China. This phenomenon can be gleaned in all the major anthologies on modern Chinese literature. For instance, while all three of the post-1949 texts in C. T. Hsia's *Twentieth-Century Chinese Stories* (1971) come from Taiwan and two of the three authors are "residents [if not citizens] of the United States," they are found to be "characteristically Chinese in their nostalgia for their lost homeland and in their intense awareness of their frustration or lack of identity in Taiwan or abroad as a 'rootless generation'" (xi). Even when limited, regional autonomy is granted in a subtitle such as Joseph S. M. Lau's *The Unbroken Chain: An Anthology of Taiwan Fiction Since 1926* (1983), which includes at least three U.S. resident contributors and one specific piece on overseas Taiwanese Chinese, the book title, nonetheless, implies a contiguous Chinese tradition from early Taiwanese writers' resistance against Japanese colonialism to the struggle with identity in later pieces.

Indeed, that C. T. Hsia's seminal essay "Obsession with

China: The Moral Burden of Modern Chinese Literature" (1971), which draws from texts prior to the Communist takeover of China in 1949, would continue to function as the framework for many critics to interpret overseas student literature derives as much from internal evidence within such texts as from a myopic critical vision. If not dismissing them offhandedly as stories with "formulaic, tired" endings (Yang Mu iii), the meager scholarly examination of overseas student literature then closely follows the ethnocentric tone set by Hsia and others. One of the major practitioners of this genre, Pai Hsien-yung, traces the exilic legacy in Chinese literature to Chu Yuan's "Li Sao" ("Elegy of Departure," the fourth-century B.C.) and then elucidates the genesis of present-day "wandering Chinese," whose membership he claims:

> To circumvent possible government censorship, these new writers [second-generation mainland émigrés in Taiwan], unlike their May Fourth predecessors, have avoided frontal attacks on burning social and political issues. Instead, they turn to the study of the individual psyche: their problem of identity in Taiwan; their cultural deprivation; their sense of insecurity; their claustrophobic fears on a small island; and the bewilderment that comes with being used as hostages for the sins of their fathers. ("The Wandering Chinese" 207)

Striking an oedipal pose against the patriarchal order, Pai attributes the rise of the modernist movement in Taiwan—compared to the May Fourth movement in the 1910s[2] and championed by him and other "new writers"—to an urge for self-expression in the stifling political system. It is interesting that almost all of these writers extend their search for alternatives across the Pacific Ocean and eventually establish themselves in the United States.[3] Pai proceeds in this essay to support his subtitle, "The Theme of Exile in Taiwan Fiction," by an analysis of the writings of his fellow expatriates, Yu Li-hua and Nieh Hua-ling. Another writer of this genre, Chang Hsi-kuo, also sees "*lang-tzu wen-hsueh* (literature of the wanderer)," facetiously dubbed "airport literature," as a major direction in Taiwan's realist fictions, a strand reflecting the "rootlessness" of the islanders ("Realism in Taiwan Fiction: Two Directions" 32). These critical attempts posit at the core of Taiwan literature, of which overseas student literature is an integral part, a gaping absence, a desire for "Chineseness" once possessed.

Even as recent scholarship in China studies begins to broaden its interpretation of "Chineseness" either to Tu Wei-ming's "Cultural China: The Periphery as the Center" (*Daedalus*, Spring 1990) or to the "Greater China" espoused in *The China Quarterly* (December 1993), the ideology of mainland China as the center is only expanded to include the peripheries inhabited by people of Chinese descent, a contingency plan in scholarship to keep up with the changes brought about by the booming economy of the Pacific Rim yet no less a move tainted with age-old cultural chauvinism. Tu celebrates the "discouse of cultural China," a discursive formation involving "three symbolic universes," all concentric circles centered in China. The first consists of mainland China, Taiwan, Hong Kong, Singapore—"populated predominantly by cultural and ethnic Chinese" (12). The second refers to the "twenty to thirty million . . . huaqiao (overseas Chinese)" (12–13) throughout the world. The third domain includes individuals "who try to understand China intellectually and bring their conceptions of China to their own linguistic communities," a site which has shaped the "international discourse on cultural China" for "the past four decades" (13). Harry Harding in "The Concept of 'Greater China': Themes, Variations and Reservations" takes issue with Tu, who is described as "defin[ing] the membership of a global Chinese culture culturally, rather than ethnically: it consists of all of those, from whatever ethnic background, who . . . join in the creation of a modern Chinese identity" (674).

Moreover, Tu's geographic and cultural elaborations veil the neo-Confucian hegemony he implicitly promotes—"the so-called Third Epoch of Confucian Humanism," which is only ostensibly dimissed as "wishful thinking" (27). Tu seeks to reterritorialize Confucianism, inspired by the striking examples of Hong Kong, Singapore, Taiwan, and south China where capitalism is wedded to the Confucian work ethic and social hierarchy. Embedded in such a philosophy is the traditional elitist preoccupation with Confucian "Shih" (literati), which prompts him to designate the third circle formed by overseas Chinese and non-Chinese intellectuals as instrumental in constructing the "international discourse on cultural China." In other words, the claim of marginal status in Tu's title is a mere rhetorical strategy; those intellectuals geographically removed from the hub of China occupy nonetheless metropolitian centers in the West where the international discourse on China is produced, circulated, and consumed.

The rhetorical claim of marginalization is repeatedly made in the same issue of *Daedalus*, for instance by Leo Ou-fan Lee, a figure no less central than Tu in modern Chinese intellectual history. In "On the Margins of the Chinese Discourse: Some Personal Thoughts on the Cultural Meaning of the Periphery," he summons authors supposedly "on the margins," who, in fact, are monumental figures in Taiwan fiction—Pai Hsien-yung, Yu Li-hua, and Nieh Hua-ling—and submits his "personal thoughts," which are published in a prestigious journal in public discourse. Finding the existential angst and nostalgia associated with the aforementioned authors unsatisfying, Lee advances the "stance of Chinese cosmopolitanism," embracing "both a fundamental intellectual commitment to Chinese culture and a multicultural receptivity, which effectively cuts across all conventional national boundaries" (215). It remains unresolved, however, as to how one is to negotiate the diverging pulls of Chineseness and multiculturalism in the midst of transnational capitalism.

This drive to be more inclusive does have an impact on recent anthologies. Michael Duke's *Worlds of Modern Chinese Fiction* (1990) represents perhaps the first attempt to anthologize modern Chinese fiction on a global scale. David Der-wei Wang and Jeanne Tai's *Running Wild: New Chinese Writers* (1994) presents a collection of short stories and novellas from the late eighties and early nineties by writers scattered all over the world and intends to project "a new image of China, a China defined not by geopolitical boundaries and ideological closures but by overlapping cultures and shared imaginative resources" (238). Wang further challenges the long-held characterization of Chinese writers—their "obsession with China"—and coins the phrase "flirtation with China" in its stead (252–58).

What continues to haunt modern China studies from New Criticism practiced by Hsia in the 1960s to cultural studies in the present is, in Zhang Longxi's term, the willingness to inhabit a "cultural ghetto." Zhang welcomes the introduction of Western theory into this field because it offers "an opportunity for us to open up *the self-enclosure of specialization* and to make the study of Chinese literature relevant to the interest and concerns of people outside the narrow circle of China specialists" (78; emphasis mine). As such, one of the most glaring blind spots in modern China studies involving Taiwan is its ignorance of the island's inherent ties to recent development in postcolonial theory. For example, though proclaiming that China's "semicolonial status severely damaged her spiritual life and her ability to tap indigenous symbolic resources," Tu Wei-ming fails to examine postcoloniality closely other than its deprivation of the "Confucian haven" (2). In terms of Taiwan specifically, Tu astutely comments on the distinct colonial "sedimentations of Taiwanese history"; he finds that "Dutch, Japanese, and American strata superimposed on the Chinese substratum since the eighteenth century—not to mention the upsurge of the Polynesian aborigines—make the claim of Taiwan's Chineseness problematic" (9–10). Yet again, even as Tu delineates, in Antonio Gramsci's words, "the historical process to date which has deposited in you [Taiwan] an infinity of traces, without leaving an inventory," his shrewd insights perennially return to the trumpeting of a neo-Confucian renaissance. Similarly, Sung-sheng Yvonne Chang mentions in passing that the Taiwanese writer Chen Yingchen acquired a heightened awareness of the "unique postcolonial phenomenon" in Taiwan as well as its Pacific Rim neighbors subsequent to his 1983 visit to the International Writing Program at the University of Iowa. But Chang refrains from exploring this not so unique amalgamation of "the expansion of capitalism" and "the spread of modernism" in the global context of postcolonialism (*Modernism and the Nativist Resistance* 161).

This postcolonial phenomenon did not, however, escape the notice of some Marxist critics. The most frequently cited example comes from Fredric Jameson's controversial essay "Third-World Literature in the Era of Multinational Capitalism" (1986), in which Jameson states:

> In the gradual expansion of capitalism across the globe, then, our economic system confronts two very distinct modes of production that pose two very different types of social and cultural resistance to its influence. These are so-called primitive, or tribal society on the one hand, and the Asiatic mode of production, or the great bureaucratic imperial systems, on the other. (68)

According to Jameson, the two modes of resistance are epitomized by the works of Ousmane Sembène of Senegal and Lu Xun of China. Jameson collapses the sites of these two resistances into the third world and argues that "All third-world texts are . . . to be read as what I will call *national allegories*" (69), as opposed to texts in capitalist culture marked by Freudian psychologization and privatization. Hence, Jameson views Lu Xun's "Diary of a Madman" (1918) as illustrating not only an individual's psychosis but also the malaise of China. Where C. T. Hsia finds an "obsession with

China," lapsing in less skillful hands than Lu Xun's into trite patriotism, Jameson uncovers a refreshing third-world national allegory. If as central a Chinese writer as Lu Xun is creating representative third-world literature, then overseas student literature coming into being during the sixties in the underdeveloped Taiwan under U.S. cultural imperialism certainly is.

Indeed, the modernist movement in Taiwan since the 1960s, launched and sustained by Pai Hsien-yung, Ou-yang Tzu, and a number of other prominent expatriate writers, is an enterprise conducted by, in Frantz Fanon's term, "the national bourgeoisie."[4] A case in point is one of the tenets of Taiwan's modernist poetry advocated by Chi Hsien, "'horizontal transplantation' [from the West] rather than 'vertical inheritance' [of Chinese tradition],"[5] which bears an uncanny resemblance to Thomas Babington Macaulay's recommendation for Britain's "civilizing mission" in India in the nineteenth century:

> We must at present do our best to form a class who may be interpreters between us and the millions whom we govern; a class of persons, Indian in blood and colour, but English in taste, in opinions, in morals, and in intellect. (729)

The only difference is that Macaulay tried to create a class of cultural comprador, whereas that elite in Taiwan was already-made. This modernist strand with its emphasis on middle-class individual psyche and aesthetic value travels with the immigrant writers and is reborn as overseas student literature from the 1960s onward. Even though subjectivities in most overseas student literature are interwoven with capitalist, bourgeois conditions, traces of Jamesonian national allegory—the intrinsic third-world postcoloniality and the nomadic subjects' minority status in the United States—reveal themselves to undercut the suprastructure of middle-class romance and nostalgia.

It may not be due entirely to expatriate Chinese writers' lack of global awareness that they unwittingly sever themselves from their postcolonial counterpart; postcolonial theorists in Western metropolitan centers are as much at fault. Despite the claim of anti-Eurocentrism and counterhegemonic resistance, postcolonial intellectuals remain deeply Eurocentric in their vision. As a result of its Commonwealth legacy, postcolonial studies has focused almost exclusively on Anglophone and Francophone literatures. Akin to the "cultural ghetto" of China studies, postcolonial studies suffers from cultural and linguistic self-containment. This disciplinary limitation can be traced back to Edward Said's *Orientalism* (1978), which, to some critics, inaugurated postcolonial theory.[6] Not only is Said repeatedly criticized for not heeding native voices contending colonial discourse but Said himself acknowledges in *Culture and Imperialism* (1993) his earlier flaw in using such a Foucauldian discourse theory. "What I left out of *Orientalism* was that response ["resistance and opposition"] to Western dominance," confesses Said, "which culminated in the great movement of decolonization" (Introduction xii). The practical obstacle is that Said, a Western-trained intellectual, could master several Western languages but probably not the non-Western languages in which "resistance and opposition" are constantly deployed. Yet by focusing on former colonies of Britain, France, and Portugal as well as their languages, Said has de facto rendered European colonial discourse the "master narrative," totally ignoring, for instance, Japanese colonialism of Asia.

In a similar vein, *The Empire Writes Back: Theory and Practice in Post-Colonial Literatures* (1989) announces its project: "This book is concerned with writing by those peoples formerly colonized by Britain, though much of what it deals with is of interest and relevance to countries colonized by other European powers, such as France, Portugal, and Spain" (1). *After Europe: Critical Theory and Post-Colonial Writing* (1989) likewise defines itself as focusing on "writing that is grounded in the cultural realities of those societies whose subjectivity has been constituted at least in part by the subordinating power of European colonialism" (Introduction ix). The editors of both works agree in using the term "postcolonial" to designate former colonies and white settler cultures. *After Europe* includes in this term's domain a third discursive formation—a "horizon of expectation" of imminent "actuations of a specific form of discursive resistance to colonialist power" (xix–xx).

These pioneering works are clearly charged with the mission of mapping the terrain of postcolonialism, but the postcolonial cartography, impressive in its opening inclusion of "[m]ore than three-quarters of the people living in the world today" (*The Empire Writes Back* 1), remains exclusionary by its nature. The contour of postcolonialism derives as much from its practitioners' vested linguistic and cultural self-interests as from any coherent logic within postcolonialism itself. In fact, severe charges of self-serving compradorism have been leveled against these critics. For instance,

Kwame Anthony Appiah contends that postcoloniality signals "the condition of what we might ungenerously call a *comprador* intelligentsia: a relatively small, Western-style, Western-trained group of writers and thinkers, who mediate the trade in cultural commodities of world capitalism at the periphery" (348). Ketu H. Katrak also calls for "decolonizing postcolonial theory," for postcolonial texts are either dismissed or used as "raw material for the theory producers and consumers of Western academia" (158). Samir Dayal sounds a similar warning: "We need to ask whether or to what extent diaspora postcolonial observers participate in the cultural or socioeconomic structure they evidently seek to unmask or undermine" (17). Finally, Arif Dirlik defines the postcolonial as "[w]hen Third World intellectuals have arrived in First World academe" (329). Dirlik undoubtedly sees postcolonialism not only as some reality existing elsewhere but as a distinct institutional development in North America and Europe. While such harsh criticisms certainly do not apply to every postcolonial project, the so-called "*comprador* intelligentsia" indeed resort to third-world texts that are culturally and linguistically accessible to the West and then repackage them with Western theories, hence in this process reaffirming rather than subverting the supremacy of European languages and Continental philosophy. Western languages and epistemology become a given in postcolonial theory, which, as Hayden White describes criticism in general, proves to be most "imperialistic" and Eurocentric.[7]

One of the pitfalls of postcolonial theory's Eurocentric obsession is, evident from the aforementioned critics' Marxist approach, its neglect of the urgent issue of neocolonialism or multinational capitalism, a phenomenon by no means confined to former European colonies. Gareth Griffiths and David Moody maintain that what truly challenges "the post-colonial world today is less that of dismantling colonialist criticism than of addressing the more complex, insidious and hidden controls which characterise contemporary neo-colonial practice and the operation of multi-national capital which it sustains" (84). Madhava Prasad also feels disenchanted with the Fanonian legacy of the Manichean division in postcolonial theories adopted by Edward Said, Benita Parry, Abdul JanMohamed, and others. Prasad suggests that these critics are

> only marginally receptive to the transformations in global political economy and their relation to the psychodrama of the colonial encounter. In other words, the East/West axis and

> the advanced/primitive axis which were developed by a rationalising philosophy of imperialism have not been rethought, in these analyses, with reference to the 'Third World', North/South, centre/periphery models which emphasise the exploitation relation. (87)

Prasad's characterization certainly holds true for the Pacific Rim where capital and control often extend from developed countries to developing ones, *all in the same region*—from Taiwan, Singapore, and Hong Kong to the Philippines, Thailand, and elsewhere. Such a movement defies the binary paradigm between East and West utilized both by colonial and by postcolonial discourse. Gayatri Chakravorty Spivak echoes this observation and boldly generalizes the situation in her interview with Howard Winant:

> I see postcoloniality as precisely the trajectory which has brought us to planetary transnational capitalism, the break-up of space-based imperialisms. . . . In that sense, the whole world is postcolonial. Even this trajectory of non-metropolitan transnational capitalism is a postcolonial phenomenon. (94–95)

The paradox remains that their arguments on global transformations are grounded in local specificities of areas they know best—India, Africa, the Caribbean, and Australia. None of them seem to indicate a willingness to move beyond their local specificities to other areas manifesting multinational capitalism, inhibited by, like those they criticize, the difficulty of surmounting foreign languages and cultures. In this sense, the current academic fixation on literatures in English from the third world and from minorities within the first world is a contingency plan employed by traditional English studics practitioners to survive in this globalizing economy and culture, without becoming overtaxed by, say, the utopia of the Department of Literature.

An extreme reaction to Western cultural and linguistic hegemony in postcolonial writings is registered in Ngugi wa Thiong'o, who switches to his native tongue of Gikuyu after four successful novels in English. He maintains that with the passage of time, "[t]he Europhone would occupy its proper place; as an appendage of European literature or as a footnote in African literature" (23). Ngugi's drastic change of the medium of his work results from the realization that African writers who opt for European languages—

English, French, and Portuguese—are utilizing languages "spoken by only about 5 per cent of the population [in Africa]" and are "set aside from people by [the writers'] education and language choice" (107). It is ironic that while Anglophone literature written and read by so small an elite in Africa is embraced so fervently in the West, overseas student literature written by Chinese immigrants and enjoyed by an immense Chinese readership at home and abroad is studied by a mere handful of sinologists in the United States. Language rather than historical colonization is the key to a text's inclusion or exclusion in postcolonial discourse.

In Asian American studies, critics at one time overlooked immigrant subjectivities, a negligence stemming from the understandably urgent task of "claiming America." Asian Americans suffer perennially from a double bind: Americans see them as unassimilable Asians; immigrants view them as unduly Americanized. Reacting to these layers of denial and, occasionally, self-denial, Asian Americans set forth to claim America. The preface to *Aiiieeeee!* (1974), the first anthology of Asian American literature edited by American-born Asians, defines Asian Americans as distinctly different from Euro-Americans and Asians. In the fervor of a minority's self-fashioning, however, the anthology editors risk misrepresenting another minority—Asian immigrants. Frank Chin, the most vocal of the four editors, behaves at times quite belligerently toward immigrants (see chapter 2). Chin's anger, in fact, is directed toward privileged Asian sojourners such as Lin Yutang, a prominent cultural comprador who trades in stereotypical images of China. To counteract this aristocratic tradition, Chin wishes to retrieve a working-class heritage of Chinese Americans through the life stories of those coolies who built the Transcontinental Railroad on the West Coast. Elaine Kim in her ground-breaking *Asian American Literature: An Introduction to the Writings and Their Social Context* (1982) characterizes Chin's endeavor as a construction of "Chinatown Cowboys" (173–213). Chin's self-empowering venture finds successors in texts such as David Henry Hwang's "The Dance and the Railroad" (1981).

In a far more prudent fashion than Chin's creative outburst, some Asian American critics have been indefatigably engaged in archival research to establish a claim on America other than the writings of upper-class Asians. This archival endeavor results in excellent collections such as *Island: Poetry and History of Chinese Immigrants on Angel Island, 1910–1940* (1991) and *Songs of Gold Mountain: Cantonese Rhymes from San Francisco Chinatown*

(1987). But then, the poems of these two collections may have been left behind primarily by a literate, educated group amongst the illiterate masses stranded on Angel Island or in San Francisco's Chinatown. Despite this potential problem, Asian American critics such as the editors of these books contribute greatly to the decentering of "Chineseness" and the construction of alternative immigrant subjectivities. In recent years, Asian Americanists have tried to accommodate in their works the explosion of Asian immigrant population since the 1960s as well as their concerns.

Another self-empowering Asian American tradition is distinctly feminist, initiated in the not-too-distant past by Maxine Hong Kingston's *The Woman Warrior: Memoirs of a Girlhood among Ghosts* (1976), an event in Asian American literary history of the seventies surpassing in magnitude the publication of *Aiiieeee!*. A similar sense of being constrained by one's Asian heritage surfaces poignantly in *The Woman Warrior*: "Even now [to the grown-up narrator] China wraps double binds around my feet" (57). While the metaphor of foot-binding sharply epitomizes the gap between the immigrant lineage and the American-born generation, it reinforces Orientalist stereotypes of the unjust and tyrannical Asian ways. As such, things Asian as well as Asian immigrants serve as the oppressive or at least oppositional "other," against which an Asian American self begins to take shape, a strategy shared by Kingston's feminist and Chin's masculinist texts. One hastens to add that such a combative cultural stance has softened and mellowed with time, as I have discussed elsewhere the qualitative differences between Kingston's and Amy Tan's uses of the ethnic past.[8]

To return to *The Woman Warrior*, however, the Asian other is embodied by the narrator's mother, Brave Orchid, a subaltern informant who provides precious raw materials for the construction of a past against which the narrator defines herself. Both the geographical site of China and the physical existence of an immigrant mother character are rendered plastic and subject to the author's manipulation. Indeed, as the narrator confesses after having dozed off during her mother's "talk-stories" that she "couldn't tell where the stories left off and where the dreams began" (24), "the stories" and "the dreams" interweave into a narrative of dreamscape—an exteriority of the other, which serves the purpose of forging the self.

The indictment made by Ngugi wa Thiong'o concerning the exploitation of colonialism may be evoked here to gauge Kingston's representation of the alien other:

> In the area of economics and geography, it is the raw materials of gold, diamonds, coffee, tea, which are taken from Africa and processed in Europe and then resold to Africa. In the area of culture, the raw material of African orature and histories developed by African languages are taken, repackaged through English or French or Portuguese and then resold back to Africa. (20)

Simply put, Kingston, as a preeminent Asian American teller, recycles alien stories and resells them to American consumers. These alien stories are presented as transcripts out of the mouths of subaltern informants such as Brave Orchid and supposedly authentic. Sophisticated Kingston apologists have regularly stressed the novel's imaginative dimension to deflect criticism of misrepresentation, yet the controversy hinges not on whether *The Woman Warrior* is mimetic of the objective reality of China and Chinese but on the means of ascension to power—polarizing and exploiting the other.

Lisa Lowe's point in "Heterogeneity, Hybridity, Multiplicity: Marking Asian American Differences" may shed light on the Kingston problematics. Lowe holds that "immigration and relocation to the Unites States" in Asian American texts are often cast as "a loss of the 'original' culture in exchange for the new 'American' culture," which in turn takes the form of generational conflicts between immigrant parents and their American-born or -educated children. This approach essentializes Asian American culture as a conflict between nativism and assimilationism. Lowe proposes to "avoid this homogenizing of Asian Americans as exclusively hierarchical and familial" by "contextualiz[ing] the 'vertical' generational model of culture with the more 'horizontal' relationship" (26). This horizontal relationship would involve, as stated earlier, a consideration of Kingston as an ethnic writer in an American market eager for politically correct yet exotic voices drawn from Orientalism.

To return to the motif of the generational strife in Kingston, Elaine Kim has on more than one occasion since her monumental work *Asian American Literature* (1982) noted a gradual acceptance of immigrants by Asian Americans due to the influx of immigrants into the United States and the globalization of the economy. Noticing an obscuring of the "lines between Asian and Asian American" (xiii), Kim proceeds in the foreword to *Reading the Literatures of Asian America* (1992) to link the phenomenon specifically to

"'Third World solidarity'—a solidarity that frees them from 'minority status,' endowing them, instead, with an empowering global identity" (xv). Despite the euphoria of joining forces between the third world and the U.S. minority, Kim continues to share the sense of urgency over identity formation of many Asian American authors. Kim defines Asian American literature as

> written primarily by American-born, American-educated Asians whose first language is English. . . . The Asian American writer exists on the margins of his or her own marginal community, wedged between the hegemonic culture and the non-English-speaking communities largely unconcerned with self-definition. ("Defining Asian American Realities through Literature" 147)

The in-between status of Asian Americans presupposes the fixed identities of two polarities—Euro-Americans and Asians—a strategy not unlike the assumption in the preface to *Aiiieeeee!*. To suggest that Asian immigrant subjectivities are already-made and thus "unconcerned with self-definition" betrays a profound ignorance of the immigrant condition. In fact, immigrant subjectivities have not been considered absolutely indispensable in Asian American literary criticism. Kim excludes in *Asian American Literature* Asian-language texts where immigrant subjectivities are most likely located: "[Writings in Asian languages] are simply beyond the purview of this study, and I am confident that they will be presented elsewhere" (Preface xi–xii).

It remains to be seen whether in the subsequent works of immigrant-generation Asian American specialists, the prospect of including Asian-language texts can be realized. King-Kok Cheung in her *Articulate Silences: Hisaye Yamamoto, Maxine Hong Kingston, Joy Kogawa* (1993) studies exclusively Asian American female writers. Sau-ling Cynthia Wong in *Reading Asian American Literature: From Necessity to Extravagance* (1993) declares her intention to eschew the "rampant" phenomenon of "de-Americaniz[ing]" Asian American Literature and to anchor Asian American texts in "American historical experiences" (9). Kim's confidence in presentation "elsewhere" does appear, for instance, in some of Wong's Chinese essays and her teaching of Chinese American immigrant writings ("Teaching Chinese Immigrant Literature: Some Principles of Syllabus Design"), both of which, however, seem supplementary to her English writings on Asian American literature.

The secondary status of immigrant literature in the careers of most Asian Americanists may be due in part to institutional constraints.[9] These specialists, after all, work in English departments in the U.S. academe, where tenure, promotion, and reputation depend on peer recognition—a recognition harder to come by if one's subject matter were to be texts written in an unfamiliar language on issues strange to mainstream Americans. The reverse of this argument is also true, though: the fact that these Asian Americans are immigrants themselves probably well versed in at least one Asian language furnishes them with a certain aura of authenticity *as* Asian Americanists. Especially at this early stage of the evolution of Asian American literature where many writers are seeking ethnic roots, an intimate knowledge of an Asian culture and language most likely provides the scholars' commentaries with certain tacit weight and prestige.

This project of salvaging immigrant subjectivities by no means should be dominated by the bourgeois condition of much of the sources, both Asian American literature and overseas student literature. In fact, with a slight variation, the opening question of this chapter becomes "can the *subaltern* immigrant speak?" Spivak's seminal essay that gives rise to both of my queries bespeaks the necessity and the impossibility in retrieving immigrant subjectivities and, particularly, subaltern immigrant subjectivities. Following Ranaji Guha's definition of the "subaltern" in *Selected Subaltern Studies* (1988): "*The demographic difference between the total Indian population and all those whom we have described as the 'elite'*" (44, italics in the original), Spivak presents the subaltern project in a deconstructive fashion. While Subaltern studies "investigate[s] . . . a subaltern or peasant consciousness [which] seems at first to be a positivistic project," leading "to some *thing* that can be disclosed" (10), she believes that the problem lies in the fact that "it is only the texts of counter-insurgency or elite documentation that give us the news of the consciousness of the subaltern" (12). This prompts one of the contributors to this collection to lament: "The peasants' view of the struggle will probably never be recovered, and whatever we say at this stage must be very tentative" (volume 1.50). To negotiate the provisionality and the gravity of its task, Subaltern studies deliberately adopts "strategic essentializing" in trying to reclaim the subaltern consciousness, that is, these historians approach the elite and imperial materials from the perspective of the peasants in revolt.

By the same token, to retrieve from Asian American and

Asian Diaspora literatures the voice of the *subaltern* rather than the *bourgeois* immigrant in the United States may be as much an exercise in futility as Guha's pursuit of subalternity, for the simple fact that the submerged subaltern immigrant probably never had a voice in these texts. But a "strategic essentializing" is in order to interrogate the existing bourgeois texts with an eye to reconstructing the *totality* of immigrant subjectivities rather than a mere middle-class portion of it.

To this end of possible retrieval of immigrant voices, disciplinary boundaries amongst China, Postcolonial, and Minority studies have to be crossed. Such a transgression is urged by Edward Said in his foreword to *Selected Subaltern Studies*:

> The rigid boundaries between academic specializations has produced a whole gamut of jargons, of self-serving attitudes, of unattractive provincialisms. But such boundaries are an extension of the imperialism that decreed the principle of "divide-and-rule." (x)

To follow disciplinary demarcations would be tantamount to succumbing to the residual hold of imperialism institutionalized in academe. The second half of this chapter, therefore, will examine from the triple critical angles of China, Postcolonial, and Minority studies two pivotal texts in overseas student literature. While a comprehensive review of this genre would at least include Pai Hsien-yung's mid- to late-1960s short stories set in Chicago and New York, Yu Li-hua's *Again the Palm Trees!* (1967), Nieh Hua-ling's *Mulberry and Peach* (1976), Chang Hsi-kuo's *Rage of Yesteryear* (1978), and Chen Jo-hsi's immigrant novels published in the mid-1980s, I select only Yu and Chang for further analysis; Pai and Nieh are examined in chapter 3.

Such intersecting critical perspectives are apt to bring out the long-muffled hybridity of these texts. For as immigrant subjectivities and desires are intertwined inextricably with what Homi K. Bhabha terms as "nation and narration," the immigrant body in these texts becomes the site where cultural forces and social formations clash. The middle-class universe of Pai Hsien-yung, Yu Li-hua, and Nieh Hua-ling presents the prototype of immigrant subjectivities and desires, where wistfulness for home converges with exoticization of the West, where the urge to stay virginal and nativist coalesces with the drive to experience, culturally and sexually. The immigrant's nostalgia for a romanticized homeland is thus complicated by a fetishized America. This conflict finds expression in the immigrant's initially guarded and subsequently depraved or emancipated sexuality.

Chen Jo-hsi and Chang Hsi-kuo politicize the prototype of individual identity by reconfiguring it in relation to massive public events, such as the Tiao-yu-t'ai incident and the Cultural Revolution, throughout the 1970s and 80s. Though adroitly eschewing the self-indulgent style of Yu and Nieh, both writers continue to thrive on and be circumscribed by a Chinese-centered consciousness. Their nationalism and ethnocentrism threaten to suppress the ever-shifting multiplicity of immigrant subjectivities.

Immigrant Subjectivities and Desires in Overseas Student Literature

If sinologists suppress the postcolonial and U.S. minority conditions in favor of a nationalist impulse in overseas student literature, they do so at the behest of diaspora texts. Since its inception in Taiwan in the 1960s, overseas student literature invariably focuses on individual alienation both from the Chinese roots and from the American environment, resulting in a permeating sense of deterioration—physically, psychologically, and sexually. There exists an utter obliviousness to the larger cultural forces shaping this private dilemma. Three kinds of cultural forces, like underground waters, surface and join in these texts: the Chinese tradition, the global postcolonial movement, and the minority problematics. These three magnets exert opposite pulls on immigrant subjectivities, rendering them nostalgic for China while eagerly Westernizing themselves, busily putting down roots on American soil yet apathetic to their own marginalized status.

With respect to the Chinese literary heritage, immigrant texts continue the age-old exile tradition. Pai Hsien-yung, for instance, designates Chu Yuan's "Li Sao" as one of the likely originating points for the exile tradition which he himself inherits. These texts produced away from the center circulate, nevertheless, in the center; by virtue of the textual absence of and longing for China, they serve to consolidate a sense of the nation's uniqueness. After all, Chu Yuan composes elegies mourning his banishment *in order to* prove his loyalty to the emperor. By the same token, diaspora texts are perennially predicated on a lost origin—home or identity—which the characters try in vain to retrieve. This sense of rootlessness felt by mainland Chinese in Taiwan must be historicized within the cataclysmic change of the Communist takeover of China and the retreat of Kuomingtang (the Nationalist party) to the island in 1949. These mainlanders consider themselves temporary passengers in Taiwan, yet they grow increasingly skeptical as to whether they could return to China, despite political propaganda to the contrary. The popularity of overseas student literature in Taiwan derives, in part, from the textual construct of idealized "Chineseness," which honors readers as ethnic Chinese and assuages their longing for home.

Falling in line with the long genealogy of ethnocentric texts in Chinese history, overseas student literature evokes a most striking precedent: *Pien-sai-shih* (the frontier poetry) from the Tang dynasty (618–906 A.D.). This genre consists of texts composed by poet-soldiers stationed in the remote frontier defending Tang's territory against possible invasion from the "barbarian" tribes in the north and is marked by bleak landscape, resigned heroism, and racial pride.[10] The poet's proximity to "the other" and, hence, precarious existence serve to strengthen one's Chinese identity—for the poet and for the reader. Such texts sediment in the Chinese consciousness, valorizing the nation as opposed to the wicked other. What was once labeled as the "Hu" tribe (northern "barbarians") in Tang dynasty is now transformed into the marauding, shadowy modern landscape of the U.S. metropolis—with one important variation. While the frontier poets tried to contain the aliens along the border to preserve Chinese integrity, present-day expatriate writers must do so as they venture into the aliens. But the *physical* territory of China may not be as critical as the *mental* one (under)girding the Chinese consciousness. Both genres seek to suppress foreign elements in their midst in favor of a fabricated racial identity.

The second of the three cultural forces shaping overseas student literature is the postcolonial magnetic field whereby middle-class intellectuals in Taiwan are drawn to metropolitan areas in the West, initially as international students and subsequently as white-collar professionals. In the first half of this chapter, I have demonstrated how China experts such as Tu Wei-ming and C. T. Hsia gloss over the importance of postcolonialism in the study of Taiwan by subsuming it under an essentialist pan-Chinese ethos. Writers and critics alike routinely put Taiwan under erasure, with a perfunctory gesture toward the colonial histories of the Dutch, Japanese, American, and, of course, the Chinese against the culture of the aborigines. Yet a total reliance on postcolonial theories only aggravates the obstacles of recuperating overseas student literature, as these theories arise from the specific conditions of India, Latin America, Australia, and other places where most postcolonial scholars originate.

To truly comprehend immigrant subjectivities embodied in overseas student literature, critics must go against the grain of the widespread essentialist sentiment which views immigrants as first and foremost a continuum of some Chinese core of being. In fact, a postcolonial reading would see the Chinese presence on the island since 1949 as another colonizing power, contributing to what eventually evolves into an immigrant culture. The alleged Chinese core of existence resembles the British civilizing mission in that both forms of colonialist thinking assume an ontological higher ground, masking diverse origins and realities of the location by assigning them an inferior position.[11]

Lastly, the immigrants' minority status in the United States in the wake of the civil rights movement also informs immigrant subjectivities, which find themselves situated currently in a global economy with tight links to their Asian origins. However, both forces are concealed in diaspora texts to privilege the Chinese component. Failing to anchor immigrant subjectivities along these triple axes results in a dead-end obsession with the individual psyche. For instance, immigrant characters are portrayed as associating almost exclusively with other Chinese. Outside the ethnic circle, there is scarcely any in-depth depiction of Americans, except in stereotypes verging at times on racism—voluptuous blondes, black hoodlums, Hispanic alcoholics, and the like. If the intended audience goes beyond Chinese, the authors would be hard pressed to justify such biased presentations of this multiracial society. While this may be a faithful reflection of Chinese immigrants' unflattering views of their host society and their unduly romanticized view of the home community, it must be understood as a defensive ethnocentrism in reaction to the postcolonial and minority conditions.

Having originated from the neocolonial Taiwan where identity may rest on a relation with the West, these immigrants continue to be marginalized in the New World. Their disillusionment triggers a retreat to nativist ethnocentrism over China for psychological relief. This yearning for an imaginary Chineseness stems not only from a culture awaiting "the decolonization of the mind" but from the writers' own class background. In other words, overseas Chinese writers' withdrawal to Chineseness is heavily inflected by their middle-class origin, evidenced by how they, on the one hand, define themselves *as opposed to* the underclass and, on the other, by how they define themselves *for* their middle-class readers. This is a common dual strategy employed by what Gail Hershatter calls "nested" subalterns:

> [I]t is important to keep in mind the possibility of multiple, relational degrees of subalternity. I am tempted to label these as "nested" subaltern statuses, in which some groups go to great pains to distinguish themselves from and speaking for those "below," while allying themselves with and speaking to those "above." The problem with nesting, of course, is that it is too linear an image to convey all of the cross-cutting, overlapping, unstable ways in which subalternity can be constituted and dissolved in particular historical times and places. At least, however, it frees us from the monolithic category of *the* subaltern. (111)

"Nested" middle-class immigrant writers, therefore, locate themselves in a complex nexus of their middle-class Chinese readers as well as the American setting with its popular image of affluence highlighted by some representation of the disenfranchised. The danger of the *possibility* of degenerating from their bourgeois Chinese self into a dispossessed member of the U.S. minorities, in an eerie way, intensifies their sense of Chineseness. The following close reading of two key texts in overseas student literature over two decades seeks to bring into sharp focus a genre largely ignored and to destabilize the ethnocentric critical consensus regarding this genre by introducing the as yet suppressed ingredients in immigrant subjectivities. Since neither Yu Lu-hua nor Chang Hsi-kuo has been translated into English, a brief summary of each text is thus called for.

Yu Li-hua's "The Rootless Generation": Nostalgia, Postcolonial Critique, and Social Class

Born in Shanghai in 1931, Yu Li-hua went to Taiwan with her family in 1947. She came to the States to attend the University of California, Los Angeles, in 1954. Having received her master's degree in journalism in 1956, Yu is currently teaching at the State University of New York, Albany. Yu Li-hua's *Yiu-chien tsung-lu! Yiu-chien tsung-lu!* (Again the palm trees! 1967) is instrumental in initiating the genre of overseas student literature and manifests many of the problematics of immigrant subjectivities, including direct criticism of immigrants' postcolonial and minority conditions. The novel opens with the protagonist, Mou Tien-lei, returning to Taiwan after a ten-year sojourn in the United States, where he obtained his doctorate in journalism and is presently a university professor teaching the Chinese language. He intends a short homecoming to marry a young woman with whom he has regularly corresponded. The novel shuttles amongst several time frames: bittersweet memories of his traditional girlfriend, Mei-li, who married a few years after he went abroad; a thwarted extramarital romance with Lu Chia-li, an independent overseas writer; and, finally, the present courtship of Chen Yi-shan, his pen pal who wishes to escape through marriage from the "cage" of the island of Taiwan to the United States.

Like a *bildungsroman* in reverse, Mou Tien-lei reminisces about his regression in the New World—the loss of his youthful spirit after a series of disenchantments and compromises. Professionally, for example, he trims back his ambition to study English literature and to become a writer, settling with a degree in journalism, and then he abandons news reporting altogether to teach the Chinese language. As a result of his experience, Mou constantly undercuts his family and friends' grandiose, untested illusions about the West. But as a witness to contest popular images of the United States, he is not particularly convincing and his critique rather pathetic. Scarred by the decade of hardship in the Promised Land, he wavers whenever called upon to make a monumental decision. First he promises Professor Chiu, his college mentor, to take up teaching at his alma mater and to co-edit a literary journal charged with redressing their compatriots' mistaken notion of "ts'ung-yang" (worshipping the West). Soon Mou reverses himself and vows to take Yi-shan abroad in order to win her hand in marriage. After Professor Chiu's sudden death (a facile solution to Mou's dilemma), Mou again promises the chair of the department to stay on and, implicitly, to continue Chiu's mission. When Yi-shan learns of his decision, she immediately begins dating another returned overseas Chinese scholar to pursue her own immigration dream, and Mou is plunged into depression. The open-ended conclusion depicts Mou Tien-lei, braced by his resourceful sister Tien-mei, in a scene redolent of his youthful college days, riding his bicycle over to the Chens to try and convince Yi-shan to reconsider. With his track record, however, nothing is certain as the book closes with the image of palm trees leading him onward.

Beyond perpetual vacillations, Mou behaves at times downright mean-spiritedly, such as when he visits Tien-mei's husband at the sugar refinery in Tainan. After a boring luncheon with the colleagues at the refinery, Mou comments, "Since I came back from America, everyone wanted to see me to make sure I'm still human and don't have three heads and six arms" (280; translation mine unless otherwise noted). Such thinly-veiled sarcasm does not escape the attention of everyone present. Other times, he is absurdly childish and domineering. For instance, when he meets his former girlfriend, he petulantly orders her to remove her jiggling ear rings, as if he wielded supreme power over this traditional woman years after their estrangement.

Mou's fluctuation and instability contrast with the central metaphor of the book, palm trees, which symbolize rootedness and moral integrity:

> He [Mou] follows the little gravel road to the front gate [of the university where he graduated]. He turns around to gaze up at those huge, tall palm trees, stretching unflinchingly into the night sky. He remembers how before he left Taiwan, he had come to this front gate to bid them farewell. He had sworn a vow to these trees, promising to be as righteous and upstanding as they. He walks back in silence, head bowed. For the past decade, he has not emerged in triumph; instead, he has become mousy and timid. (101–102)

On the contrary, Professor Chiu had given up an excellent opportunity at Stanford University because he could not bear leaving his "den," an unkempt apartment in a bachelor dormitory where he was most firmly anchored. Mou's longing to stay in Taiwan and to work with Chiu bespeaks the need for regrounding.

Indeed, the notion of rootlessness is inherent in overseas student literature, and in *Again the Palm Trees!* it surfaces conspicuously through an intertextual reference to the story of "Su Wu the Shepherd." A crucial figure in an earlier ethnocentric project, Su Wu, a Chinese envoy to the northern "barbarians," had allegedly suffered nineteen years of exile due to his steadfast loyalty to the Han emperor. Listening to the song depicting Su Wu's devotion to China, Tien-lei breaks down and weeps in front of Chia-li, hence bringing about the romance of the two forlorn souls (105). In his introduction to the novel, C. T. Hsia finds the historical allusion evoking "endless sorrow"; Hsia is clearly in sympathy with the nostalgic sentiment emanating from Su Wu (13).

This reference to Su Wu is just one in a constellation of metaphors constructing nostalgia for "Chineseness," whether mainland China for Chinese emigres or Taiwan for overseas students and professionals. Nostalgia presupposes a prior uprooting, and *Again the Palm Trees!* is usually credited with the coinage of "the rootless generation," which conveys the sense of loss accompanying the exodus of young men and women from Taiwan to the West. Critics have repeatedly pointed out that the Chinese diaspora to Taiwan in 1949 continued in the ceaseless waves of emigrating Taiwanese students, but few have ever analyzed the postcoloniality inherent in Yu's point of reference for rootlessness. Tien-lei says to Tien-mei in the novel:

> Gertrude Stein [her name appearing in English in the original] told Hemingway that he was part of the lost generation. What about us? Isn't our generation another rootless generation? Yes, you guessed it right, I will go back [to America], not for Dad and Mom . . . not for Yi-shan . . . I'll go back—for my own sake. (176–77)

The Chinese diaspora is legitimized via the precedent of American intellectuals' pilgrimage to Europe, despite the widely diverging contexts of the two flights. Tien-lei resembles what Homi K. Bhabha calls the colonial "mimic man,"[12] whose identity consists of an imitating of the West, and, in Tien-lei's case specifically, the high modernist angst. Tien-lei, nonetheless, epitomizes his times, exposing Taiwan's restless and self-doubting collective unconscious, prompting him to return to the United States in spite of his instinctive reluctance.

The protagonist's inadequacies notwithstanding, he does offer critiques of Taiwan's postcolonial mentality and does relate his own disenfranchized minority position in the United States. Throughout the novel, whereas Tien-lei devours Chinese food, Yi-shan chooses Western food only. In his typically satirical way, Tien-lei mocks her: "The moon in America is rounder than that in China; American watermelons are surely sweeter than those in China" (149). More directly, he repeatedly describes the "other" America submerged under the facade of affluence, a point that fails to register in the minds of his family and friends. For instance, Tien-lei's weekly letters are filled with depressing notes on Chicago slums, claustrophobic winters, homogeneous and consumerist metropolises, lonely compatriots, and numerous self-denigrating remarks (138–40, 162), yet Yi-shan is most thrilled when Tien-lei promises to take her on a tour across the United States. Ultimately, it is because Yi-shan sees Taiwan as a "cage," "a barren land surrounded by the sea" that she so desperately wishes "to find out what's on the other side of the sea," even though Tien-lei assures her that "it is still a cage out there" (340–41).

Tien-lei is doomed to fail in trying to change the views of Yi-shan, his parents, and others because, fundamentally, his own understanding of the phenomenon is half-baked. The social phenomenon is identified as "ts'ung-yang" (worshipping the West), a banal interpretation closing off any probing of root causes. Tien-lei admits to Tien-mei his inability to inquire into it: "Don't ask me why they [the parents] think this way. I've never analyzed it. I think it's the time the place the environment making everybody feel that America is the only way to become somebody" (175). The slight breathlessness of the last sentence betrays the speaker's own frustration, but Tien-lei does provide some insight into the postcolonial state of mind when he points to vanity or the herding instinct (219). But Tien-lei's failure to comprehend this as a general social phenomenon signals a blindness of the times, one repeated by critics studying Yu Li-hua.

In "The Wandering Chinese: The Theme of Exile in Taiwan Fiction," Pai Hsien-yung elucidates "rootlessness" by way of references not just to Yu's "Lost Generation" but to Joyce's *Ulysses*, Camus' *L'Etranger*, and John Osborne's "Angry Young Man" (209), an identical move as Yu's allusion to Gertrude Stein. Yu and other writers' elegies of exile are highly dubious—until one locates the impulse squarely in the postcolonial mindset. The unbalanced structure of power since the cold war between the periphery of Taiwan and the center of the West propels these postcolonial writers to leave home and simultaneously to construct an imaginary home in the essentialized China. The result is that while they complicitously graft themselves to other cultures in pursuit of "more" happiness, they mourn the severance from their assumed origin. This contradiction is borne out by the fact that as nostalgia for China surfaces poignantly when Tien-lei and other returned overseas Chinese visit Quemoy and look across the Taiwan Strait at their place of origin (215), they do not see that their having this moment of homesickness is predicated on their status as privileged guests from the United States to which they will soon return.

When they are in the States, they are not much happier, as Tien-lei testifies repeatedly: "I can't describe the agony in a concrete way. It's not the kind of agony from my working as a manual laborer, of selling my physical strength cheaply. That pain is an invisible thing, a feeling. With Americans, you feel you're not one of them" (145). Theoretically, Tien-lei's distance from the white majority might have brought him closer to American minorities of similar fate, but he alienates himself from them as well. Almost all American minorities are harshly stereotyped: "In the tramcar are obese, dumb black women with thick, perked-up lips . . . and drunken, hairy Puerto Ricans, and Jews holding a detective story and smoking cigarettes under their Jewish nose" (267). Amazingly, a self-proclaimed stranger, Tien-lei becomes quite acculturated in internalizing white stereotypes of peoples of color. The "Jewish nose," for instance, has always been a marker for the Jewish race in the tradition of Western pseudo-science which culminates in the Nazi Holocaust against the "degenerate" and "Asiatic" Jews (Gilman's *The Jew's Body* 169–93). Yu evidently deploys stereotypical images of various ethnic groups: shrewd, cerebral Jews reading detective stories; ignorant, working-class blacks; alcoholic, animalistic Hispanics. C. T. Hsia in his introduction to the novel approvingly quotes these very descriptions of minorities as examples of Yu's superb craftsmanship in bringing alive scenes and characters (14). No critique is offered because Yu's representations of races might have been shared by Chinese readers and critics in the late 1960s when, ironically, the civil rights movement was underway.

The use of racial stereotypes by the author clearly stems from Tien-lei's reactions to a precipitous descent in his social class in the United States. The only solace this middle-class protagonist can find as he loses control over his life is to further disempower those below him by allying himself with the majority white culture, including its worst xenophobic instincts. Both Yu's readers and critics approve of this approach, as it somehow alleviates their precarious positions either as minorities in the United States or as postcolonial subjects living outside the American boundaries. This sense of amelioration comes via passing glimpses of the underclass in the American as well as Taiwanese society. The slums and the poor are viewed with pity and aloofness. Tien-lei recalls the rundown Chicago neighborhood he once chanced upon:

> Rows and rows of dilapidated, collapsing apartments . . . dust-covered rear windows, broken carpets piled up in the back cor-

> ridor, legless tables and chairs, springless mattresses. On the rickety railings are laid out women's panties, bras with holes, baby's diapers. Looking down, one sees a plot of dry yellow lawn like dry tofu. Papers flutter on the lawn, some smeared with snot, some drawn with human heads, some scrawled with obscenities. (268)

This quick peek of the subaltern from a Chicago tram corresponds to Tien-lei's awful impression of the subaltern at the Cheng Chenkung Temple in Tainan:

> The thing that Tien-lei can least tolerate is filth and clutter. . . . Climbing up the stone stairs [of the Temple], they encounter filthy, naked children staring at Yi-shan in her high-heeled shoes and sunshades. Papers and fruit rinds are strewn all over the stairs. Once up the stairs, crafts and food stands are arrayed before the temple. A mother with bare breasts feeds her child with one arm and shoos away flies with the other. A coating of yellow sand covers the food stands; some persistent red-head flies perch on them. (287)

Tien-lei's glimpses of Chicago poor and Taiwanese poor resemble each other in their brevity, forgettability, and the tinge of aversion. The disdain for the subaltern population crosses national lines. The underclass is marked by, among other things, repulsive sexuality in terms of displayed panties in Chicago or bare breasts in Tainan, both silhouetted against scenes of decay.

Tien-lei's class position also accounts for many of his bitter memories of working menial jobs in the United States. Upon his return to Taiwan, he notices photographs of himself exhibited on the living room wall chronologically, from the first one taken on the ship to the States, to the second against the backdrop of the Golden Gate Bridge, to the third at the driver's seat in a borrowed Buick, and to the final one with himself in full academic costume receiving his Ph.D. Disrupting this sanitized version of his struggle in the States, however, is his vivid recollection of the summer frenzy of job search, "like a stray dog squiggling everywhere, seeking shelter." Specifically, he recalls

> driving a truck of frozen ice from San Francisco to Carmel nightly, a semi as long as a freight car, from midnight to five o'clock in the morning. The world slept soundly, but he was

> awake in total despair, his bloodshot eyes fixed on the winding mountain road. . . . Behind his back were thousands of *ching* of chilling ice; before him were layers and layers of terrifying precipices. Inside him was burning the fire of desperation, rage, and discontent. Slowly crawling, driving, laboring along the loneliest road on earth. (33–34)

Hsia again commends this passage for its graphic depiction (Introduction 14), an assessment requiring readers' acquiescence to the presentation of labor jobs as beastly and condescending to overseas students. As such, the characters and readers' class position is indisputably bourgeois, which entails an obliviousness to the intersection of their comfortable life with the immediate surrounding as well as with past history. A case in point is when Tien-lei and his girlfriend pay a visit to sugar refineries in Taitung and Tainan, they take for granted their Japanese-style accommodations and the entire operation of the sugar industry, unaware of their entrance into the very heart of the Japanese colonial empire in Taiwan from 1895 through 1945. Nor do they—the author included, for that matter—register the fact that Tien-lei's brother-in-law, a division head at the sugar refinery, speaks with a "northern Chekiang [a province of China] accent" (272)—a possible signifier of racial difference between mainland Chinese management and Taiwanese labor force, a partition also receiving some minimal but more conscious reflection in Chang Hsi-kuo's novel.

Chang Hsi-kuo: Elegy on the Politicization of Passion

Chang Hsi-kuo was born in Chungking, China, in 1944. After obtaining his B.S. from National Taiwan University in 1965, he came to the States to attend a graduate program in electrical engineering at the University of California, Berkeley. He received his Ph.D. in 1969 and has taught at Cornell University, Taiwan's Chiao-tung University, and the University of Illinois in Chicago, and is presently teaching at the University of Pittsburgh. Though a scientist, he has been active in Taiwan's literary scene since his college days.[13] Characterized by his lucid, crisp, and versatile style, *Tso-jih chih nu* (Rage of yesteryear 1978) proceeds in five chapters following seasonal changes. In this novel, Chang parts company with Pai's modernist preoccupation with individual anxiety, Yu's bourgeois romance of a Chinese hamlet, and Nieh's allegorical portrayal of a schizophrenic woman; instead, he offers explicit handling of political events—the "Protect Tiao-yü-t'ai Movement," or simply Pao-tiao, across the United States in the early 1970s.

The backdrop leading to Pao-tiao is Taiwan's increasingly beleaguered international relationships caused primarily by the opening of its ideological arch-enemy—China. On April 9, 1971, the U.S. State Department announced that it would "return the Chien-kuo (Senkaku in Japanese) Islands, about 100 kilometers northeast of Keelung, Taiwan, to the jurisdiction of Japan in 1972. Tiao Yü T'ai is the largest of this group of islands" (Lau's Preface to *The Unbroken Chain* xii), which touched off a series of protests by overseas Chinese. This diplomatic setback is compounded by Taiwan's expulsion from the United Nations in 1971, President Nixon's visit to China in 1972, Japan's termination of its diplomatic relationship with Taiwan in 1972, and President Carter's recognition of the mainland as the only legitimate China in 1978. The decade was fraught with many more such gloomy political news; however, Taiwan meanwhile fared well economically and emerged as one of the four so-called "little dragons of the Pacific Rim."

Pao-tiao seems to be a personal obsession of Chang's due to his involvement with the movement; no other overseas Chinese writers focus on this incident as much as Chang, who devotes *Rage of Yesteryear*, "Red Boy," and other works to memorialize it. Joseph S. M. Lau in "Obsession with Taiwan: The Fiction of Chang Hsi-kuo" attributes this to C. T. Hsia's long-established thesis of "Obsession with China," coincidentally reflected in the author's name *Hsi-kuo*—"concerned with one's country" (152). Clearly, in the mental geography of both Hsia and Lau, mainland China and Taiwan are collapsed together, so it is for Chang as well. Chang writes in the postscript to *Journey to the Heavenly City* (1977): "When the earth shook in tremor in Peking, Tientsin and T'ang Shan, I was there [in China]. When the Gang of Four was being purged, I was there" (201). Hyperboles aside, Chang embraces ethnic Chinese both from China and from Taiwan, an attachment rooted in an abstract, historically constructed "Chineseness." This intense yet ill-defined loyalty comes under severe test during the Tiao-yü-t'ai Incident, when both political entities that seemingly embody "Chineseness" collide. Ultimately, the return of Tiao-yü-t'ai to Japan is dictated by international circumstances beyond the overseas students' control; the irreversible trajectory of the islands' sovereignty thus punctuates the crevices of the so-called Chinese identity. A patriotic campaign upholding *China*'s territorial integrity is launched from *over-*

seas over islands close to and claimed by *Taiwan*'s regime. The passion of many overseas Taiwanese Chinese activists, in this tumultuous chain reaction, is rapidly politicized and their allegiance shifted to Beijing when Nixon declares his imminent visit to China and when the Nationalist government capitulates to the U.S.-Japan arrangement. "The aborted youth movement" (221) can be attributed, insofar as immigrant subjectivities are concerned, to the participants' fused allegiance to China and Taiwan, to the historic animosity between China/Taiwan and Japan, and to the immigrant dilemma of residing in the United States yet longing for an imagined homeland.

Despite the disclaimer in Chang's afterword that the reader should "not treat *Rage of Yesteryear* as literature," but a mere "personal interpretation of the Chinese youth political movement" (300), this novel's political import is manifested by way of well-wrought literary strategies. From shifting perspectives, it delineates various types of overseas Chinese: sheltered, dreamy college students; a history professor lusting for young women; a political activist clinging to passion and idealism; vulgar Taiwanese businessmen; an editor of Chinese-language newspaper in New York's Chinatown. Due to the political and economic circumstances of the time, these overseas Chinese are exclusively from Taiwan and Hong Kong rather than China.

The various strands of the story revolving around the historical incident are woven together through a limited narrator, Chen Tze-hsiung, an ordinary businessman in Taiwan. Chen's gorgeous cousin, Wang Ya-nan, marries Hung Hsien-tsu during her brief visit to the States as a representive of Taiwan's college youths. Their marriage is unstable and Wang eventually divorces Hung to live with Ko Jih-hsin, a Pao-tiao activist and an incorrigible idealist. Two minor characters are Wu Han-shan, a professor of history and Chen's brother-in-law, who is bent upon starting some business venture and having affairs with college students, and Shih Ping, newspaper editor in New York's Chinatown as well as Ko's classmate in college in Taiwan and at the University of California, Berkeley.

The overseas activists' nationalist zeal and disillusionment over Pao-tiao must be contextualized in Taiwanese youths' education. Taiwan's college students are represented in the novel by members of a University Philosophy Club, including Ko Jih-hsin, Shih Ping, and the chair, Hu Wei-kang. Hu is a handsome, melancholic young man prone to pulling his hair in agony over existentialist reveries such as "None of you understand me! . . . For me, existence itself is the greatest burden of all. I simply have no idea how to go on living the next moment. . . . We were all thrust into this world" (92), while waiting—in a separate villa built for his exclusive use in the family garden—for the attractive maid to deliver his next meal. Chang's satire of the privileged elite also taunts the fad over French existentialism in Taiwan during those decades as well as modernism's engrossment with the self. When Hu travels to Los Angeles to attend graduate school, Shih Ping describes him as a changed person, one who "has worked as a dish washer and tasted the bitterness in life" (122). Menial jobs represent "the bitterness in life" to the educated from Taiwan, for such part-time, temporary occupations symbolize a fall from their Confucian "Shih" (literati) background whereby all things requiring strenuous or repetitious physical labor are relegated to the working class and to women. Even though working—preferably nonmenial jobs—to support oneself through graduate school is a common phenomenon in the States, overseas students have not been Americanized in this regard. For them, such experiences signal a plunge in social status and self-esteem. In a similar vein, while working for their doctorate, Wu Han-hun in Pai's "Death in Chicago" delivers laundry for the Jim Wong Laundry and Mou Tien-lei in Yu's *Again the Palm Trees!* drives a truck along the California coast. Candidacy for an advanced degree should not in theory prevent anyone from taking on low-paying jobs to make a living; however, Wu and Mou's grievances may in fact suggest the discrimination they suffer over not being able to receive appointments more in line with their capabilities. The prejudice is at least implied in Wu's job at the laundry, one of the few occupations in which Chinese immigrants are frequently stereotyped as engaging in the nineteenth-century American West.[14] At any rate, such a working experience for overseas students invariably contributes to their melancholy and self-depreciation.[15]

The most conscientious member of the club is Ko Jih-hsin, who matures from debating Hu on Western philosophy in Hu's garden villa to patriotic actions in the United States during Pao-tiao. Ko's growth begins as he witnesses the antiwar demonstrations at Berkeley and awakens to his and other young Taiwanese students' sheltered, constricted life. Experiences on campus are reinforced by Ko's voracious reading at Berkeley's library of heretofore inaccessible materials in Taiwan; Ko is thus prepared to dedicate himself to Pao-tiao as a way of erasing past sins and reaffirming his present commitment to be an *engagé* intellectual. His research into China's past furnishes him with Nationalist rhetoric throughout the campaign. Specifically, Ko evokes the anti-Japanese War (1937–45) and other disgraceful chapters in modern Chinese history to rally his audience. Ko is certainly too passionate and patriotic to be agitating the normally apathetic masses in such a calculating way, but many other student leaders are manipulative for self-gain, eventually causing the "aborted youth movement."

To inspire his fellow expatriates during the movement, Ko at one point refers to the invasion of the Ching dynasty by European imperialist powers, while "passing around photographs of the Nanking Massacre [committed by the Japanese Royal Army after they enter the capital city on 12 December 1937] and the Boxer Rebellion [in 1900 which leads to the Allied Expedition]" (130). The historic misalignment of incidents decades apart as well as the obfuscated connection between the past and the present are subsumed in Ko's "flushed face, trembling voice" and his audience's subsequent heated discussion. Such strategies are consistently used by Ko throughout Pao-tiao. When Shih Ping fails to see any personal relevance in the Berkeley Peace Demonstration, Ko urges him to read an anthology from the 1930s on how deeply Chinese youths then were dedicated to saving the nation. When another friend wavers on the eve of a Pao-tiao rally for fear of retaliation after he returns to Taiwan, Ko admonishes: "Do we rise up in revolt only after the Japanese have already occupied half of our river and mountain [an endearing classical term for China]" (162). Even slogans chanted during the demonstrations resonate with the Sino-Japanese War: "Defeat Japanese Imperialism!" (169), "Resist Foreign Powers, Eliminate Chinese Traitors!" (177). The latter incantation at a commemorative ceremony for the May Fourth movement of the 1910s harks back to another historic precedent of resistance against Japanese aggression. The anti-Japanese attitude post-Pao-tiao is not always so pure and exalted; it on occasion lapses into vulgar jokes. A group of Taiwanese businessmen visiting Detroit flaunt the fact that they deliberately change their hotel room from one floor below the Japanese to one floor above:

> Why do we have to live under [punning with "in the crotch of"] the Japanese? Besides, they love to pee on the floor. If we're not careful . . . Ha, ha! I personally have strong national consciousness. Since I represent my country in this meeting, I'll never give in to the Japanese. (228)

Though the businessmen's jest is a corrupt version of Pao-tiao's ardor, it illustrates that Pao-tiao grows out of an intensely nativist sentiment most Chinese seem to share vis-à-vis the Japanese.

In the post-Pao-tiao years, the failed mass movement provokes an excruciating soul-searching for erstwhile activists. One character indicts the Chinese culture as being plagued by "ideological egotism" which insists on hegemonic domination and does not tolerate any dissenting views (239). Moreover, only Shih Ping who has undergone the thrills and the agonies of the movement can perceive, upon his return to Taiwan, a nativist movement sprouting on the island and rejuvenating the Pao-tiao spirit (290). Of all those involved, only the idealistic Ko clings to the memories of the mass movement and refuses to allow the "small I" (egotistic concerns) to overwhelm the "big I" (collective consciousness) (161, 164). Not compromising with the capitalist society, Ko makes a living by peddling *pao-tze* (stuffed dumplings) on the streets of Berkeley while continuing his futile nationalist campaign. His love for Wang Yanan, nevertheless, compels him to contemplate looking for a job with his doctorate in chemistry. Like the idealist Professor Chiu in Yu's *Again the Palm Trees!* Ko dies in a traffic accident before any major change in life could materialize (298). It would appear that both novelists sense the herculean yet fruitless attempt of their quixotic characters, who are made, therefore, to meet an early, unexpected death.[16] Otherwise, Chang Hsi-kuo would most likely conclude with Ko taking an office job and Yu Li-hua with Mou and Chiu co-editing a journal dedicated to altering the pro-West ethos. The former ending appears to be, as Lau puts it in "Obsession with Taiwan: The Fiction of Chang Hsi-kuo," "a mocking commentary on the futility of patriotic impulse." Lau thus defends Ko's accident as "a *coup de grâce* rather than a failure of imagination" (156). The latter ending becomes excessively didactic, jarring with the postcolonial reality. Hsia in his introduction to Yu's novel likewise justifies Professor Chiu's accident as having its "inevitability in terms of the story's logic" and further adds that such incidents are entirely possible in the congested Taipei. In his typically cavalier fashion when addressing the Chinese readership, Hsia even provides the following as proof: "I heard that a Professor of History at National Taiwan University was run over by a car" (22). Both Lau and Hsia's apologies for the convenient deaths prove that the critics are in cahoots with the novelists in constructing a tragic yet "untainted" finale for China-centered idealism. The demise of the *flawed* hero Ko saves him from becoming a *corrupted* one, whereas that of Chiu ceases all further interrogation of Taiwan's immigrant culture. The denouements made possible in this manner avoid delving into Ko's minority status in the United States and Chiu's postcolonial environment. Accordingly, Chang ends with the widow Wang Ya-nan returning to Taipei holding in her arms Ko's newborn baby, in whom the nativist hope is once again invested. Yu similarly closes with the cliffhanger of Mou suspended between his late professor's miserable utopianism and his girlfriend's West-bound happiness, a perfect epitome of Taiwan's postcolonial condition.

Scattered throughout *Rage of Yesteryear*, however, are pieces of evidence of Chang's consciousness of postcoloniality and the immigrant's minority status. For instance, the impetuous Wang Ya-nan agrees to marry Hung Hsien-tsu because all the male guests at a certain banquet, including her suitor Hung, are captivated by "a local student, eighteen or nineteen, the daughter of a diplomat, a senior at the University of Michigan. She speaks fluent English and Chinese. Before the banquet, she even played several piano pieces" (176). Far from a mere case of female jealousy, this Michigan student enjoys tremendous popularity not only due to her beauty and competence but for her exalted social status. Few college-age Taiwanese youths in those decades could *live* and study abroad, a privilege rendering Wang who could only *visit* the States pale in comparison.

The severest attack against this postcolonial hierarchy based on one's proximity to the West is launched by the conscience of the novel, Ko Jih-hsin. In addition to his actions, Ko diagnoses this mentality as "cultural compradorism" (126). In a more composed and wistful tone, Shih Ping, the Chinese-language newspaper editor, muses over the inevitable fate of such compradors, who are severed both from their origin and from their progeny: "The younger generation of Chinatown . . . will no longer harbor a deep attachment to China like the older generation" and must struggle for their own rights in the American society (72–73). This generation gap is revealed in a line from Tang poetry recited by a Chinese professor in response to his American-born son's question about a Chinese record. "A Hu [barbarian] youngster/person first hearing a Han [Chinese] family/empire tune," says the professor caressing his son's head (126). The dual translation brings out the ambiguity in the original, treating the supposedly uncultivated foreigner both as a protege of Chinese culture and as a junior member of the Chinese family and empire.

Eschewing the extremes of Ko's selfless idealism and Hung's selfish materialism, Shih Ping provides a wider view of New York's Chinese immigrants, particularly the subaltern population. For example, a worker at the Chinese newspaper is depicted as an inveterate gambler, a family tradition passed down by his father who died in poverty in Hong Kong (138). More detailed are Shih Ping's childhood memories of an employee at his father's factory in the rural Taiwan. This worker had lost an arm on the job and stood outside Shih Ping's home for days seeking justice. The child Shih Ping was fascinated by the lonely figure standing guard day and night, but the adult recalls that the families' response was to find a watch dog to protect themselves. Such reminiscences overwhelm Shih Ping with remorse and guilt, especially the scene when Shih Ping, looking for the dog, hears the worker say "with a shy smile": "Gone away. I have go chase. Didn't catch it" (285), as if he were a family servant responsible for the retrieval of the dog. The awkward literal translation of the second sentence—which may well read "I have given chase"—tries to retain the worker's Taiwanese accent. Such subtle references to the collusion of ethnicity and social position in terms of characters' Taiwanese or mainland accent permeate Taiwanese literature, so much so that one begins to discern a veiled, or perhaps unconscious, pattern of subversion of the Nationalist party's unwritten ethnic hierarchy of those years.[17] Therefore, through the fleeting image of a diffident, dismembered, and largely mute Taiwanese, Chang exposes the social stratification at the time of mainland managerial staff versus Taiwanese laborers. Nonetheless, it is noteworthy that when the dispossessed in the United States or in Taiwan come alive momentarily in the hands of a conscientious writer such as Chang Hsi-kuo, they are cast either as addicts to gambling or as silent sufferers, both popular images of the helpless, pitiable underclass. Such strategies of representation perhaps betray the novelist's marginal understanding of that marginal segment of the society, but these images have at least improved from downright contempt of the wretched of the earth in Yu Li-hua to patronizing sympathy in Chang Hsi-kuo.

Conclusion: Toward the Future of Immigrant Subjectivities

What continues to characterize overseas student literature, however, is the genre's entrenched bourgeois condition, giving rise to an ethnocentric defensiveness on the part of those whose class interests are under siege through migration and by U.S. imperialism. This defensiveness, however, is rather misplaced, as it manifests itself as nostalgia for the lost homeland and disdain for the adopted land. The subaltern element in immigrant subjectivities remains largely elided, except for occasional, scattered glimpses of the disenfranchised in the United States and Taiwan. This glaring omission is inextricably tied to the nature of overseas student literature. The brief biographical sketches of Yu and Chang show that these two practitioners of the genre—and, by extension, Pai, Nieh, and Chen mentioned earlier—are middle-class intellectuals. Of the five, Chen Jo-hsi is the only one from a disadvantaged Taiwanese background, but she comes to espouse the pan-Chinese ethos, proven by her return to China during the Maoist era and her recurring focus on Chinese intellectuals. Some shared biographical details bear witness to their middle-class consciousness. Four out of the five writers were graduates of supposedly the most prestigious university in Taiwan, and the more senior Nieh taught creative writing there. Each journeyed to the States for advanced degrees in the 1960s (Yu did so in the 50s but did not publish her magnum opus until a decade later) and continued since to operate amongst American academicians and Chinese writers and publishers. Of course, one's class background does not dictate one's class position, but these writers seem completely immersed in their specific social stratum.

These writers are equally obsessed, to return to C. T. Hsia, with China. This nationalist sentiment is originally produced by what Louis Althusser terms as the "Ideological State Apparatuses"—education in particular. Their education in the Chinese and Taiwanese mold saturates them with ethnocentrism so thoroughly that even their advanced education in American institutions and, ultimately, their naturalized American citizenship fail to decenter their ideology. In fact, the ideology based on an allegiance to "Chineseness" frequently neutralizes and absorbs alien elements in immigrant subjectivities, such as Taiwan's postcolonial, hence un-Chinese, condition—which contributes to the exodus to the West—as well as immigrants' ensuing minority status in a foreign land—which threatens to besmirch pure "Chineseness." These writers eventually become not only products of "Ideological State Apparatuses" but re-producers of that structure. In Homi K. Bhabha's terms, these writers create the "nation" through their "narration." For instance, Chu Yuan's "Li Sao" cited by Pai Hsien-yung, the legendary figure of Su Wu deployed by Yu Li-hua and hailed by C. T. Hsia, the paradoxical celebration of an immigrant's Chinese half by her American other in Nieh Hua-ling, the elegy on nationalist fervor in Chang Hsi-kuo, the stoic, self-effacing Chinese intellectuals in Chen Jo-hsi, and many other such cultural monuments converge to construct the nostalgia for "Chineseness."

Indeed, "nations" are "imagined communities," as Benedict Anderson puts it, but such imagination exacts a heavy toll on immigrant subjectivities, obliging them to relinquish whatever within themselves that seem at odds with the nationalist project. It appears to be almost a betrayal of their Chinese origin for immigrants either to acknowledge that they are postcolonial subjects no less than those from ex-colonies or to accept that they belong under the umbrella term of Asian American minority. But both are prerequisites to a more comprehensive fashioning of immigrant subjectivities informed yet unbound by national affiliation. Practitioners of overseas student literature may do well to heed the arguments of Fredric Jameson, John Tomlinson, Arjun Appadurai, and others;[18] it is perhaps time for them to conceive their texts globally and "postnationally," attending to rather than dismissing the nonnationalist ingredients in their immigrant characters. The genre of film appears to embody this future trend most promisingly because it crosses national and cultural boundaries with minimal distress and because it befits the late capitalist epoch whereby subjectivities are manifested less through the relative fixity of the printed word than through the proliferating kaleidoscopic images of the electronic media.[19]

But before this leap from literature to film can be performed, immigrant writers and intellectuals need to step out of the intricate web of their own "overseas" "nationalist bourgeois" condition. To chart the course of future immigrant subjectivities, they must interrogate cultural compradorism from which their migration and mentality often originate. This can be achieved by analyzing how compradorism is resisted by Taiwan's *hsiang-t'u* (home-soil or nativist) literature. Underpinned with a similar sense of nostalgia as overseas student literature, nativist literature launches its critique of compradorism from the disintegrating utopia of rural Taiwan, one lamented as being engulfed by multinational capitalism and its concomitant urbanization, Americanization, and vulgarization.

SEVEN

An Island of Immigrants: Nativist Critique of Taiwan's Compradorism

That so many Taiwanese writers converge in the United States and in the genre of overseas student literature is no mere accident. It reflects the comprador culture in postwar Taiwan—an island of immigrants whose values and desires are dictated by the West. But the present neocolonial phenomenon should be historicized in the ebb and flow of forces in Taiwan. Such a historicization reveals the island as a site where power rather than any essentialist core of being dictates the location's allegiance at any given time. First of all, the aborigines in Taiwan are of Malayan-Polynesian, hence non-Chinese, origin, sharing biological and cultural characteristics with the original inhabitants of Southeast Asia and the Pacific Islands region. The earliest reference to Taiwan in Chinese texts seems to be to the island of "Yichou" in Chen Shou's *San-kuo-chi* (Chronicle of the three kingdoms) in the third century A.D. Various Chinese dynasties claimed Taiwan as part of their territory over many centuries. In 1544, the Portuguese reached Taiwan and named it "Formosa." The Japanese had tried taking over Taiwan since the sixteenth century. In 1622, a Dutch fleet landed in the Pescadores, islands offshore of Taiwan, and, two years later, began constructing the city of Zeelandia in Tainan in southern Taiwan. In 1629, Spanish troops built the city of Santo Domingo (today's Hung Mao [red hair] City) in Tamsui in northern Taiwan. Cheng Ch'eng-kung, loyal to the collapsing Ming dynasty, occupied Taiwan in the seventeenth century as his home base to launch a campaign against the Ching dynasty. The Opium War between the British and the Chinese commenced in 1840, prompting the British to plan an attack on Taiwan. In 1854, Commodore Matthew Calbraith Perry of the United States, having opened Japan to foreign trade, sent ships to Taiwan to investigate its mineral deposits.[1] The Sino-Japanese War ended in 1895 and the Treaty of Shimonoseki ceded Taiwan to Japan. Taiwan was not returned to China until 1945 at the close of World War II. The Nationalist party (Kuomingtang) led by Chiang Kai-shek fled to Taiwan in 1949, after having been defeated by the Communists.

It is evident from this brief schematic review of Taiwan's history that the island is regarded by whatever power of the time as a temporary refuge to prepare for an eventual departure for a more ambitious enterprise. Cheng Ch'eng-kung crusaded against the Ching dynasty in the mainland; Western countries exploited the island's natural resources and geopolitical location; Japan used it as the headquarters for its operation to invade Southeast Asia in World War II. The majority of Chinese immigrants since 1949 share this kind of sojourner mentality, except that their final destination lies increasingly not in China, a country behind the "iron curtain," but in the United States. To accomplish the goal of exiting the island, they have to be of the social class that enables them to emigrate, particularly in terms of educational background and economic resources. Taiwanese immigrant texts, such as overseas student literature, therefore, are produced by what Frantz Fanon calls the "national bourgeoisie," a class deeply embroiled in and profiting from Westernization and modernization. As a consequence, these immigrant texts seldom offer critiques of their own inherent postcoloniality.

Hsiang-t'u wen-hsueh (home-soil or nativist literature) rises in the 1970s as a counterhegemonic resistance against cultural imperialism. Yet the problematic choice of "nativist" in translation unwittingly touches on this movement's entanglement with the complex colonial history. To launch a veiled political resistance against the West as well as its mainland Chinese compradors in the Kuomingtang regime, nativist writers try to retrieve an unsullied Taiwan, a strategy echoing the nativist streak of the assumption of a certain Chinese essence in overseas student literature. In addition to this resemblance to overseas student literature, nativist literature erases the aborigines of the island, eliding the differences between these earliest settlers with Fukien, Canton, and Hakka immigrants arriving one or two centuries ago. Since the term *nativist* alludes to the *genesis* of a particular culture, nativist writers likewise err in duplicating the mainland Chinese immigrants' truncation of history. In the case of nativist literature, the "authentic" Taiwan is located in the waves of pre-1949 migration to Taiwan from southern China.

A third point of the problematics of naming derives entirely from the American context where these pages of commentary on Taiwan's literary history are to be received. The term "Nativism" has a distinct odious ring in U.S. history. Rampant in the latter half of the nineteenth century and the early decades of the twentieth century, the xenophobic, anti-Asian nativist sentiment manifested itself in racial discrimination and crimes. A nationwide legalization of such nativist hatred against Asians crystalizes in the 1882 Chinese Exclusion Act. The fear over "the Yellow Peril" was first publicized, according to historian Roger Daniels, by Henry George in an article in the *New York Tribune* on 1 May 1869 ("Majority Images-Minority Realities" 232) and continues even today in the renewed vigor pursuing anti-immigration legislation in Congress in the 1990s. To approach nativism in Taiwan since the 1970s, one needs to detach the unfortunate choice of translation from its association in U.S. history.

Viewed in Taiwan's cultural context, the power of nativist literature lies in its sympathetic portrayal of rural Taiwan and its dispossessed inhabitants. Taiwan's countryside, particularly in the southern and eastern parts of the island, becomes an Eden in the process of being infected by metropolitan culture, particularly that of Taipei in the north. Subsequently, nativist literature turns its attention from the dystopias of rice paddies and fishing ports to the grotesques of the island's city dwellers. This shift in focus involves the foregrounding or suppressing of three types of characters: Americans, urban(ized) compradors, and rural *hsiao-jen-wu* ("little people"). In its inception, nativist texts such as Huang Chung-ming's "The Son's Big Toy" and "Drowning an Old Cat" feature as the antagonist not Americans but rather a metropolitan, Western lifestyle—advertisement and the swimming pool, respectively. Gradually, this form of nativist presentation focusing on the plight of rural residents gives way to a preoccupation with the global expansion of American power, ranging from the neocolonial Vietnam War to the corporate penetration around the world, from soldiers with guns to businessmen with dollars. While the depiction of

American GIs decreases with the end of the war, stories on transnational capitalism have grown into a subgenre.[2] At times, nonetheless, American soldiers and businessmen come to occupy the center stage of nativist texts. These Americans are invariably accompanied by urban or urbanized compradors who epitomize the immigrant culture. The satire against these Rabelaisian-Bakhtinian middlemen sans the earthy, regenerating energy of the Renaissance concentrates on their urbanization, Americanization, and barbarization. Such criticism of the compradors' corruption of the body is often launched by rural observers, whose "grotesque" or "carnivalesque" folk humor that celebrates all that is low, as Bakhtin sees it, is in danger of vanishing amidst Westernized degeneration.

In addition to Bakhtin's reading of Renaissance "grotesque realism" and its gradual disappearance, another fundamental paragidm in which the complex cultural interface situates itself within nativist texts seems to be the Foucauldian-Saidian one of gender and power. In the West, the long lineage of Orientalism deploying the alleged power relationship of the two genders is conspicuous in Puccini's *Madama Butterfly* (1904) and is revived in the recent broadway show *Miss Saigon* on the Vietnam conflict. Even Asian American playwright David Henry Hwang, bent upon composing a "deconstructivist" *M. Butterfly* (1986), continues to draw from Orientalist stereotypes; one is not sure whether Hwang succeeds in debunking or reinforcing the "exotic Orient."[3] It is time, however, to see how "the other" reacts to this paradigm, how nativist literature in Taiwan "writes back." Nativist literature offers an intriguing revision of the Orientalist notion of the penetration of the Western phallus into Eastern femininity, militarily or monetarily. The reaction of nativist literature to Western domination is threefold, closely linked to the three types of characters mentioned earlier: it laments the fate of rural *hsiao-jen-wu*; it satirizes Chinese compradors, presented as "fake" Americans; and it problematizes American presence on the island.

All War and No Play Makes Jack a Dead Boy: American GIs on Furlough and the Sex Trade in Nativist Literature

Nativist literature problematizes the American presence on the island, first as innocent, shellshocked American GIs on furlough from the Vietnam War; subsequently as unpalatable, profiteering businessmen of transnational corporations; and finally as tropes, which, by virtue of their absence in the text, become the island compradors' object of desire. This part of the chapter explores the first type of representation, namely, the intersection in nativist texts of American military personnel on leave in Taiwan and the mushrooming sex trade.

This interrogation begins with Chen Ying-chen's "Ho-ta-ko" ("Brother Ho"). The narrator is a female college student, embarrassingly maudlin, enthralled by fantasies of love and idealism. She grows increasingly enamoured with Brother Ho, a mysterious, self-sacrificing American. His volunteer work at a handicapped children's sanatorium in rural Taiwan is motivated by a sense of guilt. In fact, he turns out to be mentally disturbed due to his implication in the My Lai Massacre and other atrocities. Brother Ho, in all likelihood, identifies subconsciously with the handicapped children; after all, he has been maimed psychologically in the war as well. "To help these children is in fact to help myself" (*Night Freight* 160; translation mine unless specified otherwise), he confides.

In the protagonist's adolescent attempt to reach him, she uses the excuse of wishing to learn English. He commends her English, to which she responds: "But some of the things Brother Ho says I don't understand completely" (163). Her juvenile bashfulness comes through the third-person address of "Brother Ho," which follows the standard etiquette in referring to one's elders in the Chinese language. Unwittingly, however, this answer touches on his secret of the massacre. The protagonist's youth, so well manifested in the story's self-consciously sentimental style, begins to be unsettled not only by the horror of war but also by the stylistic shift to the reportage section consisting of transcripts of psychoanalytic sessions and correspondence in which Brother Ho confronts the atrocities.

Brother Ho is diagnosed as schizophrenic and presented as a pawn of nationalism. Blame is laid squarely on nationalism rather than on individuals. "Behind them [the executioners of the My Lai Massacre] stands a giant—the country. Those children in Vietnam are all victims of nationalism" (189). "Those children" most likely refers to American soldiers, not to the Vietnamese people. Chen's story demonstrates how American involvement in Vietnam is viewed by many nativist writers with distrust and misgiving, but the attitude toward individual American soldiers is one of sympathy. This might be evading the ethical issue of the connection between the agents of evil and evil itself, for, after all, there were cases whereby ordinary soldiers defied the order of murdering innocent civilians in My Lai and elsewhere. Moreover, the ending of "Brother Ho" jives with the expedient division between innocent American soldiers and an evil U.S. government. While the youthful narrator matures after having learned of Brother Ho's suffering, she finds herself summoned by the disciplinary officers of her school and interviewed by what appears to be Taiwan's secret police on her involvement with Brother Ho. This commentary on Taiwanese politics by the dissident-author[4] suggests political intervention into and manipulation of private lives similar to Brother Ho's experience. Since representatives of the apparatus of oppression in Taiwan are exposed in closing, then who are their counterparts in My Lai, if not Brother Ho and others like him? Herein lies a deep-seated contestation of realism and romanticism within nativist literature.[5] While this body of texts is certainly realistic in its depiction of social ills, it tends to romanticize the disenfranchised—American soldiers or Taiwanese "little people"—in the midst of an adverse environment.

This contradiction is shared by Huang Chung-ming's "Hsiao-kua-fu" ("Little widow") and "P'ing-kuo-te-tzu-wei" ("The taste of apple" 1972). Huang's satires, however, move Chen's story from individuals' emotions to their material conditions. "The Taste of Apple" depicts a Colonel Ker-lei (Gray?), well-intentioned but ignorant, running over and incapacitating a poor Taiwanese laborer, who slowly realizes that this victimization by an American miraculously frees his family from financial burdens. This seems to be an apt allegory for Taiwan's modernization, which threatens to demolish the self in order to construct a new one. Secretly overjoyed, the family tastes the colonel's gift of a basket of apples, a rarity in the subtropical island at that time. This foreshadows Taiwan's future as a U.S. beneficiary with some degree of prosperity but a mutilated psyche.

"Little Widow" is the story among those examined thus far with the fullest portrayal of American GIs on furlough and the most blatant manifestation of the financial arrangement of the sex trade. This novella opens with Manager Ma introducing new publicity stunts to the board members of a prostitution ring. Ma's innovative ideas consist of cashing in on the already-existing Orientalist stereotypes of Madame Butterflies. Ma proposes that Taiwan's sex trade distinguish itself from those in other parts of Asia by catering to American soldiers' thirst for exoticism. Their brothel is then to be renamed "Little Widow," purportedly featuring recently bereaved traditional Chinese women sporting turn-of-the-century costume, sewing and waiting amidst Chinese screens. Said to be tortured by strict mores governing Chinese widows' conduct, these "widows" are "an iceberg on the outside, a volcano inside" (*Little Widow* 120). The harlots are advised, for lack of a better phrase, to "play hard to catch" with an Orientalist twist. Ma understands Western stereotypes and popular images of Asian women so thoroughly because of his past experiences in the United States.

Ma's promotional strategies also include advertisements in the media arousing American soldiers' sense of curiosity and adventure, further testifying to his facility in the capitalist system. A depraved comprador, Ma sees cultures, politics, human bodies as merely expediting monetary transactions. Profiting from cross-cultural *mis*understanding, he exploits Taiwanese bar girls' bodies as well as American soldiers' loneliness and guilt. The ultimate irony stems from the fact that Ma's sheer commercialism fails to crush other characters' souls. The humanitarian undercurrent of nativism percolates through the unfolding of the kindness of hookers and customers in the thick of business exchange. All three of the GI characters—Louie, Tom, and Billy—are traumatized by their own brutality, which is presented as inevitable in the war. Louie becomes impotent, plagued by memories of his compulsive shooting of a female corpse whose vagina is overrun with maggots. Both Tom and Billy are shown to be lost boys, dearly loved by the prostitutes who spend the night with them more as their elder sisters than as lovers. The story ends with Tom losing his life and Billy his left arm. Billy is the only survivor of his unit because, according to him, the incense necklace the bar girl gave him stands guard over him. It is significant that, despite its purely marketing purpose, the name "Little Widow" does characterize these prostitutes who have become widows to their dead and maimed American customers. However, the women are not mere sex objects providing services to their clients. They are delineated as maternal figures granting solace to frightened American boys who seek oblivion in alcohol, drugs, and intimacy. One prostitue, Ah Ching, is literally the mother to a "Hsiao Hei" ("darkie"), a common nickname (without the derogatory connotation in its English translation) for interracial children; Hsiao Hei is the testimony of her devotion to an African American sergeant.

Postcolonial Compradors in Nativist Satire: Urbanization, Americanization, Vulgarization

With the withdrawal of American troops from Vietnam, the representation of American GIs dwindles in nativist texts, replaced by the presence of U.S.-based transnational corporations and, of course, that of foreign businessmen and tourists. Chen Ying-chen's "Night Freight" ("Yeh-hsin-huo-ch'e") and Huang Chung-ming's "I Love Mary" ("Wu-ai-ma-li")[6] revolve around how Western capitalism threatens to transform into compradors those Taiwanese who come under its spell.[7] Such characters are readily noticeable in Manager Ma in "Little Widow," but they seem to proliferate rapidly as material interests begin to mount.

In Chen Ying-chen's "Night Freight," a triangular relationship develops among three employees of the Taiwanese branch of the Malamud International Company: Li Jung-p'ing, known as "J. P." to his colleagues; Liu Hsiao-ling or Linda, J. P.'s secretary and ex-lover; and Chan I-hung or James, an intense young man whose passion often turns abusive toward Liu, his lover. While J. P. is a typical cultural comprador with "a slave mentality" (*The Unbroken Chain* 106), Chen Ying-chen's stylistic "high-seriousness" prevents him from making a clown out of this natural candidate. Instead, J. P. is tortured by his love for Liu, on the one hand, and his family responsibility and career in the foreign company, on the other. The real antagonists being relentlessly ridiculed are the American executives. Mr. Morgenthau, the head of the Taiwanese branch, turns out to be an unscrupulous man, despite initial exoticism associated with him—his "deep, vigorous voice" (103) and "pale blue eyes, decorated with golden eyelashes," resembling "the vacant gray eyes of the cougar in an American T.V. commercial promoting automobiles" (105). As a secretly repulsed J. P. recalls his employer's animalistic eyes, it is telling that the image from an American commercial flows through his mind, which is circumscribed by the business world. The other kind of vulgar characters, described only in passing, are the rowdy Japanese tourists urinating in public. The portrayal of Morgenthau, however, is flawed by the fact that he speaks British rather than American English. The constant usage of "*old Boy*" (English words in italics in the original Chinese version) by Morgenthau, supposedly an American, bespeaks a confusion of the two dialects. Moreover, the romantic vein of nativism lapses into a melodrama between Liu and Chan. During one of Chan's routine beatings of Liu on the eve of her departure for the United States, Liu deviates from her usual resignation and protects herself with a fruit knife, while solemnly declaring to a drunken Chan: "'I'm carrying this one [Chan's child] because—' her voice was a little quivery, 'because—I love you'" (123). Straight out of a soap opera, this sentimental scene follows the formula of a teary yet maternal woman, a tempestuous yet repentent man, and a third party—J. P.

How this disaster of an affair is averted requires special attention. During a company banquet after their ambiguous farewell tryst, Chan's personal frustration clashes with Morgenthau's racial slurs in public—"*And you fucking Chinese think the United States is a fucking paradise*" (131). While comprador characters at the banquet, such as J. P., endure the insult in silence, Chan explodes and meaningfully switches to Taiwanese as he addresses J. P.: "Let's not quarrel in front of the barbarians" (131), the traditional Chinese term of contempt for all aliens. This revolt not only empowers Chan but wins him the heart of his lover, who agrees not to go abroad. Flashing through Chan's mind at this moment of triumph is the childhood memory of "a long line of immense, black freight cars rumbling before him, moving toward the south. Oh, toward the south, his hometown" (129). Nativism based in southern Taiwan and nationalist pride against cultural and economic imperialism transcend and resolve personal dilemmas, sexual or patriotic, in a heavy-handed manner. But contrary to the postcolonial subjects' predicament of inhabiting the United States while wistful over an imaginary homeland in overseas student literature, these nativist characters relinquish, simultaneously, the trip to the New World and the sojourn in Taipei.

Chen's didactism and rage over self-denigrating collaboration with the West become biting satire against full-fledged slavish compradors in Huang Chung-ming's "I Love Mary." The protagonist Ta-wei (transliterating "David," but synonymous with "potbelly" in Chinese) Chen exhibits the classic postcolonial complex; his sense of self-worth derives from a servile approximation of the West, exemplified in this story by the Raymonds. Mr. Raymond is the head of the foreign company where Ta-wei is employed. Despised as "a pig or a dog" (*The Unbroken Chain* 144) by the Raymonds, Ta-wei finds even their mongrel dog, Mary, which he enthusiastically inherits upon their departure from the island, a symbol of American lifestyle and of the close ties with his former superior. Ta-wei's conversations in the office thus constantly turn to "how he and his family had to wait upon [Mary]" (148). Indeed, Mary becomes Ta-wei's substitute spouse at one point when he subconsciously scratches her erogenous zone with gusto, causing "her bright red tongue to loll lazily to the side as she stared at the magic fingers that were bringing such pleasure to her" (155). So perverted is his thinking that he scolds his wife, Yu-yun, when she sinologizes

"Mary" as "Mei-li"; he takes it out on her again when Mary demolishes his beloved orchids; he even abuses Yu-yun physically when Mary mates with a stray. The reversal of wife and dog is complete as Ta-wei wishes Yu-yun dead and declares that he loves Mary instead.

Cultural compradors such as Ta-wei Chen are most pronouncedly abominable in that their servitude to transnational capitalism is practiced as a way of life, practiced despite a total absence of representatives of American or foreign interests. Put another way, compradors serve intuitively at the pleasure of the West, even though no Westerner is there to be pleased. Americans become a conceptual trope whose very absence and distance escalate its desirability, a postcolonial paradox underpinning both of Wang Chen-ho's hilarious satires, *Mei-jen T'u* (Portrait of beautiful/Americanized people 1982; henceforth referred to as *Portrait*) and *Mei-kuei Mei-kuei Wu-ai-ni* (Rose, Rose, I love you 1984; henceforth referred to as *Rose*). After all, the global economic and cultural systems implicit in both texts have largely predetermined the compradors' eagerness to perpetuate American interests, which coalesces with self-interests, at the expense of crushing rural characters.

It is no surprise that Wang Chen-ho is rarely translated; these two texts under examination are virtually untranslatable. Wang's later style is so characterized by a festive heteroglossia of voices and dialects that he integrates Mandarin, Taiwanese, English, Japanese, Hakanese, Cantonese, Shanghainese, and Taiwan's aboriginal language in the speeches of his characters. Bakhtin's definition of heteroglossia helps shed light on Wang's texts:

> Authorial speech, the speeches of narrators, inserted genres, the speech of characters are merely those fundamental compositional unities with whose help heteroglossia [*raznorecie*] can enter the novel; each of them permits a multiplicity of social voices and a wide variety of their links and interrelationships (always more or less dialogized). (*The Dialogic Imagination* 263)

To suggest the linguistic complexity of Wang's novels—of how the dialogized "multiplicity of social voices" is enacted, a minor example will have to suffice. A city councilman in *Rose* offers a short speech to a group of prostitutes and then yields the floor by saying: "A speech should be like women's miniskirt, the shorter the better, so I will S-To-Pu here" (222). The simile of short skirt comes from the humorist Lin Yutang and it is, more or less, a literary or Mandarin reference. Yet "S-To-Pu" is originally the Japanese pronunciation of an English word, both of which have been incorporated into Taiwanese idioms. From this brief instance, one can catch a glimpse of the polyglot-novelist's style. What is more significant, Wang's multilinguistic talents are complemented by his folk humor. When the councilman brings up this analogy, a prostitute immediately rejoins, "How good can this be!? . . . Stripping naked is better." She is echoed by another prostitute: "Ha Ha Ha! Right, just like councilman you yourself stripping naked" (221). This refers to the councilman's sensational campaign tactic to prove how much more daring he is than other candidates. The bantering revolves around "the naked body," which of course bespeaks the audience's profession but, more importantly, signals a folk humor celebrating the "lowly" flesh, one that is superbly explicated by Bakhtin in the context of Rabelais and the Renaissance. Bakhtin asserts in *Rabelais and His World* (1968):

> [T]he images of the material bodily principle in the work of Rabelais (and of the other writers of the Renaissance) are the heritage, only somewhat modified by the Renaissance, of the culture of folk humor. . . . We shall call it conditionally the concept of grotesque realism. . . . The essential principle of grotesque realism is degradation, that is, the lowering of all that is high, spiritual, ideal, abstract; it is a transfer to the material level, to the sphere of earth and body in their indissoluble unity. . . . To degrade is to bury, to sow, and to kill simultaneously, in order to bring forth something more and better. To degrade also means to concern oneself with the lower stratum of the body, the life of the belly and the reproductive organs; it therefore relates to acts of defecation and copulation, conception, pregnancy, and birth. (18–21)

But unlike Bakhtin's interpretation of the rejuvenating flesh, Wang's universe presents a decomposing body beyond redemption. From a nativist standpoint, Wang sharply satirizes Taiwan's compradors for their urbanization, Americanization, and barbarization, all of which are manifested in the compradors' unsavory body. The fundamental problematic is that, due primarily to Taiwan's sense of cultural inferiority, a faraway America comes to exert an immense magnetic force over the postcolonial subjects' physical yearnings. For instance, in *Portrait*, the American-owned Taiwanese travel agency is staffed by "fake" Americans—people eager to become "Mei-kuo-jen" ("Americans," synonymous with "beautiful people"). These "mimic men" are bent upon sexual desires and material interests as they seek to Americanize/beautify themselves. Each of the employees goes by an American name, which is transliterated back into a Chinese phrase involving bodily functions, especially defecation and sexual intercourse. Most female travel agents are promiscuous and pathetically obsequious to the West, including overseas Chinese professionals, whereas most male clerks and managers are lascivious and androgenous. Taken symbolically, the travel agency in *Portrait* epitomizes the metropolitan culture in Taiwan which treats the island as a transit stop, with a large segment of the population anxious to move out.

The glamorized exit out of the island cherished by the compradors often exacts sacrifices from the rural or un-urbanized characters: Hsiao Lin from southern Taiwan, an orderly at the travel agency, is exploited and loses his naivete; Old Chang, a decent senior employee who can not speak English, is so disgusted that he gives up his job and pension; Hsiao Kuang from Hong Kong dies of heart failure. While humanity is generally corrupt and sexuality perverse in the urban setting, these marginalized characters offer some heart-warming episodes. Part 1 of *Portrait* revolves around Hsiao Lin's dilemma of not being able to help pay for his brother's wedding in the country. Hsiao Lin's father pays him a brief visit in Taipei, hoping to impress upon him the urgent need, for that impending wedding is the only way to tie down the brother to the ancestral land before the brother also leaves for the big city, like Hsiao Lin, for a more "rewarding" job. The union is a sorrowful one; what saves the meeting from becoming sentimental is the precise Taiwanese dialect and meticulous psychological description. Analyzing the father's Taiwanese reveals the irony that this working-class dialect spoken by the wretched of the earth on the island in fact retains traces of the elegant Wen-yen (classical Chinese), with syntactic structure much denser and usages more archaic than Pai-hua (standard vernacular Chinese or Mandarin). In other words, an aging, shabby peasant speaks in a way closer to the literary language of yesteryear than does the sophisticated city dweller.

True emotion and affection exist solely amongst these disenfranchized country people. Even one who is well versed in the ways of the metropolis, such as Hsiao Lin's roommate Hsiao Kuo, also from southern Taiwan, still proves to be humane. Hsiao Kuo, like most city inhabitants, emulates what appears to be the myth of the

Western lifestyle. He sleeps naked; he showers in the morning only; he even refuses to wear underpants for fear of creating creases on his jeans. But the other side of his personality emerges in the fact that when Japanese tourists pay him, a tour guide, he gives the money to prostitutes. In addition, learning of his friend's difficulty in financing the wedding, Hsiao Kuo, with no hesitation at all, offers Hsiao Lin a hard-earned check of NT$25,000. In the urban setting where materialism reigns supreme, Hsiao Kuo's generosity testifies to the kindness of country folk. To endow certain rural characters with an essentialist virtue bespeaks, once again, the romantic core of nativism—even in Wang's social satire. Hsiao Kuo's sacrifice can be appreciated only in the context of how he obtains the huge check: he prostitutes himself. Subjecting himself to sexual advances from his homosexual employer, he hopes, originally, to purchase a car with that money. Both sexual depravity and materialistic egotism come to an abrupt halt once a desperate friend seeks assistance.

The interface of Americans "under erasure" and prostitution culminates in Wang Chen-ho's *Rose*. Wang sets the parody in Hualien, a seaboard town in eastern Taiwan famous for its natural beauty. This novel caricatures a horde of cultural compradors grooming their bar girls for the imminent arrival of American GIs on furlough. These soldiers, in their absence, become the originary trope, the *raison d'être* for the comedy. In preparation for "Mei-jin" (Taiwanese Mandarin for "American soldiers" and "American dollars"), the principal comprador, Tuen Sse-wen, the English teacher at the local school and graduate from a Taipei university, conducts a cram school of English and other matters for prostitutes. Wang once again reverses the celebration of the primitive life force Bakhtin finds so precious in Rabelais; instead, it is the denigration of folk and nativist culture by Taiwanese compradors that renders their corporeality and utterance irrevocably repulsive. Tuen, for instance, is overweight and abject, releasing gas whenever he is excited. This English teacher is flanked by equally vile and money-grubbing city officials and prostitution bosses in the gallery of compradors. While only the English instructor embodies urbanization and Americanization so prominently displayed by the travel agents in *Portrait*, *Rose* reveals the general desire to imitate the ways and language of Taipei and, ultimately, of the West in the attempt to better serve American masters. The heart-warming episodes of oppressed rural characters seem somehow missing in *Rose*. The coarse prostitutes from rural Taiwan, nonetheless, continue to exhibit an earthy, folk resilience. The resourceful body of these women is the remnant of the nativist romanticism which desecrates the high—the city and the West, while sanctifying the low—the body and the rustic.

Coda

The transaction of money and sex American GIs from the Vietnam War contributed in founding across the Pacific Rim continues unchecked today, though in far more complex formations than ever before. In fact, this trading of dollars and bodies is thriving rather dramatically as transnational corporations expand throughout the area. No longer a simple matter of military or political imperialism, such capitalist exchanges—business ventures, investments, tourism, blue- and white-collar migrant workers, and even the vibrant enterprise of international adoption—are conducted in a pseudo-voluntary rather than a blatantly coercive manner, blending cultural and economic practices, yet the fundamental power structure seems unchanged from the one described and satirized in nativist texts. Invariably, it involves the intrusion of foreign cultures with advanced technology, the collusion of local Westernized or Nipponized compradors, and the decimation of native *hsiao-jen-wu* and their lifestyle. As late capitalism envelops the world, one turns almost nostalgically to nativist literature in Taiwan for the critique of postcolonial compradorism.

EIGHT

Ang Lee's Domestic Tragicomedy: Immigrant Nostalgia, Exotic/Ethnic Tour, Global Market

I.

The Taiwanese immigrant filmmaker Ang Lee's award-winning trilogy, *Pushing Hands* (1992), *Wedding Banquet* (1993), and *Eat Drink Man Woman* (1994),[1] represent the most recent phase in the evolution of *Liu-shueh-shen wen-shueh* (overseas student literature) since the 1960s. While narrative strategies of immigrant texts linger, while traditional filmic techniques prevail, Lee advances overseas student/immigrant discourse by conceiving his films globally, with an eye to commodifying both the nationalist and the non-nationalist ingredients in the immigrant, Asian American, and American characters. Instead of simply dwelling on nostalgia for a bygone era, these films elaborate the immigrant's present dilemma in the United States and, in *Eat*, the immigrant culture in Taipei. Most significantly, Lee increasingly undermines fixed categories in racial, cultural, and sexual identities through interjecting into immigrant subjectivities, among other things, ludic sexuality and deracination, both elements being utterly missing in Lee's literary predecessors on Chinese immigration. Though retaining some melancholic tone of overseas student literature, all three of Lee's films challenge sexual orientation, traditional romance, and marital suitability, whereby gender, race, and age seamlessly intersect.

The material conditions of Lee's films betoken boundary-crossing in a globalized film culture. Despite being financed chiefly by Central Motion Picture in Taiwan and representing Taiwan in various international film festivals, Lee's films are self-consciously produced and consumed in the world market, with multinational crew, storyline, and marketing strategies. Lee collaborates with a New York production company, Good Machine, headed by James Schamus and Ted Hope (Comer 63). The scripts for the trilogy grow out of the concerted effort of Hui-ling Wang, Lee, and Schamus. Despite the fact that the last member of the team does not even speak Mandarin, Lee calls Schamus "one of the best script doctors in the world" (64) and is unstinting in his praise of Schamus' contribution. Schamus, quoted by Chen Pao-shu in his interview of Lee, forces the script-writing trio to examine the focus of *Eat* and they subsequently decide to zoom in on "filial-piety" and "family." On Schamus' advice, they also resolve to produce the finale to what appears to be a trilogy—*Pushing*, *Wedding*, and *Eat* (147). Schamus suggests as well that *Eat* reverse the trend of the first two and allow the father to disappoint the children (148).[2] In addition to Good Machine, the credits to all three films indicate that Western technicians as well as performers play a crucial role in this joint venture.[3]

While the production side is unequivocally multinational, Lee's consumption strategies are no less global. Few aspiring filmmakers nowadays can afford not to think globally. Elizabeth B. Buck in "Asia and the Global Film Industry" offers a cogent analysis of the necessary promotion in the world film market:

> While Hollywood is still dominant in terms of exports (U.S. films command roughly two-thirds of the box offices in the majority of countries around the world), the dynamics of the film industry are changing rapidly, moving toward a more international product that has creative and financial roots in several countries. Now the industry talks about a 'global cinema' where any single film may have stars, producers, director, scriptwriters, and financing from various countries, all aimed at a global cinema audience of two hundred million people. (122)

Lee's aggressive promotion tour at international film festivals testifies to his appreciation of global cinema. Box office success around the world, Lee knows all too well, corresponds to nominations and awards at film festivals, particularly those garnered from Western Europe and the United States. In sum, both the production and the consumption of Lee's films are practiced in a capitalist framework, whereby "Third-World international or festival films," as Fredric Jameson puts it in *The Geopolitical Aesthetic: Cinema and Space in the World System* (1992), are obliged to be packaged "in national, cultural and one is tempted to say, *tourist-friendly* ways, in which it is the fact of a brand-new locale and unprecedented national provenance that is stressed and marketed" (119; emphasis mine). In his ensuing exegesis of Taiwanese "New Wave" films, Jameson also points out that films on Taipei urban spaces engage "a kind of Third-World situation we have rarely until now included in that (rather traditional) category: namely, the developing Third World or the newly industrializing First-World tier of the Third World or Pacific Rim (excluding Japan)" (155).

Ang Lee's oeuvre goes beyond what Jameson calls for—a close examination of the "Pacific Rim"—because Lee's leading roles customarily possess immigrant subjectivities so perpetually shuttling between the first and the third world that the barriers raised between them are nearly collapsed to reveal *one* world.[4] Nevertheless, Lee does present his films in a "tourist-friendly" way in terms of the appeal to bourgeois taste and the subsuming of class, to which this chapter will return. Similar to a great number of overseas Taiwanese Chinese students/immigrants, Lee originally came to the U.S. to pursue an advanced degree, earning an MFA from New York University (Comer 63). Two salient factors prevent his art from falling into the formula of dejection and homesickness of overseas student literature: compared to Pai Hsien-yung and other overseas Chinese writers, he belongs to a younger generation whose art comes of age in recent years in the United States. The context from which Lee emerges, therefore, differs drastically from that of overseas student literature decades ago in Taiwan and other Chinese-speaking areas. Secondly, his medium of art is cinema which, increasingly, is conceived in and consumed by a larger audience than just the Chinese, who have remained the target group for literature in Chinese. Lee's generation and profession suggest the possibility of transgression of established parameters concerning nationality, race, gender, and age differences.

II.

The title of this chapter categorizes Lee's trilogy as "domestic tragicomedy." The term "domestic" is usually linked in Western literary discourse, particularly of the feminist vein, to melodrama. But melodrama is highly inappropriate in characterizing Lee. Western theater historians often designate the French Revolution as the beginning of melodrama, which comes to epitomize the "democratic impulse" in satisfying "the popular audience's demands for a vulgar, sensual, and emotional theatrical experience" (Heather Jones 6). E. Ann Kaplan likewise quotes Peter Brooks in locating the advent of the European/North American melodrama in the eighteenth century when "the drive for melodrama in this period was a drive [felt by the bourgeoisie] for moral meaning in a post Enlightenment world in which prior religious and transcendent values no longer gave significance to people's lives" (9). Kaplan proceeds to define "domestic melodrama":

> This sphere [of European/North American melodrama] may loosely be called that of the "domestic," entailing the level of love/sex, marriage/motherhood, jealousy, loss, murder or other violences, infidelity, pre-oedipal/oedipal relations. Other qualities have to do with (a) exaggeration/excess; (b) allegorical or stereotypical good versus evil forces; (c) the individual shown as at the mercy of forces beyond his or her control. (7)

Some of these traits are clearly visible in Lee, especially the element of bourgeois entertainment. Though describing his works as "comedies that are somewhat romantic, bourgeois," and "commercial," Lee seems to be rather torn by his failure, on the one hand, to produce "high brow" films and, on the other, to stamp out any aspiration for his films other than as successful recreation (Chen Paoshu 176, 168–69). The similarity of entertainment notwithstanding, the historical context and tradition of "melodrama" jar with Lee's films. One main disjunction comes from the Western feminist tradition of associating melodrama with domesticity and hence with femininity. This is evident in Kaplan's distinction within melodrama: "I thus distinguish between domestic melodramas that seem *complicit* with dominant, patriarchal ideology (calling these 'women's *melodrama*') and those that contain elements that *resist* dominant ideology (calling these 'women's *films*')" (10). Heather Jones makes an almost identical point in characterizing critics as gendering melodrama into "domestic melodrama (unavoidably profeminine)" and "heroic melodrama (re-articulated as promasculine)" (7).

The term "Domestic melodrama" describes more aptly the "Mandarin Ducks and Butterflies" Literature (*yuan-yang hu-t'ie pai wen-hsueh*) which flourished in Chinese cities around the turn of the century.[5] Replete with sentimental romances, such literature finds present-day reincarnations in popular writers such as Ch'iung Yau and Yi Shu, whose novels, incidentally, can be located in quantity in any Chinatown bookstore in the United States.[6] Consistently in this genre, nonetheless, woman seems to be submerged, as Rey Chow phrases it in *Woman and Chinese Modernity* (1991), "under the 'larger' headings of history, society, tradition, and the like" (50). The focus is invariably on the male protagonists' struggle against the entrenched, extended family system and other social formations. This antipatriarchal legacy by *male* characters differs drastically from what Kaplan and Jones delineate as a feminine or feminist penchant within domestic melodrama. This incarcerating of male characters by Chinese tradition continues to obsess Ang Lee, who trains his lens on the father figure in all three films—in part due to his own experience. During his interview with Chen Pao-shu, Lee offers a personal anecdote in response to the observation of the recurring father character in the trilogy. He recalls that his authoritative, ex-principal father had become so frail that he "slept all the way through" the son's honeymoon trip (Chen 190). It dawns on him then that the immutable and permanent family, one symbolized by his father, is in fact transient. Though it may be dismissed as peculiarly Chinese to bring along parents and parents-in-law on one's honeymoon, as Ang Lee purportedly did, one would appreciate this arrangement as nearly inevitable considering the cross-Pacific journey the parents undertake to attend the wedding in the United States and perhaps to tour the wonders of the New World on the side. This personal account on the aging father helps illuminate Ang Lee's unwavering scrutiny of the father figure and, specifically, the father's repeated dozing off in *Wedding*. Metaphorically, Lee sees the father as epitomizing Chinese culture in the process of disintegration. The crumbling of Chinese tradition paradoxically furnishes a comic end both to *Wedding* and to *Eat*, culminating in the closing twist of *Eat* when the father announces his imminent unconventional remarriage and hence violates the Confucian family ethics (Chen 153). *Eat* contains as well the only variation to the thread of father-son relationship when three daughters replace the son figure.

The term "Domestic tragicomedy" is more appropriate for Lee's trilogy because of the existence of the Chinese term Chia-t'ing Pei-hsi-chu (family tragicomedy) with its suggestion of Chia-t'ing Lun-li (family ethics), which is exactly one of the axes on which the films are constructed. Family ethics revolving around a patriarchal figure is, after all, the foundation of Confucian cosmology. Moreover, the word "domestic" is exceptionally enlightening, for its intrinsic ambiguity serves to shed light on Ang Lee's cross-cultural, multinational texts. "Domestic" refers not just to family but to nation or culture. Furthermore, it can be taken to mean the cultures both of Taiwan and of the United States, a duality contributing to the films' global success, for an international moviegoer, whatever his or her subjectivity in approaching the film, is able to find some appeal. The complex duality at times renders the same episode evoking nostalgia in some audience and exoticism in others. For instance, what a Chinese (immigrant) audience considers a nostalgic moment over an irretrievable Chineseness may turn out to be an exotic/ethnic tour for a Westerner venturing into an alien culture. Conversely, what a Chinese audience finds exotic becomes, for a Westerner, comforting, contextualizing markers for what might otherwise be a Brechtian "alienation effect" that threatens to disorient or even repulse the middle-class moviegoers. Above all, the designation of "domestic *tragicomedy*" brings out the distinctive movement of the trilogy. The initial, potential tragedy on immigrant predicament and nostalgia is transformed into a comedy as an exotic/ethnic tour is extended to the audience in a global market.

III.

Lee's trilogy are widely available at major video stores across the United States. Of the three, *Pushing* is less polished technically and far more intense in featuring immigrant nostalgia. Some characters reappear in the three films, such as the father figure played by Lang Hsiung, who becomes a crucial link stringing together the trilogy. *Pushing* describes how a retired Tai Chi master moves from China to New York to live with his son and American daughter-in-law, Martha. All three are trapped by their cultural and linguistic differences, and the master feels especially humiliated when he and Mrs. Chu, also from Beijing, perceive that they are being brought together as a match by their children. The father "runs away from home" in a rather adolescent manner and degenerates into a dishwasher in Chinatown. This melodramatic episode later leads to the ethnocentric myth of Chi Kung (Chinese Kung Fu, manipulating the inner "breath"). When fired by the ruthless restauranteur, the master shows his true grit: he remains immobile on the premises and bounces off anyone trying to remove him—Chinatown gangsters and policemen alike—with his Chi Kung, which is as much a commentary on his power as it is on his ineffective stasis. His son finally locates him in prison and, following the master's request, rents a unit for him in a retirement complex in Chinatown, where the master chances upon Mrs. Chu. She has moved into a nearby apartment due to problems similar to his.

The comic plot of *Wedding* stems from a series of mistakes and miscalculations. A homosexual Taiwanese, Gao Wai-tung, lives with his Caucasian lover, Simon, in New York and collects rent from the various apartments he owns. His traditional parents in Taipei are so anxious to have grandchildren that they practically send a bride-to-be from Taiwan to meet Wai-tung. Desperate "to get them off [his] back," Simon and Wai-tung orchestrate a sham marriage between Wai-tung and Wei-wei, a Shanghai painter of abstract art stranded in one of Wai-tung's rundown apartments. Wei-wei is to benefit from the arrangement by acquiring a "green card" or permanent residence. The plan derails as the parents unexpectedly travel to New York to attend the wedding. It goes even further awry when Wai-tung and Wei-wei, exhausted and intoxicated from the banquet and subsequent Nao-tung-fang (friends disrupting the bridal chamber), have intercourse and Wei-wei becomes pregnant. The tense, triangular relationship explodes as a jealous, enraged Simon storms away from the breakfast table. The parents, who supposedly do not speak English, are dumbfounded. The breakup is saved only when Wei-wei decides against an abortion, when Simon agrees to maintain a ménage à trois, and when the retired general-father, in a vintage Ang Lee comic twist, privately reveals to Simon, *in English*, that he understands their morning brawl and accepts him as another son.

The leading role of *Eat* is a widower-father and master chef at Taipei's Grand Hotel. Chef Chu has mysteriously lost his taste buds and is losing his three daughters—Chia-jen the spinster Christian who allegedly turned religious because she was jilted by Li Kai in college, Chia-chien the airline executive yuppie, and Chia-ning an adolescent who works part-time at McDonald's. The rents in the fabric of the family show through the meaningless, ritualistic Sunday night banquet the father prepares for the daughters. In addition to his professed wish to present Chinese cuisine cinematographically, Ang Lee explains the banquet as follows: "Sometimes the things children need to hear most are the things parents find hardest to say, and vice versa. When that happens, we resort to rituals" (Comer 62). Food, as "a metaphor of love," is poorly produced as the chef can no longer control the right amount of seasoning and is poorly received as the daughters contemplate a move away from the family prison. Four anouncements of imminent move out of the family are made by each of the family members at four separate Sunday dinners, but Ang Lee's trademark comic resolution occurs when the chef-father discloses his impending marriage with a family friend decades younger than himself and long regarded as "a fourth daughter" of the Chus.

Considered individually, each of the trilogy contains both immigrant nostalgia leading to melodrama or even tragedy and exotic/ethnic tour suggesting a comic denouement. But taken chronologically in the order of their release, the trilogy reveals an increasing propensity toward exotic travel in search of the Other rather than nostalgic lamentation over the loss of the Self. Specifically, *Pushing* opens with the claustrophobic impasse felt by the immigrant father, the film's acute nostalgia only slightly mitigated by the sight and sound of the ethnic community in Manhattan. *Wedding* seeks to balance melancholy felt by the retired general-father over lost lineage and comic components derived from gender-transgression, that is, homosexuality, and from culture-transgression, that is, parody of Chinese and American values. Finally, *Eat* concludes with an unreservedly exotic/ethnic tour of Taiwan for a Western audience, with the chef-father's predicament offering some indigenous flavor to the "tourist-friendly" film. As a result of the lessening of immigrant nostalgia, which only strikes the chord of a specific kind of audience anyway, and the highlighting of the exotic other, which is favored by moviegoers around the world, Lee's later films receive much more global recognition and are more commercially successful than the first film.

The opening of *Pushing* illustrates how the immigrant father and his American daughter-in-law, Martha—and, by extension, the Americanized son/husband and the Asian American grandson—are straitjacketed in the same space. A repeated pattern of the mise en scene for the film's credit contrasts, on the one hand, the father-in-law practicing Tai Chi or Chinese calligraphy in studied and silent movement with, on the other, Martha, in the opposite background or foreground, staring at the computer screen, neurotically twitching her fingers above the keyboard. The writer's block Martha experiences echoes the Tai Chi master's entanglement in a linguistic and cultural maze. The master's measured steps and breathing will not enable him to speak English, drive a car, or operate a microwave—until the aluminum foil he accidentally puts in bursts into flame. While Tai Chi, the father's traditional Chinese dress and shoes, the scroll of Chinese calligraphy on the wall, and videos of Beijing opera and Kung Fu films evoke forlorn nostalgia for Chinese and Chinese immigrants, all these denote an alien Other to a Westerner. By contrast, Martha's presence, her computer, and her typical American behavior patterns help situate the aforementioned exotic elements within a familiar context for a Western audience, yet Martha and everything about her become sheer exoticism for Chinese. These opening scenes have merged both nostalgia over the lost Self and exoticism for the Other, often in the same shot, depending on the subject position—Chinese or non-Chinese—of the audience projecting the gaze.

As a cross-cultural intermediary, the husband is woefully inadequate in negotiating the differences of the people closest to him, for instance, the divergent notions of space:

MARTHA: "I don't have space to think [for my new book]."
HUSBAND: "Not enough space! This room is big enough for four people back home [China]."

The husband's outburst over Martha's legitimate complaint is in part justified by his guilt for his parents' suffering during the Cultural Revolution, but it also betrays a weakness in characterization. They all tend to display a sudden change of path: in addition to the son's mood swings, the father behaves rather melodramatically, and Martha winds up writing a novel about early Chinese immigrants building the Transcontinental Railroad. This flaw of Lee's first major production, however, does not eclipse the ingenious juxtaposition, within the opening mise en scene of computer and Tai Chi, of two conflictual spaces where Martha's desire for future-oriented literary fame and the master's past-oriented homesickness are interlocked. Throughout his trilogy, Lee deploys such crammed urban spaces to frame tense and volatile human relationships: the crowded streets, restaurants, classrooms, the school quadrangle in New York and Taipei; the traffic jam during rush hours; the long queue at McDonald's; cats meowing in heat; a neighbor's deafening Karaoke; entangled and misplaced underwear in the drawers.

Shackled by urban space, incapacitated by their age and impotence, the three father-retirees are caught in a world beyond their control. In response, they long to return to an imaginary Chineseness, seen in terms of their Beijing dialect and their insistence on tradition, especially with regard to cuisine and/as ritual. Linguistically, the fathers' nostalgia for an alleged Chinese orthodoxy is embodied in the actor Lang Hsiung's near-perfect Beijing accent, which forms the basis for standard Mandarin. Similarly, Mrs. Chu, whom he courts in *Pushing*, is also from Beijing and enunciates every syllable with the same crispness. These characters representing an older generation in fact *verbalize* an idealized Chineseness totally unadulterated by other Chinese dialects and, above all, by English. By contrast, all the younger, white-collar Taiwanese immigrant-children speak Taiwanese Mandarin and English, symbolizing their distance from the imagined Chinese core. Lastly, the American-born grandchildren—such as Martha's son, Li Kai's son, and, conceivably, the child of the "triangular" marriage in *Eat*—speak English primarily or exclusively, illustrating their severance from Chineseness.

The culinary art, regarded as one of the great achievements of the Chinese civilization, likewise epitomizes the dissipation of the tradition. Meals have always been important social occasions whereby Chinese family members or acquaintances strengthen the bond. However, arguments abound in the trilogy as a result of hidden hostility. The strained relationship in *Pushing* explodes over the dinner table, where two languages, two kinds of dishes, and two mentalities clash. The deception no longer holds in *Wedding* over breakfast when the couple and Simon exchange obscenities, oblivious to the stupefied parents and eventually causing the father's second stroke. In *Eat*, the family's routine Sunday night banquet has become such a meaningless and torturous ritual that each member uses it to announce his or her intended exit from the family.

Increasingly in the trilogy, however, is a tendency for the tragic to be attenuated and ultimately overwhelmed by the comic light-heartedness of an exotic/ethnic tour. Food in the trilogy, for example, has grown from, in *Pushing*, the master's uncouthly huge rice bowl of Chinese "home cooking," which suggests his disjunction with the family members who prefer Western food,[7] to the lavish banquet in *Wedding* as well as to the chef's "star tour" of Grand Hotel's mammoth kitchen and his sumptuous family feast in *Eat*. Chinese cuisine becomes less a marker of immigrant dilemma than an exotic tour of the taste for a foreign audience. The wedding banquet in *Wedding*, in fact, is punctuated not only by elaborate courses but also by carnivalesque "performances" designed for the express purpose of public humiliation of the newlyweds. The filmmaker, during his cameo appearance in that scene, rationalizes this intricate ritual: these titillating and embarrassing practical jokes suffered by the newlyweds, claims Lee the guest to two baffled Americans, reflect "five thousand years of sexual repression" (Galbraith 33). Surely a tongue-in-cheek hyperbole based on the stereotype of the asexual Chinese, it comes to justify an exotic filmic spectacle of what is supposedly the prevailing Chinese custom. To his credit, nonetheless, Lee meticulously shows that the mastermind of the games does seek approval from the general-father before wrecking havoc. The father's slight nod and grin sanction all the subsequent excesses. These games consist of forcing the couple to drink immoderately and of having the blindfolded bride receive kisses from male guests, culminating in a multitude of indecent acts in public. Even if non-Chinese viewers do not find these bewildering, what follows in the bridal suite is, to be sure, exotic.

Such pranks intensify during the traditional Nao-tung-fang, where the crowd becomes more intoxicated and rowdy and the performances required of the newlyweds more lewd. Only a Bakhtinian interpretation of the wedding banquet as a carnivalesque transgression suffices to account for the extravaganza. The license to shed the daily Confucian code of conduct gives rise to a communal ritual of Bacchus-like drunkenness and cavorting. However, being a product consciously packaged for the world market, it would be disingenuous to deny that such exaggeration during the banquet sequence comes to satiate the urge for exoticism, as the Western audience is treated to a puzzling but not terribly disorienting alien culture.

This exotic tour is found in the preparation of the Sunday night banquet during the opening moments of *Eat* as well. The chef slaughters fish, chicken, frogs, displaying superb dexterity and a wall of knives of different sizes. At one point, the chef even uses a heavy axe to crack open some solid object wrapped in huge lotus leaves on the elegant dining table. Another striking juxtaposition occurs when the lovemaking of Chia-chien cuts to the chef blowing into a duck's raw, headless throat to prepare perhaps the famed Peking duck. Lee consciously choreographs these scenes as a strange blending of the aesthetic and the abhorrent; the chef's metier comes to fuse beauty and brutality. The Asian American playwright Frank Chin has long called this kind of gastronomic tourism "food pornography," aptly defined by Sau-ling Cynthia Wong as

> making a living [in Lee's case, a film] by exploiting the 'exotic' aspects of one's ethnic foodways. In cultural terms it translates to reifying perceived cultural differences and exaggerating one's otherness in order to gain a foothold in a white-dominated social system. (*Reading Asian American Literature* 55)

Even though Lee has asserted that part of his intention in *Eat* is to demonstrate the sophisticated Chinese civilization in cuisine (*Eat Drink* in the title) blended with the primitive sex drive (*Man Woman* in the title) (Chen 164), the filmmaker has yielded to the stereotype of an artistic yet unfathomably inhuman Orient. The result is box office success since the film confirms the global audience's preconceived notion of a mysterious and inviting East.

Tragicomedy must end, more or less, happily, and the evolution of the trilogy's concluding moments demonstrates, yet again, the proclivity to move immigrant nostalgia to exotic tour for consumerist societies. *Pushing* closes with the Tai Chi master and Mrs. Chu standing on a dingy Chinatown street, shadowed by skyscrapers on all sides. The master rather awkwardly inquires: "Anything to do this afternoon?" She hesitates and replies while lowering her eyes: "Nothing." Both are frozen after this exchange, and their paralysis is prolonged by the gradual fade-out, the bleakness of this scene only somewhat redeemed by the possible union of the two. Some melancholic tone does continue in the closure of *Wedding*. When the parents board the departing flight, the sadness of parting is crystalized in the father's helplessness of the final shot—the victim of two strokes raising his arms in slow motion to be frisked by the airport security. It is, however, a highly ambiguous gesture since his arms suggest as much a surrender to life by a frail retiree as a possible sign of victory for gaining an heir—a grandson (despite the mistranslation of "grandchild" throughout the film)—to the Gaos. After all, shortly before the departure, the father, a typical Chinese male who makes little physical contact, holds tightly Simon's hand rather than Wei-wei's to bid farewell, fully acknowledging Simon as a member of the family. The father seems to give his blessing to the formation of a happy yet nonconventional family. His acceptance of an alternative marriage may derive from a rather conservative reason, though, namely, the prospect of carrying on the family name through the homosexual son. Put another way, the exotic/ethnic tour into the gay interracial lifestyle is normalized and mainstreamed by a traditional premise.[8] In addition, the vintage Ang Lee comic twist of an English-speaking father confiding in Simon dissolves some of the gloom gathered over his recent stroke and the impending breakup of the sham marriage. By the same token, *Eat* concludes with yet another comic twist when the father announces at the banquet that he will marry a family friend considerably younger than himself. This totally unexpected turn of events provides comic relief to the anticipation that he will marry the family friend's obnoxious mother, who has been actively wooing him. This happy ending is compounded by the chef's miraculous recovery of the sense of taste as he savors his daughter's soup, a further sign that the traditional family has been restructured rather than demolished. Such wish-fulfillments in the endings both of *Wedding* and of *Eat* attest to the bourgeois tendency to subsume immigrant nostalgia in exotic travelogue.

IV.

To consider Ang Lee as the most recent phase in the evolution of the discourse of overseas Taiwanese Chinese student/immigrant provides an intriguing angle with which to examine what Jameson calls the "geopolitical aesthetic" or "cinema and space" of the trilogy. As globalization radically transforms demographics and politics, not much currency is now allotted by the homogenized consumerist culture to a desperate, uncompromising clinging to the past. Rather, exploration of the "domesticated unknown" is encouraged by the popular taste, a change readily noticeable in Ang Lee. The intense immigrant nostalgia in *Pushing* is formulated in the stifling New York Chinatown, where the Tai Chi master finds himself ensnared. Beijing wafts through the retiree's mind merely as an object of longing, for, however reluctantly, he finally settles into the Chinese community—a niche of some sort. A frequent exchange across the Pacific becomes commonplace in *Wedding*. Physical movement certainly does not define all the dynamics involved; cultural and gender borders are constantly traversed as well. A Taiwanese opera singer has a "white boy friend"; Wai-tung's lover is not only Caucasian but also male. Finally, despite the fact that *Eat* shifts its space to Taipei, a logical move since most immigrant characters in *Pushing* and *Wedding* originate there, the representation of that metropolis strikes a delicate balance between "global" and "national" in order to make it a captivating site to foreign gazes. To all intents and purposes, the exotic tour in *Eat* is the most thorough one in the trilogy, evident not only through its emphasis on Chinese cuisine but also in specific characterization and setting, which are always fashioned with great "tourist-friendliness." Many characters have explicit overseas connections. The chef's suitor recently returns from California; Li Kai's ex-wife and son live in the United States; his career as well as Chia-chien's involve foreign markets. Indeed, the omnivorous corporate culture claims almost all the characters and sites amongst its ranks. A case in point is that Li Kai the ex-chemist and Chia-chien the chef-to-be turn out to work for an airline company. Had they pursued their real interests, they might still find themselves in the same immense bureaucracy of capitalism.

In terms of food, The master chef works at Taipei's Grand Hotel, a state-run tourist resort perched on a hill overlooking the Taipei Basin. The exhilarating "star tour" of the Grand Hotel's massive kitchen only augments the reputation of the locale. As for the opening wonders of elaborate food preparation, Lee follows the sequence with three segments introducing the daughters—a Christian who listens to Handel's *Messiah* on her faulty Walkman, an airline executive with an expansive view of Taipei's skyline, and a McDonald's staff wearing the universally identifiable uniform. These familiar postmodernist symbols for a late capitalist culture more than agree with the Western audience; the three daughters serve to package the previous exotic tour of the eyes and the tongue in an entertaining, middle-class context.

Just as aspiring young men and women such as Li Kai and Chia-chien find it necessary to mainstream and commodify their youthful idealism, Ang Lee does the same with his art. Global capitalism becomes an invisible totality from which no character or his/her creator can escape. The world market demands, for instance, that the filmmaker downplay immigrant nostalgia preoccupying the first installment of the trilogy in favor of an exotic tour in the latter two. The commodification on a global scale entails some mildly shocking transgressions—but within the permissible bourgeois parameters. Therefore, deracination is exhibited in terms of interracial romance and upwardly mobile naturalized professionals in *Pushing* and *Wedding*. Excessive nationalism and nativism are shunned. Secondly, differences of sexual orientation and lifestyle are tolerated, seen in the homosexual affair and the nonconventional ménage à trois in *Wedding*. Thirdly, age differences in marriage are minimized as in the intergenerational marriage in *Eat*. Lastly, a complete embourgeoisement envelops the trilogy; nowhere does the audience see the remains of those crushed by the wheel of homogenizing capitalism. Industrialization and commercialization in the Pacific Rim appear to produce, exclusively, middle-class subjectivities, which, at worst, are afflicted with immigrant nostalgia and which, at best, are conduits—"tour guides" for domestic and foreign customers alike—of adventures abroad.

Yet even the most ironclad embourgeoisement is bound to have ruptures; glimpses of the huddled masses flash through even bourgeois art. This occurs in *Eat* when Chia-ning and her boyfriend ride to his apartment in suburban Taipei. He lives alone, as his parents busy themselves buying real estate in mainland China and California and his Ah-ma (grandmother) is in the nursing home, suffering from what seems to be the late stages of Alzheimer's disease. He apparently is the only one in the family who cares for Ah-ma. Periodically photographing her, he explains that camera flashes are the sole stimulus to which Ah-ma still responds. Chia-ning, perhaps too quickly, says: "Maybe she doesn't want to be photographed!" "Maybe—" he hesitates in some confusion but immediately calls her attention to the image of an old woman taking shape gradually in the tray of solution, "Look, here she comes." Wishful thinking, alas, the old woman is gone. The revolutionary potential of this scene is further diluted by the shot subsequent to the one on the aged matron: anticipating the full image, the young lovers gently join hands. What might have been a searing indictment of the hegemony lapses into a catalyst for youthful romance. The double silence of Ah-ma's infirmity and photographic existence, nevertheless, registers her irrelevance to today's world. Deprived of a home by entrepreneurial children, that segment of the population is doomed to vanish without a trace. Yet if indeed the term "domestic tragicomedy," with its middle-class implications, characterizes the trilogy, Ang Lee has tentatively punctured the overarching bourgeois ideology through Ah-ma's hauntingly white, as if hollowed-out, pupils staring back at her sons and daughters.

Notes

Chapter 1

1. Aunt Emily in Joy Kogawa's *Obasan* makes a sobering contrast on how Canada and, by association, the United States, treated different groups of "enemy alien" during World War II. Aunt Emily indefatigably reminds other characters that the Canadian government chose to imprison Canadian-born Canadians and not German-born Germans.

2. The birth of *Aiiieeeee!*, the first Asian American anthology, was greatly indebted to the editors of *Yardbird Reader*, Ishmael Reed and Al Young, who invited Chin and others to edit a special issue of the journal on Asian American literature. While editing this special issue, Chin and others were asked by Howard University Press to produce *Aiiieeeee!*. The genesis of Asian American literature was clearly tied to the African American struggle and the civil rights movement.

3. By "ethnographic feminism," I do not mean anthropologists who adopt feminist approaches. This term is coined to call attention to the literary strategy of converging ethnographic materials and feminist concerns in Maxine Hong Kingston's *The Woman Warrior* and other texts.

4. See the following chapter, "Orientalism in Chinese American Discourse: Body and Pidgin."

5. Kazuo Ishiguro is further canonized with the huge success of his third novel, *The Remains of the Day* (1989), winner of the Booker Prize—Britain's top literay award. After his first two novels which suggest

through plot, characterization, and other dimensions the writer's own ethnicity, Ishiguro has achieved a "universalist" reputation in *Remains* by choosing to focus on the epitome of a bygone era in the British Empire—a butler. But is this sense of nostalgia truly cosmopolitan or simply a self-erasing drive toward becoming more British than the British? Whatever the answer, the reception of *Remains* has proven that Ishiguro is now a celebrated writer, at least in the English-speaking world. It is equally telling that *Remains* has been adapted since for cinema by the Merchant-Ivory team. The leading roles are played by Anthony Hopkins and Emma Thompson.

6. Yueh Fei was a male general who fought against the invading northern tribes during the Sung dynasty. In Chinese legends, his back was tattooed by his parents with patriotic sayings to spur him on in the battle. Kingston has merged the two historical figures, Yueh Fei and Fa Mu Lan, to create her own story.

7. By analyzing reviews of *The Woman Warrior*, Kingston herself has inferred this possible assumption on the part of reviewers and readers. In "Cultural Mis-readings by American Reviewers," she criticizes the otherwise fine reviews of her novel by Peter S. Beagle and Jane Kramer in *Harper's Bookletter* and *The New York Times Book Review* because they exploit her interracial marriage. Kingston believes that these reviewers singled out the fact "that I had 'married an American' . . . [to imply] that I somehow became *more* American through marriage, and that marriage is the way to assimilation" (60).

8. This persistent image of an immigrant with split life and personality can be found both in Asian immigrant and in Asian American texts. For the schizophrenic in Asian immigrant writings, see chapter 3, "Immigrant Schizophrenic in Asian Diaspora Literature."

9. Frank Chin with three other editors of *Aiiieeeee!* (1974) have discussed many Chinese historical-mythical figures in the 1991 preface to the Mentor Edition of that anthology. The editors focus on the genealogy of heroism in "Confucius . . . Sun Tzu's *Art of War* . . . [Kwan Kung in] *Romance of the Three Kingdoms*" (xxxviii). A reaction to Kingston's lineage of Chinese heroines, Chin and others assert their masculinity via borrowings from ancient China, a culture which they set out to dispute in the first place. This paradoxical attitude exposes Asian Americans' simultaneous self-hatred and self-empowerment. Kingston's use of Fa Mu Lan, Amy Tan's female-exclusive "Joy Luck Club," and other texts come under direct attack in the introduction (penned by the same editorial board) to *The Big Aiiieeeee!* (1991).

10. I am paraphrasing Jean Amery's "On the Necessity and Impossibility of Being a Jew" in *At the Mind's Limits* (1980).

Chapter 2

1. Feminist film criticism has done a great deal in analyzing the implied audience of a given work. The male or phallic gaze at the female body on the screen is transformed in this chapter into the white gaze at the nonwhite object. Both relationships are constructed on a power structure, with one side viewing and the other being viewed.

2. I have drawn heavily from Sander Gilman's analysis in *Jewish Self-Hatred* of the psychological processes any minority group undergoes in the attempt to be, or at least to feel, assimilated.

3. Foucault describes J. Bentham's *Panopticon* as a prison compound with a central tower with wide windows surrounded by annular prison cells. The effect of backlighting allows a guard on the tower to observe "the captive shadows in the cells of the periphery" and to remain unseen by standing out against the light. In this structure, inmates constantly live under a sense of being supervised, whether there is a guard or not on the watchtower. For a more detailed depiction, see Michel Foucault's chapter on "Panopticism" in *Discipline and Punish*, pp. 195–228.

4. For an example of such criticism, refer to Helena Michie's *The Flesh Made Word*, p. 6.

5. The best example of the proximity of Orientalism and sexism is David Henry Hwang's *M. Butterfly* (1986), which dramatizes the homosexual affair between a female impersonator in the Peking Opera and a French diplomat. The female impersonator is also a spy for Communist China, gathering intelligence by selling his androgynous body.

6. Marlon K. Hom, in his introduction to *Songs of Gold Mountain* (1987), lists other useful studies of the image of Chinese in American literature.

7. Frank Chin has repaid the honor by having one of the main characters in his *Gunga Din Highway* (1994) modeled after Maxine Hong Kingston.

Chapter 3

1. See "Images of Asians in Anglo-American Literature" in Elaine Kim's *Asian American Literature*, particularly the discussion on "the Unassimilable Aliens" (9–11).

2. The protagonist in *Jasmine* is not so much marked by "skewed perception of the external world and of themselves" as by an utter lack of affect in the killing of the rapist Half-Face. Jasmine exhibits, first of all,

nothing but numbness as she slices her tongue after being raped and, subsequently, calculated precision as she stabs Half-Face to death.

3. Collected in *Chi-mo te Shih-chi-ts'ui* (Lonely seventeen 1976), these stories are "Death in Chicago" (1964), "Up the Soaring Tower" (1964), "A Day in Pleasantville" (1964), "Excursion to Fire Island," "The Tale of a Fallen Angel" (1965), and "Lamentation on a Fallen Angel" (1969). "A Day in Pleasantville" is included in *Born of the Same Roots: Stories of Modern Chinese Women* (1981). "Hong Kong—1960" (1964) is the only story not set in the United States and therefore is excluded from my discussion.

4. Considering Pai's homosexuality, which is the central theme of many of his short stories and of a long novel, one begins to discern the linkages between "The Tale of a Fallen Angel" and Thomas Mann's *Death in Venice*. Pai's story can be facetiously subtitled "China's Death in Venice."

5. Sau-ling Cynthia Wong points out the irony of Nieh's retracing of the American westward myth in "Ethnicizing Gender: An Exploration of Sexuality as Sign in Chinese Immigrant Literature." Wong further expands the exegesis on "the Politics of Mobility" in *Reading Asian American Literature*. Pai Hsien-yung, however, misrepresents Peach Red's movement as "from the Midwest to New York" (210).

6. S. Pandya points out in the context of Mukherjee's short stories that many of her characters speak "Indian English" such as "hot-hot" and "I am loving this country" (71).

7. Though Mukherjee claims in her interview with Hancock that her "mother tongue is still Bengali. . . . I think of North American English as my step-mother-tongue" (38), I am not aware of any work by Mukherjee written in her "mother tongue." She seems rather accustomed to composing in her adopted language.

Chapter 4

1. Yung Wing's remarks are representative of early immigrants' attitude toward Caucasian women. He is quoted because of his prominent status as the first Asian graduate of a distinguished American institution of higher education. If an intellectual harbors such an inferiority complex, one wonders how less priviledged immigrants might feel. Reference to Yung Wing's statement is found in Thomas E. La Fargue's *China's First Hundred* (1942), p. 42, and Lowell Chun-Hoon's "Teaching the Asian American Experience: Alternative to the Neglect and Racism in Textbooks," p. 40.

2. I am indebted to Sander Gilman for the line of thinking deriving from the term "White Bodies," which is used in his "Black Bodies, White

Bodies: Toward an Iconography of Female Sexuality in Late Nineteenth-Century Art, Medicine, and Literature."

3. Critics such as Gayatri Chakravorty Spivak, Sara Suleri, Trinh Minh-ha, bell hooks, Hazel V. Carby, and others have explored this critical juncture from a largely feminist perspective—quite different from the angle of Asian American male writers.

4. In a recent MLA publication, Donald Marshall's *Contemporary Critical Theory: A Selective Bibliography* (1993), Marshall combines the two disciplines into one chapter: "Ethnic and Postcolonial Studies."

5. See, for instance, Peggy Pascoe's "Race, Gender, and Intercultural Relations: The Case of Interracial Marriage."

6. See the case study in Pascoe, 10–11.

7. Some of the most representative pieces of writing exposing this racist aspect of American culture are Elaine Kim's "Images of Asians in Anglo-American Literature," the first chapter in her *Asian American Literature: An Introduction to the Writings and Their Social Context* and the two prefaces to *Aiiieeeee!: An Anthology of Asian American Writers*.

8. *Eroticism* is also translated as *Death and Sensuality*, in which Bataille separates the world into the realm of work and the realm of taboos. The realm of work is the ordinary world of profane time, when people carry out their duty as stipulated. The realm of taboos belongs to sacred time, when people celebrate, often with sexual and other behavioral license, by transgressing against social taboos. The fact that something is forbidden makes the offense of it much more sinful and pleasurable. Bataille calls such behavior of violating the taboos "eroticism," a term with broader definition than is commonly supposed.

9. "Occidental Madame Butterfly" is, of course, a deliberate reversal of Giacomo Puccini's *Madame Butterfly* (1904). See also how David Henry Hwang rewrites Puccini's opera into a deconstructionist *M. Butterfly* (1986).

10. Two most frequently used translations of this ficiton are Arthur Waley's *Monkey* (1943), which is highly popularized and radically abridged, and Anthony C. Yu's thorough, four-volume *Journey to the West* (1980).

11. In the Indonesian writer Pramoedya Anata Toer's *This Earth of Mankind* (1991), for instance, the female protagonist, Annelies Mellema, is introduced as follows: "In front of us stood a girl, white-skinned, refined, European face, hair and eyes of a Native" (25). The colonial history of Indonesia under the Dutch plays a crucial role in determining this standard of feminine beauty. While Pramoedya was orally composing—during his fourteen-year imprisonment—a text to undermine colonial hold and

nationalist excesses of his country, his idealized female remained, however, "white-skinned, refined, European."

12. Frantz Fanon, *Black Skin, White Mask* (1967). See especially the chapter "The So-Called Dependency Complex of Colonized Peoples."

Chapter 5

1. Originally *"Isang magandang señora, libot na libot ng espada,"* this Tagalog riddle is taken from Ronald Takaki's *Strangers from a Different Shore.* Takaki asserts that this riddle serves to "warn the newcomers" to America (316).

2. This chapter uses the term "America" to indicate the idealized image of the United States, which immigrants long to attain. "The United States" becomes more of a geopolitical term signifying the nation.

3. Based on the historical fact that most Filipinos in the United States around the time Bulosan composed his works are males, this chapter concentrates solely on the male psyche of *manongs.*

4. Benedict Anderson defines "nations" as "imagined communities" in his pioneering work, *Imagined Communities* (1983). While he seeks to reconfigure nationalism from within each state and its tradition, I borrow his concept to describe how it is done from without, how "aliens" such as Bulosan conceive "America."

5. Most case studies in *Nationalisms and Sexualities* (1992) investigate how nationhood is conceived and crafted from within, by that nation's own members. It does not focus on the subject of this chapter—the fact that "aliens" such as Bulosan in a host country similarly labor to conceptualize the nation-ness of that state. In this particular instance, Bulosan deliberately feminizes America to embolden the alien protagonist's masculinity.

6. I want to thank my colleague Roger Bresnahan at Michigan State University for bringing to my attention the comparison between Bulosan and Rizal, especially Maria Clara in Rizal's novel.

7. As I suggest in an endnote in chapter 4, Indonesia's nationalist-dissident writer Pramoedya Ananta Toer also chooses to have a mestiza as the heroine in *This Earth of Mankind,* despite the author's anti-Dutch colonial position and the consequent imprisonment.

8. "As Long as the Grass Shall Grow" was analyzed by Lina B. Diaz de Rivera, who utilized feminist theories, but de Rivera's high praise for the story was refuted by L. M. Grow.

9. Originally titled *The Cry and the Dedication, The Power of the People* was written circa 1955 and was initially published in Canada in 1977. The 1986 edition came out in the Philippines.

Chapter 6

1. Perry Link in "Ideology and Theory in the Study of Modern Chinese Literature: An Introduction" traces the genesis of modern China studies in "about five major university centers" in the 1960s to the funding from "the Ford Foundation and National Defense Foreign Languages" of the U.S. government. These were "indirect results of the shock of *Sputnik* and the vision of an expanding Communist bloc" (4).

2. Though the student demonstration in Beijing against Japan was held on May 4, 1919 (hence its name), the term May Fourth movement as used today covers the period roughly from 1917 through 1921. See Chow's *The May Fourth Movement: Intellectual Revolution in Modern China* (1960: 1–15). It stands to reason that Pai alludes more to the literary revolution launched by Hu Shi and others in 1917 than to its political counterpart. The May Fourth movement always serves as a reference point for modernists in Taiwan whenever they describe their literary endeavor, as Pai clearly attempts to do here while glossing over the difference between the social dimension of the previous movement and their own aesthetic preoccupation.

3. Many of these expatriate writers had already been somewhat established before they went abroad. Pai, for instance, had been a regular contributor to *Hsien-tai wen-hsueh* (Modern literature; 1960–73; 1976–) and other modernist journals before he went to the United States in 1962 to attend the International Writing Program at the University of Iowa. See Lee's "'Modernism' and 'Romanticism' in Taiwan Literature" (13–21) and Chang's *Modernism and the Nativist Resistance* (1993). The fact remains, nevertheless, that these writers' careers were truly institutionalized in Taiwan concurrent with their absence in Taiwan. A case in point is that Pai's fame soared only after he published *Tai-pei jen* (Taipei residents, 1971).

4. Frantz Fanon predicts that "the Pitfalls of National Consciousness" will come about when "the national bourgeoisie" usurps the Proletarian revolution of decolonization and becomes a new generation of colonial masters.

5. See Lee's "'Modernism' and 'Romanticism' in Taiwan Literature" (10) for the six basic tenets laid down by Chi Hsien in the 1950s in the journal *Hsien-tai Shih* (Contemporary poetry, 1953–63).

6. Patrick Williams and Laura Chrisman, editors of *Colonial Discourse and Post-Colonial Theory: A Reader* (1994), thus assess Said's con-

tribution to postcolonialism: "It is perhaps no exaggeration to say that Edward Said's *Orientalism*, published in 1978, single-handedly inaugurates a new area of academic inquiry: colonial discourse" (5).

7. Hayden White in *Tropics of Discourse* (1978): "The contours of criticism are unclear, its geography unspecified, and its topography therefore uncertain. As a form of intellectual practice, no field is more imperialistic" (ix).

8. See Chapter 1, "Native Informants and Ethnographic Feminism in Asian American Texts."

9. I am indebted to King-Kok Cheung for this observation. Cheung very graciously pointed this out to me after reviewing an early draft of the abstract to *Immigrant Subjectivities in Asian American and Asian Diaspora Literatures*.

10. Some most famous frontier poets are Wang Ch'ang-ling (?–756), Kao Shih (702?–65), and Ts'en Shen (715–70).

11. For an analysis of Taiwan's colonial past and neocolonial present, see also my commentary on the problematic choice of "nativist" in the genre of *Hsiang-t'u* (home-soil or nativist) literature in chapter 7, "An Island of Immigrants: Nativist Critique of Taiwan's Compradorism."

12. The term "mimic man" derives from V. S. Naipaul's novel of that title.

13. According to Joseph S. M. Lau's "Obsession with Taiwan: The Fiction of Chang Hsi-kuo," Chang published his first piece of fiction, *Reverend Pi*, in 1963 when he was a sophomore at National Taiwan Univeristy (148). All the biographical information came from Lau's essay.

14. Amy Ling in *Between Worlds: Women Writers of Chinese Ancestry* (1990) claims that Chinese men have long been emasculated in the New World due to the professions they are allowed to enter: they "serve the white master through the demeaning work usually relegated to women—cooking, washing, and ironing" (145).

15. The sense of shame and self-depreciation felt by Asian immigrants when they engage in menial jobs is reflected even in Asian American literature written for young adults. The teenage Korean character Yoon Jun in Marie G. Lee's *If It Hadn't Been for Yoon Jun* (1993) is embarrassed when his classmates discover that he works at a restaurant.

16. Another such quixotic character doomed to vanish without a trace is Chang Hsi-kuo's protagonist in "Red Boy" (1972), another Pao-tiao activist who remains absent throughout the story and is declared missing by the Federal Bureau of Investogation at the end. A translation of this story can be found in Lau's *The Unbroken Chain*.

17. Another example of this type of disguised protest against the ethnic division under the Nationalist rule in Taiwan is found in Chung Li-ho's "Together through Thick and Thin," also included in Lau's *The Unbroken Chain*. When the Taiwanese protagonist's wife makes away with a stolen log from a state forest, she is intercepted by a man speaking "Mandarin with a heavy southern accent" (65).

18. See Jameson's *Postmodernism; or, the Logic of Late Capitalism* (1991), Tomlinson's *Cultural Imperialism* (1991), and Appadurai's "Patriotism and Its Futures" (1993).

19. For an example of this development of immigrant subjectivities in cinema, see chapter 8, "Ang Lee's Domestic Tragicomedy: Immigrant Nostalgia, Exotic/Ethnic Tour, Global Market."

Chapter 7

1. Commodore Perry was particularly interested in looking for coal in Taiwan, or Formosa as the island was called at the time. Perry thus "ordered the Macedonian and Supply to that island" (Perry's *Narrative of an Expedition* 565).

2. Sung-sheng Yvonne Chang in *Modernism and Its Nativist Resistance* maintains that Chen Ying-chen's fiction on "transnational corporation has created a popular genre" (163).

3. For mixed reviews and critical opinions on *M. Butterfly*, see Angela Pao's "The Critic and the Butterfly."

4. Chen had been imprisoned for "subversive activities" from June 1968 to September 1975. He was tried in a secret military trial, and the charges against him were never made public. His original ten-year sentence was commuted during the amnesty honoring the death of Chiang Kai-shek. For details of Chen's dissident past, see Lucien Miller's introduction to *Exiles at Home* (1986).

5. Jing Wang in "Taiwan *Hsiang-t'u* Literature: Perspectives in the Evolution of a Literary Movement" makes the same observation concerning the realist and romanticist blendings in Taiwan's nativist literature: "And the new literature [nativist literature], in the flagellation of social injustice, and in its heroic but sometimes awkward efforts to depict the contradictions within such an economic mode, revived the romantic spirit of humanitarianism, a legacy from the May Fourth movement, as well as the pseudo-scientific objectivity of realism" (44).

6. These two texts are drawn from an English anthology of Chinese short stories, *The Unbroken Chain*, so their English titles are given first, followed by the Chinese titles in parenthesis.

7. Huang Chung-ming's "Saiyonara, Good-bye" (1973) depicts a group of Japanese tourists visiting Taiwan for exotic sex. Though there are many parallels between "Saiyonara, Good-bye" and other stories analyzed in this chapter, I have decided not to include "Saiyonara, Good-bye" because it involves Japanese rather than American presence. However, the Japanese influence is connected closely to the American one, as the two countries remain the dominant economic and cultural forces throughout the Pacific Rim.

Chapter 8

1. *Wedding Banquet* (1993) won a Golden Bear for best picture at the Berlin International Film Festival in 1993 and, with Sally Potter's *Orlando*, shared the prestigious Palme d'Or at Cannes. *Eat Drink Man Woman* (1994) won the best picture award at the thirty-ninth Asia-Pacific Film Festival and was nominated for Best Foreign Film at the Oscars.

2. Lee accounts for Schamus' genius in an essentialist manner. He believes that Schamus' Jewish background provides him with a personality less inhibiting than the Chinese psyche and enables him to express fully his intuition about the Chinese script.

3. Alex Albanese's "Behind the Scenes: It's 4 AM, Do You Know Where Your Chopsticks Are?" in the August 1994 issue of *Boxoffice* demonstrates that Ang Lee also relies on the assistance of American studios and technicians not included in the credits of the films.

4. See Buell's *National Culture and the New Global System* (1994), especially chapters 4 and 5.

5. See Perry Link's *Mandarin Ducks and Butterflies* (1981) and chapter 2 of Rey Chow's *Woman and Chinese Modernity* (1991).

6. See Leo Lee's explication of Ch'iung Yau in "'Modernism' and 'Romanticism' in Taiwan Literature."

7. However, Martha experiences gastrorrhagia (bleeding in the stomach) because of the pressure of work and of living with her father-in-law. More significantly, the bleeding occurs while the Tai Chi master tries to cure her with his Chi Kung. Not only does her digestive organ rupture but the human relationship does as well.

8. *Wedding* has been criticized by various women's rights groups and gay/lesbian rights advocates in Taiwan. "On Being Gay in Taipei: An Acclaimed Film Fails to Please Everyone" in the December 1993 issue of *Asiaweek* reports that according to Lee Yuan-chen, director of the women's rights group, Awakening Foundation, in Taiwan, "The ease with which the

conflict between the parents and their son is resolved and the apparent understanding [they reach] at the end of the film differ from most true-life experiences here [in Taiwan]" (45). By the same token, Chi Chia-wei, Taiwan's gay-rights and AIDS-education advocate, complains that the resolution comes about because the baby would have "ensured that their line [lineage] would continue" (45).

Works Cited

Abe, Kobo. *The Woman in the Dunes*. 1964. Trans. E. Dale Saunders. New York: Vintage, 1991.

Althusser, Louis. "Ideology and the Ideological State Apparatuses (Notes Towards an Investigation)." *Lenin and Philosophy and Other Essays*. Trans. Ben Brewster. New York: Monthly Review P, 1971. 127–86.

Alvarez, A. *The Savage God: A Study of Suicide*. 1971. New York: Penguin, 1974.

Amery, Jean. *At the Mind's Limits: Contemplations by a Survivor on Auschwitz and Its Realities*. Trans. Sidney Rosenfeld and Stella P. Rosenfeld. Bloomington: Indiana UP, 1980.

Anderson, Benedict. *Imagined Communities: Reflections on the Origin and Spread of Nationalism*. London: Verso, 1983.

Appadurai, Arjun. "Patriotism and Its Futures." Public Culture 5 (1993): 411–29.

Appiah, Kwame Anthony. "Is the Post- in Postmodernism the Post- in Postcolonial?" *Critical Inquiry* 17.2 (Winter 1991): 336–57.

Ashcroft, Bill, Gareth Griffiths, and Helen Tiffin. *The Empire Writes Back: Theory and Practice in Post-Colonial Literatures*. New York: Routledge, 1989.

Bakhtin, M. M. *The Dialogic Imagination*. Ed. Michael Holquist. Trans. Caryl Emerson and Michael Holquist. Austin: U of Texas P, 1981.

———. *Rabelais and His World.* Trans. Helene Iswolsky. Cambridge, MA: M.I.T., 1968.

Bataille, Georges. *Death and Sensuality (Eroticism).* 1962. New York: Macmillan, 1986.

Bhabha, Homi K., ed. *Nation and Narration.* New York: Routledge, 1990.

———. "Of Mimicry and Men: The Ambivalence of Colonial Discourse." *October* 28 (1984): 125–33.

Bresnahan, Roger J. *In Time of Hesitation: American Anti-Imperialists and the Philippine-American War.* Quezon City, Philippines: New Day, 1981.

Brewster, Anne. "A Critique of Bharati Mukherjee's Neo-nationalism." *Journal of the South Pacific Association of Commonwealth Literature* 34–35 (Oct. 1992–March 1993): 50–59.

Buck, Elizabeth B. "Asia and the Global Film Industry." *East-West Film Journal* 6.2 (July 1992): 116–33.

Buell, Frederick. *National Culture and the New Global System.* Baltimore: Johns Hopkins UP, 1994.

Bulosan, Carlos. *America Is in the Heart.* 1943. Seattle: U of Washington P, 1973.

———. *The Cry and the Dedication.* Philadelphia: Temple UP, 1995.

———. *The Laughter of My Father.* New York: Harcourt, Brace and Company, 1942.

Carb, Alison B. "An Interview with Bharati Mukherjee." *Massachusetts Review* 28 (Winter 1988): 645–54.

Casper, Leonard. Introduction. *Scent of Apples: A Collection of Stories.* By Bienvenido N. Santos. Seattle: U of Washinqton P, 1979. ix–xvi.

Chan, Jeffrey Paul. "The Chinese in Haifa." *Aiiieeeee!: An Anthology of Asian American Writers.* Ed. Frank Chin, Jeffrey Paul Chan, Lawson Fusao Inada, and Shawn Wong. 1974. New York: Mentor, 1991. 70–92.

Chang Hsi-kuo. "Realism in Taiwan Fiction: Two Directions." *Chinese Fiction from Taiwan: Critical Perspectives.* Ed. Jeannette L. Faurot. Bloomington: Indiana UP, 1980. 31–42.

———. *T'ien-ch'eng chih lu (Journey to the Heavenly City).* Taipei: Hongfeng, 1977.

———. *Tso-jih chih nu (Rage of Yesteryear)*. Taipei: Hong-feng, 1978.

Chang, Sung-sheng Yvonne. *Modernism and the Nativist Resistance: Contemporary Chinese Fiction from Taiwan*. Durham: Duke UP, 1993.

Chen Jo-hsi. *Erh-hu (The Two Hus)*. Taipei: Tun-li, 1985.

———. *The Execution of Mayor Yin and Other Stories from the Great Proletarian Cultural Revolution*. Trans. Nancy Ing and Howard Goldblatt. Bloomington: Indiana UP, 1978.

———. *Tu-wei (Breaking Out)*. Taipei: Lien-ching, 1983.

———. *Yuan-chien (Foresight)*. Taipei: Yuan-ching, 1984.

Chen Pao-shu. "Interview of Ang Lee on Shooting *Eat Drink Man Woman*." *Yin-shi Nen-nu (Eat Drink Man Woman: Filmscript and Filming Process)*. Taipei: Yuan-liu, 1994. 143–91.

Chen Ying-chen. "Ho-ta-ko" ("Brother Ho"). *Yeh-hsin-huo-ch'e (Night Freight)*. Taipei: Yuan-ching, 1979. 143–94.

———. "Night Freight" ("Yeh-hsin-huo-ch'e"). *The Unbroken Chain: An Anthology of Taiwan Fiction Since 1926*. Ed. Joseph S. M. Lau. Bloomington: Indiana UP, 1983. 102–32.

Cheung, King-Kok. *Articulate Silences: Hisaye Yamamoto, Maxine Hong Kingston, Joy Kogawa*. Ithaca: Cornell UP, 1993.

Chin, Frank. *The Chickencoop Chinaman and The Year of the Dragon: Two Plays*. Seattle: U of Washington P, 1981.

———. "Come All Ye Asian American Writers of the Real and the Fake." *The Big Aiiieeeee: An Anthology of Chinese American and Japanese American Literature*. Ed. Jeffrey Paul Chan, Frank Chin, Lawson Fusao Inada, and Shawn Wong. New York: Meridian, 1991. 1–93.

———, Jeffrey Paul Chan, Lawson Fusao Inada, and Shawn Wong, eds. *Aiiieeeee!: An Anthology of Asian American Writers*. 1974. New York: Mentor, 1991.

Chow, Rey. *Woman and Chinese Modernity: The Politics of Reading between West and East*. Minneapolis: U of Minnesota P, 1991.

Chow Tse-tsung. *The May Fourth Movement: Intellectual Revolution in Modern China*. Cambridge: Harvard UP, 1960.

Chu, Louis. *Eat a Bowl of Tea*. 1961. New York: Lyle Stuart, 1990.

Chua, C. L. "Passages from India: Migrating to America in the Fiction of V. S. Naipaul and Bharati Mukherjee." *Reworlding: The Literature of the Indian Diaspora*. Ed. Emmanuel S. Nelson. New York: Greenwood, 1992. 51–61.

Chun-Hoon, Lowell. "Teaching the Asian American Experience: Alternative to the Neglect and Racism in Textbooks." *Amerasia Journal* 3.1 (1975): 40–58.

Clifford, James, and George Marcus, eds. *Writing Culture: The Poetics and Politics of Ethnography*. Berkeley: U of California P, 1986.

Comer, Brooke. "Eat Drink Man Woman: A Feast for the Eyes." *American Cinematographer* Jan. 1995: 62–67.

Connell, R. W. "The State, Gender and Sexual Politics: Theory and Appraisal." *Power/Gender: Social Relations in Theory and Practice*. Ed. H. Lorraine Radtke and Henderikus J. Stam. London: Sage, 1994. 136–73.

Daniels, Roger. "Majority Images-Minority Realities: A Perspective on Anti-Orientalism in the United States." *Prospects* 2 (1976): 209–62.

Dayal, Samir. "The Subaltern Does not Speak: Mira Nair's *Salaam Bombay!* as a Postcolonial text." *Genders* 14 (Fall 1992): 16–32.

De Rivera, Lina B. Diaz. "The Female Principle and Woman Reading in Carlos Bulosan Story." *Diliman Review* 37.3 (1989): 11–14.

Dirlik, Arif. "The Postcolonial Aura: Third World Criticism in the Age of Global Capitalism." *Critical Inquiry* 20 (Winter 1994): 328–56.

Donovan, Josephine. "Beyond the Net: Feminist Criticism as a Moral Criticism." *Denver Quarterly* 17 (1983): 40–53.

———. "Toward a Women's Poetics." *Feminist Issues in Literary Scholarship*. Ed. Shari Benstock. Bloomington: Indiana UP, 1987. 98–109.

Duke, Michael S. "Personae: Individual and Society in Three Novels by Chen Ruoxi." *Modern Chinese Women Writers: Critical Appraisals*. Ed. Michael S. Duke. Armonk, New York: M. E. Sharpe, 1989. 53–77.

———, ed. *Worlds of Modern Chinese Fiction*. Armonk, New York: M. E. Sharpe, 1990.

Espiritu, Yen Le. *Asian American Panethnicity: Bridging Institutions and Identities*. Philadelphia: Temple UP, 1992.

Estroff, Sue E. "Identity, Disability, and Schizophrenia: The Problem of Chronicity." *Knowledge, Power, and Practice: The Anthropology of Medicine and Everyday Life*. Ed. Shirley Lindenbaum and Margaret Lock. Berkeley: U of California P, 1993. 247–86.

Evangelista, Susan. *Carlos Bulosan and His Poetry: A Biography and Anthology*. Seattle: U of Washington P, 1985.

Faith, Karlene. "Resistance: Lessons from Foucault and Feminism." *Power/Gender: Social Relations in Theory and Practice*. Ed. H. Lorraine Radtke and Henderikus J. Stam. London: Sage, 1994. 36–66.

Fanon, Frantz. *Black Skin, White Masks*. 1952. Trans. Charles Lam Markman. New York: Grove, 1967.

———. "The Pitfalls of National Consciousness." *The Wretched of the Earth*. Trans. Constance Farrington. New York: Grove, 1963. 148–205.

Foucault, Michel. *Discipline and Punish*. Trans. Alan Sheridan. New York: Pantheon, 1977.

———. *The History of Sexuality*. Trans. Robert Hurley. New York: Pantheon, 1978.

Galbraith, Larry. "Culture Clash" (Interview of Ang Lee). *Outrage* Aug. 1993: 30–33.

Gates, Henry Louis, Jr., ed. *"Race," Writing, and Difference*. A Special Issue of *Critical Inquiry* 12 (Autumn 1985). Rpt. as *"Race," Writing, and Difference*. Chicago: U of Chicago P, 1986.

Gilman, Sander L. "Black Bodies, White Bodies: Toward an Iconography of Female Sexuality in Late Nineteenth-Century art, Medicine, and Literature." *Critical Inquiry* 12 (Autumn 1985): 204–42.

———. *Jewish Self-Hatred*. Baltimore: Johns Hopkins UP, 1986.

———. *The Jew's Body*. London: Routledge, 1991.

Gramsci, Antonio. *Prison Notebooks*. New York: Columbia UP, 1992.

Griffiths, Gareth, and David Moody. "Of Marx and Missionaries: Soyinka and the Survival of Universalism in Post-Colonial Literary Theory." *After Europe: Critical Theory and Post-Colonial Writing*. Ed. Stephen Slemon and Helen Tiffin. Sydney, Australia: Dangaroo P, 1989. 74–85.

Grow, L. M. "Carlos Bulosan: A Quagmire for Critics." *Pilipinas* 18 (Spring 1992): 19–37.

———. "*The Laughter of My Father:* A Survival Kit." *MELUS* 20.2 (Summer 1995): 35–46.

Guha, Ranaji, and Gayatri Chakravorty Spivak, eds. *Selected Subaltern Studies*. New York: Oxford UP, 1988.

Hancock, Geoff. "An Interview with Bharati Mukherjee." *Canadian Fiction Magazine* 59 (1987): 30–44.

Handlin, Oscar. *The Uprooted: The Epic Story of the Great Migrations that Made the American People.* New York: Grosset & Dunlap, 1951.

Harding, Harry. "The Concept of 'Greater China': Themes, Variations and Reservations." *The China Quarterly* 136 (December 1993) Special Issue: Greater China. 660–86.

Healey, Barth. "Mosaic vs. Melting Pot." *New York Times Book Review* 19 June 1988: 22.

Hershatter, Gail. "The Subaltern Talks Back: Reflections on Subaltern Theory and Chinese History." *Positions: East Asian Cultures Critique* 1.1 (Spring 1993): 103–30.

Hing, Bill Ong. *Making and Remaking Asian America through Immigration Policy 1850–1990.* Stanford: Stanford UP, 1993.

Hom, Marlon K. *Songs of Gold Mountain: Cantonese Rhymes from San Francisco Chinatown.* Berkeley: U of California P, 1987.

Horowitz, Gad, and Michael Kaufman. "Male Sexuality: Toward a Theory of Liberation." *Beyond Patriarchy: Essays by Men on Pleasure, Power, and Change.* Ed. Michael Kaufman. New York: Oxford UP, 1987. 81–102.

Hsia, C. T., ed. "Obsession with China: The Moral Burden of Modern Chinese Literature." *A History of Modern Chinese Fiction.* 2nd ed. New Haven: Yale UP, 1971. 533–54.

———, ed. *Twentieth-Century Chinese Stories.* New Haven: Yale UP, 1971.

Hsu, Kai-yu. "A Sense of History: Reading Chen Jo-hsi's Stories." *Chinese Fiction from Taiwan: Critical Perspectives.* Ed. Jeannette L. Faurot. Bloomington: Indiana UP, 1980. 206–33.

Huang Chung-ming. "Hsiao-kua-fu" ("Little Widow"). *Hsiao-kua-fu.* Taipei: Yuan-ching, 1975. 93–213.

———. "I Love Mary" ("Wu-ai-ma-li"). *The Unbroken Chain: An Anthology of Taiwan Fiction Since 1926.* Ed. Joseph S. M. Lau. Bloomington: Indiana UP, 1983. 133–74.

———. "P'ing-kuo-te-tzu-wei" ("The Taste of Apple" 1972). *Luo (Gong: The Collection of Huang Chung-ming's Fictions, 1969–1972).* Taipei: Crown, 1985. 137–72.

———. "Sai-yo-na-ra, Tsai-chien" ("Saiyonara, Good-bye"). *Sai-yo-na-ra, Tsai-chien (Saiyonara, Good-bye: The Collection of Huang Chung-ming's Fictions, 1973–1983).* Taipei: Crown, 1985. 13–82.

Hwang, David Henry. *FOB and Other Plays*. New York: Plume, 1990.

———. *M. Butterfly*. New York: Penguin, 1986.

Ishiguro, Kazuo. *An Artist of the Floating World*. 1986. New York: Vintage, 1989.

———. *A Pale View of Hills*. 1982. New York: Vintage, 1990.

———. *The Remains of the Day*. 1989. New York: Knopf, 1990.

———. *The Unconsoled*. New York: Knopf, 1995.

———, and Oe Kenzaburo. "The Novelist in Today's World: A Conversation." *Japan in the World*. Ed. Masao Miyoshi and H. D. Harootunian. Durham: Duke UP, 1993. 163–76.

Jameson, Fredric. *The Geopolitical Aesthetic: Cinema and Space in the World System*. Bloomington: Indiana UP, 1992.

———. *Postmodernism, or, the Cultural Logic of Late Capitalism*. Durham: Duke UP, 1991.

———. "Third-World Literature in the Era of Multinational Capitalism." *Social Text* 15 (1986): 65–88.

Jen, Gish. *Typical American*. New York: Plume, 1992.

Joaquin, Nick. "The Novels of Rizal: An Appreciation." *Readings in Contemporary Philippine Literature*. Compiled and ed. the Committee on the Humanities. Quezon City: Ken Incorporated, 1967. 32–40.

Jones, Heather. "Feminism and Nationalism in Domestic Melodrama: Gender, Genre, and Canadian Identity." *Essays in Theatre* 8.1 (Nov. 1989): 5–14.

Kaplan, E. Ann. "Melodrama/Subjectivity/Ideology: Western Melodrama Theories and Their Relevance to Recent Chinese Cinema." *East-West Film Journal* 5.1 (Jan. 1991): 6–27.

Katrak, Ketu H. "Decolonizing Culture: Toward a Theory for Postcolonial Women's Texts." *Modern Fiction Studies* 35.1 (Spring 1989): 157–79.

Kennedy, John F. *A Nation of Immigrants*. New York: Harper & Row, 1964.

Kim, Elaine H. *Asian American Literature: An Introduction to the Writings and Their Social Context*. Philadelphia: Temple UP, 1982.

———. "Defining Asian American Realities through Literature." *The Nature and Context of Minority Discourse*. Ed. Abdul R. JanMohamed and David Lloyd. New York: Oxford UP, 1990. 146–70.

———. Foreword. *Reading the Literatures of Asian America*. Ed. Shirley Geok-lin Lim and Amy Ling. Philadelphia: Temple UP, 1992. xi–xvii.

King, Bruce. "The New Internationalism: Shiva Naipaul, Salman Rushdie, Buchi Emecheta, Timothy Mo and Kazuo Ishiguro." *The British and Irish Novel Since 1960*. Ed. James Acheson. New York: St. Martin's, 1991. 192–211.

Kingston, Maxine Hong. *China Men*. New York: Knopf, 1980.

———. "Cultural Mis-readings by American Reviewers." *Asian and Western Writers in Dialogue: New Cultural Identities*. Ed. Guy Amirthanayagam. London: Macmillan, 1982. 55–65.

———. *Tripmaster Monkey: His Fake Book*. New York: Knopf, 1989.

———. *The Woman Warrior: Memoirs of a Girlhood among Ghosts*. New York: Knopf, 1976.

Kogawa, Joy. *Obasan*. Boston: David R. Gordon, 1982.

Kolodny, Annette. *The Lay of the Land*. Chapel Hill: U of North Carolina P, 1975.

La Fargue, Thomas E. *China's First Hundred*. Pullman: State College of Washington, 1942.

Lai, Him Mark, Genny Lim, and Judy Yung. *Island: Poetry and History of Chinese Immigrants on Angel Island, 1910–1940*. Seattle: U of Washington P, 1991.

Laing, R. D. *The Divided Self*. 1960. New York: Pantheon, 1969.

———. *The Politics of Experience*. New York: Pantheon, 1967.

Lao She. *Rickshaw*. 1936–37. Trans. Jean M. James. Honolulu: U of Hawaii P, 1979.

Lau, Joseph S. M., ed. *Chinese Stories from Taiwan: 1960–1970*. New York: Columbia UP, 1976.

———. "Obsession with Taiwan: The Fiction of Chang Hsi-kuo." *Chinese Fiction from Taiwan: Critical Perspectives*. Ed. Jeannette L. Faurot. Bloomington: Indiana UP, 1980. 148–65.

———, ed. *The Unbroken Chain: An Anthology of Taiwan Fiction since 1926*. Bloomington: Indiana UP, 1983.

Lee, Ang. Dir. *Eat Drink Man Woman*. Taipei: Central Motion Picture, 1994.

———. *Pushing Hands*. Taipei: Central Motion Picture, 1992.

———. *Wedding Banquet*. Taipei: Central Motion Picture, 1993.

Lee, Leo Ou-fan. "'Modernism' and 'Romanticism' in Taiwan Literature." *Chinese Fiction from Taiwan: Critical Perspectives*. Ed. Jeannette L. Faurot. Bloomington: Indiana UP, 1980. 6–30.

———. "On the Margins of the Chinese Discourse: Some Personal Thoughts on the Cultural Meaning of the Periphery." *Daedalus: Journal of the American Academy of Arts and Sciences* 120.2 (Spring 1990) Special Issue on "The Living Tree: The Changing Meaning of Being Chinese Today." 207–26.

Lee, Marie G. *If It Hadn't Been for Yoon Jun*. Boston: Houghton Mifflin Company, 1993.

Lim, Shirley Geok-lin. "Asians in Anglo-American Feminism: Reciprocity and Resistance." *Changing Subjects: The Making of Feminist Literary Criticism*. Ed. Gayle Greene and Coppélia Kahn. New York: Routledge, 1993. 240–52.

———. "Assaying the Gold: Or, Contesting the Ground of Asian American Literature." *New Literary History* 24 (1993): 147–69.

———. *Writing South East Asia in English: Against the Grain, Focus on Asian English-language Literature*. London: Skoob Books, 1994.

Lin, Patricia. "Clashing Constructs of Reality: Reading Maxine Hong Kingston's *Tripmaster Monkey: His Fake Book* as Indigenous Ethnography." *Reading the Literatures of Asian America*. Ed. Shirley Geok-lin Lim and Amy Ling. Philadelphia: Temple UP, 1992. 333–48.

Ling, Amy. *Between Worlds: Women Writers of Chinese Ancestry*. New York: Pergamon, 1990.

Link, Perry. "Ideology and Theory in the Study of Modern Chinese Literature: An Introduction." *Modern China* 19.1 (January 1993): 4–12.

———. *Mandarin Ducks and Butterflies: Popular Fiction in Early Twentieth-century Chinese Cities*. Berkeley: U of California P, 1981.

Lipman-Blumen, Jean. "The Existential Bases of Power Relationships: The Gender Role Case." *Power/Gender: Social Relations in Theory and Practice*. Ed. H. Lorraine Radtke and Henderikus J. Stam. London: Sage, 1994. 108–35.

Lipsitz, George. "The Possessive Investment in Whiteness: Racialized Social Democracy and the 'White' Problem in American Studies." *American Quarterly* 47.3 (September 1995): 369–87.

Liu Wu-chi. *An Introduction to Chinese Literature*. Bloomington: Indiana UP, 1966.

Louie, David Wong. "Pangs of Love." *Pangs of Love*. New York: Knopf, 1991. 75–98.

Low, Gail Ching-liang. "In a Free State: Post-Colonialism and Postmodernism in Bharati Mukherjee's Fiction." *Women: A Cultural Review* 4.1 (Spring 1993): 8–17.

Lowe, Lisa. "Heterogeneity, Hybridity, Multiplicity: Marking Asian American Differences." *Diaspora* 1.1 (Spring 1991): 24–44.

———. "On Contemporary Asian American Projects." *Amerasia Journal: Double Issue on Thinking Theory in Asian American Studies* 21.1/2 (1995): 41–52.

Macaulay, Thomas Babington. "Indian Education: Minute of the 2nd of February, 1835." *Macaulay Prose and Poetry*. Ed. G. M. Young. London: Rupert, 1952. 719–30.

Marshall, Donald. *Contemporary Critical Theory: A Selective Bibliography*. New York: MLA, 1993.

Michie, Helena. *The Flesh Made Word*. New York: Oxford UP, 1987.

Miller, Lucien. Introduction. *Exiles at Home: Short Stories by Ch'en Ying-chen*. Michigan Monographs in Chinese Studies, Vol. 57. Ann Arbor: Center for Chinese Studies, 1986. 1–26.

Miyoshi, Masao. *Off Center: Power and Culture Relations between Japan and the United States*. Cambridge: Harvard UP, 1991.

Morantte, P. C. *Remembering Carlos Bulosan: His Heart Affair with America*. Quezon City, Philippines: New Day Publishers, 1984.

Mukherjee, Bharati. *Jasmine*. New York: Fawcett Crest, 1989.

———. *Wife*. New York: Fawcett Crest, 1975.

Mura, David. *Turning Japanese: Memoirs of a Sansei*. New York: Atlantic Monthly P, 1991.

Nakpil, Carmen Guerrero. *Woman Enough and Other Essays*. Quezon City: Vibal, 1963.

Nazareth, Peter. "An Interview with Chinese Author Hualing Nieh." *World Literature Today* 55.1 (Winter 1981): 10–20.

Ngugi wa Thiong'o. *Moving the Centre: The Struggle for Cultural Freedoms*. London: James Curry, 1993.

Nieh Hua-ling. *Chianshan wai shuichangliu (Beyond the Myriad Mountains Flows the River)*. Hong Kong: San-lien, 1985.

———. *Sang-ching yu tao-hong (Mulberry and Peach: Two Women of China)*. 1976. London: The Women's P, 1981.

Okada, John. *No-No Boy*. 1957. Seattle: U of Washington P, 1979.

Olaniyan, Tejumola. "Narrativizing Postcolony: Responsibilities." *Public Culture* 5.1 (Fall 1992): 47–55.

"On Being Gay in Taipei: An Acclaimed Film Fails to Please Everyone." *Asiaweek* Dec. 1993: 45.

Pai Hsien-yung. *Chi-mo te Shih-chi-ts'ui (Lonely Seventeen)*. Taipei: Yuan-ching, 1976.

———. "A Day in Pleasantville." *Born of the Same Roots: Stories of Modern Chinese Women*. Ed. Vivian Ling Hsu. Bloomington: Indiana UP, 1981. 184–92.

———. *T'ai-pei jen (Taipei Residents)*. Taipei: Ch'en-chung, 1971.

———. "The Wandering Chinese: The Theme of Exile in Taiwan Fiction." *The Iowa Review* 7.2–3 (Spring/Summer 1974): 205–12.

Palumbo-Liu, David, ed. *The Ethnic Canon: Histories, Institutions, and Interventions*. Minneapolis: U of Minnesota P, 1995.

Pandya, Sudha. "Bharati Mukherjee's Darkness: Exploring the Hyphenated Identity." *Quill: the Asian Writers' League Journal* 2.2 (Dec. 1990): 68–73.

Pao, Angela. "The Critic and the Butterfly: Sociocultural Contexts and the Reception of David Henry Hwang's *M. Butterfly*." *Amerasia Journal* 18.3 (1992): 1–16.

Parker, Andrew, Mary Russo, Doris Aommer, and Patricia Yaeger, eds. *Nationalisms and Sexualities*. New York: Routledge, 1992.

Pascoe, Peggy. "Race, Gender, and Intercultural Relations: The Case of Interracial Marriages." *Frontiers* 12.1: 5–18.

Perry, Matthew Calbraith. *Narrative of the Expedition of an American Squadron to the China Seas and Japan*. New York: D. Appleton, 1856.

Pramoedya Anata Toer. *This Earth of Mankind*. 1975. Trans. Max Lane. New York: William Morrow, 1991.

Prasad, Madhava. "The 'Other' Worldliness of Postcolonial Discourse: A Critique." *Critical Quarterly* 34:3 (1992), 74–89.

Puccini, Giacomo. *Madama Butterfly*. New York: G. Ricordi & Company, 1940.

Rizal, José. *Noli Me Tangere (The Lost Eden)*. 1887. Trans. León Ma. Guerrero. Bloomington: Indiana UP, 1961.

Roberts, D. *Mei Mei: A Daugher's Song*. Soundprint. National Public Radio. 27 September 1989.

Said, Edward. *Culture and Imperialism*. New York: Knopf, 1993.

———. *Orientalism*. New York: Pantheon, 1978.

San Juan, Epifanio, Jr. *Bulosan: An Introduction with Selections*. Manila: National Book Store, 1983.

———, ed. and intro. *On Becoming Filipino: Selected Writings of Carlos Bulosan*. Philadelphia: Temple UP, 1995.

Santiago, Lilia Quindoza. "The Filipina as Metaphor for Crisis." *Women Reading: Feminist Perspectives on Philippine Literary Texts*. Ed. Thelma B. Kintanar. Quezon City: U of the Philippines P, 1992. 118–30.

Santos, Bienvenido N. *Scent of Apples: A Collection of Stories*. Seattle: U of Washington P, 1979.

Sass, Louis A. *Madness and Modernism: Insanity in the Light of Modern Art, Literature, and Thought*. Cambridge: Harvard UP, 1992.

Simpson, George. Editor's Introduction. *Suicide: A Study in Sociology* by Emile Durkheim. Trans. John A. Spaulding and George Simpson. Glencoe: Free P, 1951. 9–12.

Slemon, Stephen, and Helen Tiffin. Introduction. *After Europe: Critical Theory and Post-Colonial Writing*. Ed. Stephen Slemon and Helen Tiffin. Sydney, Australia: Dangaroo P, 1989. ix–xxiii.

Sollors, Werner. *Beyond Ethnicity: Consent and Descent in American Culture*. New York: Oxford UP, 1986.

Spivak, Gayatri Chakravorty. "Can the Subaltern Speak?" *Marxism and the Interpretation of Culture*. Ed. Lawrence Grossberg and Cary Nelson. Urbana: U of Illinois P, 1988. 271–313.

———. *In Other Worlds: Essays in Cultural Politics*. New York: Menthuen, 1987.

Sue, Stanley, and James K. Morishima. *The Mental Health of Asian Americans*. San Francisco: Josse-Bass, 1982.

Sui Sin Far. *Mrs. Spring Fragrance and Other Writings: Sui Sin Far*. Ed. Amy Ling and Annette White-Parks. Urbana and Chicago: U of Illinois P, 1995.

Suleri, Sara. "Woman Skin Deep: Feminism and the Postcolonial Condition." *Critical Inquiry* 18 (Summer 1992): 756–96.

Takaki, Ronald. *Strangers from a Different Shore: A History of Asian Americans*. New York: Penguin, 1989.

Tan, Amy. *The Hundred Secret Senses*. New York: Putnam, 1995.

———. *The Joy Luck Club*. New York: Putnam, 1989.

———. *The Kitchen God's Wife*. New York: Putnam, 1991.

Tomlinson, John. *Cultural Imperialism: A Critical Introduction*. Baltimore: Johns Hopkins UP, 1991.

Trinh T. Minh-ha. *When the Moon Waxes Red: Representation, Culture and Cultural Politics*. New York: Routledge, 1991.

Vorda, Allan, and Kim Herzinger. "An Interview with Kazuo Ishiguro." *Mississippi Review* 20.1/2 (1991): 131–54.

Waley, Arthur, trans. *Monkey (Hsi-yu chi)*. By Wu Cheng-en. New York: Grove, 1943.

Wang Chen-ho. *Mei-jen Tu (Portrait of Beautiful/Americanized People)*. Taipei: Hung-feng, 1982.

———. *Mei-kuei Mei-kuei Wu-ai-ni (Rose, Rose, I Love You)*. Taipei: Yuan-ching, 1984.

Wang, David Der-wei, and Jeanne Tai, eds. *Running Wild: New Chinese Writers*. New York: Columbia UP, 1994.

Wang, Jing. "Taiwan *Hsiang-t'u* Literature: Perspectives in the Evolution of a Literary Movement." *Chinese Fiction from Taiwan: Critical Perspectives*. Ed. Jeannette L. Faurot. Bloomington: Indiana UP, 1980. 43–70.

White, Hayden. *Tropics of Discourse: Essays in Cultural Criticism*. Baltimore: Johns Hopkins UP, 1978.

Williams, Patrick, and Laura Chrisman. "Colonial Discourse and Post-Colonial Theory: An Introduction." *Colonial Discourse and Post-Colonial Theory: A Reader*. Ed. Patrick Williams and Laura Chrisman. New York: Columbia UP, 1994. 1–20.

Winant, Howard. "Gayatri Spivak on the Politics of the Subaltern: Interview by Howard Winant." *Socialist Review* 20.3 (1990): 81–97.

Wong, Sau-ling Cynthia. "Denationalization Reconsidered: Asian American Cultural Criticism at a Theoretical Crossroads." *Amerasia Jour-*

nal: Double Issue on Thinking Theory in Asian American Studies 21.1/2 (1995): 1–27.

———. "Ethnicizing Gender: An Exploration of Sexuality as Sign in Chinese Immigrant Literature." *Reading the Literatures of Asian America.* Ed. Shirley Geok-lin Lim and Amy Ling. Philadelphia: Temple UP, 1992. 111–29.

———. *Reading Asian American Literature: From Necessity to Extravagance.* Princeton: Princeton UP, 1993.

———. "Teaching Chinese Immigrant Literature: Some Principles of Syllabus Design." *Reflections of Shattered Windows: Promises and Prospects for Asian American Studies.* Ed. Gary Y. Okihiro et al. Pullman: Washington State UP, 1988. 126–34.

Yamamoto, Hisaye. *Seventeen Syllables and Other Stories.* Latham, NY: Kitchen Table (Women of Color P), 1988.

Yang Mu. Preface. *Mei-kuo Yu-liang (American Moon).* By Tsao Yi-fang. Taipei: Hong-feng, 1985. i–vi.

Yu, Anthony C., trans. *Journey to the West (Hsi-yu chi).* By Wu Cheng-en. Chicago: U of Chicago P, 1980.

Yu Li-hua. *Yiu-chien tsung-lu! Yiu-chien tsung-lu! (Again the Palm Trees!).* Taipei: Crown, 1967.

Zhang Longxi. "Out of the Cultural Ghetto: Theory, Politics, and the Study of Chinese Literature." *Modern China* 19.1 (January 1993): 71–101.

Index

J

K

L

M

N

O